MICRO
BRANDING

Build a Powerful Personal Brand & Beat Your Competition

MICRO
BRANDING

Build a Powerful Personal Brand & Beat Your Competition

T. Scott Gross

Leading
Authorities **Press**

Washington, DC

Leading
Authorities Press

Leading Authorities Press
919 18th Street NW
Suite 500
Washington, DC 20006
202-783-0300

ISBN 0-9710078-2-9

Publisher's Cataloging-in-Publication
(Provided by Quality Books, Inc.)

Gross, T. Scott
    Micro branding : build a powerful personal brand &
beat your competition / T. Scott Gross — 1st ed.
    p. cm.
    Includes bibliographical references and index.
    ISBN 09710078-2-9

    1. Brand name products — Marketing — Management.
I. Title.
    HF5415.13.G76 2002   658.8'27
                   QB101-201148

Dedication

She has brown eyes that roll like one of those old-fashioned kitchen clocks. Her hair is a poof of silver. She likes to cook, and she's good at it. I don't think my airplane would fly without her sitting in the right seat being what she calls a "nagigator." But best of all, she's really good at loving me.

To my partner, best friend, editor, and love of my forever, I dedicate this and all that I do.

Her real name is Melanie, but you can call her Buns!

Contents

Contents

Introduction

When Mike Todd was shooting his motion picture masterpiece, *Around the World in 80 Days*, he needed a shot of seagulls congregating around the rear of the ship. So his assistants threw garbage over the fantail, and naturally, the seagulls were happy to do the necessary congregating.

Mike Todd, however, was unhappy. "What are you doing, feeding garbage to my actors? Throw them shrimp."

The seagull story made all the papers and was partially responsible for the enormous success of the film. Never have a couple of pounds of shrimp created so much favorable publicity.

My writing (in the ten books I have authored or co-authored) has been cold, practical, reasoned explanations of marketing strategy in all of its varied forms and permutations. Yet there is a role in marketing for emotion, for "over the top" actions that set examples for others to follow. A marketing strategy itself may be unemotional (as mine have usually been), but how you execute that strategy can call for all the passion, enthusiasm, excitement, boldness, and sensitivity you can muster. How you say something to your customers, your prospects, and your employees can be just as important as what you say.

This is the area that *MicroBranding* explores in great detail. To be a great marketing general, you have to master the emotional side of the marketing business. You can't be all logic and no feelings. You have to be willing to back up your strategy with your passions. If your marketing strategy doesn't feel right inside of you, if you can't express it in a passionate, emotional way, it probably won't work on the outside either.

When I worked for an advertising agency in New York, the office manager once came into my office dragging a credenza. "We're giving each of our account executives one of these to hold material you can't fit in your desk."

I opened the thing and tried to fit a layout for a full-page *Wall Street Journal* ad inside. It wouldn't fit. "I need a bigger one," I said.

"Nope," he replied, "everybody gets the same size unit."

Since I knew I couldn't get *The Wall Street Journal* to change its page size, I took the next best step. I picked up the credenza and threw it out in the hallway, where it sat on its side for the next couple of weeks. From that day on, everyone in the ad agency (except perhaps the office manager) thought I was the most creative person they had on the staff.

What Mike Todd achieved by throwing shrimp, I achieved by throwing a credenza. Stupid, yes. Childish, yes. But also an honest expression of personal feeling. If we wanted our client to spend $100,000 a pop to run advertisements in *The Wall Street Journal*, we should have been willing to spend $100 to buy a sideboard to hold the layouts.

When emotions are honest, when they are honestly expressed, you seldom see situations where they backfire. Quite the opposite. They tend to make a deep impression on everyone concerned. And they reinforce the position of the party involved.

When a client asked art director George Lois what a two-page advertisement would look like in a one-page format, he took the two-page layout and ripped it in half. Stupid, yes. Childish, yes. But also an effective expression of an honest opinion. The ad ran as planned in the two-page format.

Speaking of advertising, we live in an over-communicated society. The average person is bombarded with some three thousand advertising messages a day. That's only the advertising; the real overload is in the editorial and entertainment content of the media. A single Sunday newspaper can weigh five pounds or more.

Then there's the proliferation of media. The Internet is just another medium heaped on the media burdens we already bear.

There's television. Broadcast, cable, and pay.

There's radio. AM and FM.

There's newspapers. Morning, evening, daily, weekly, and Sunday.

There's magazines. Mass magazines, class magazines, enthusiast magazines, business magazines, trade magazines.

And, of course, buses, trucks, streetcars, subways, and taxicabs. Generally speaking, anything that moves today is carrying a "message from our sponsor."

Even the human body has become a walking billboard for Ralph Lauren, Tommy Hilfiger, Calvin Klein, Nike, Reebok, and hundreds of other brands.

With millions of messages floating around the ether, the problem is not just the formulation, or strategy of the message itself. The real problem is getting the message inside the mind of the prospect. MicoBranding deals with this fundamental issue in a totally new and different way.

You may or may not be able to build a brand with logic. But the fastest, cheapest, most effective way to build a brand is with emotion.

In other words, by MicroBranding it.

—AL RIES
Chairman of Ries & Ries
Roswell, Georgia

PART I

CHAPTER ONE

Branded!

In the land of the blind, the one-eyed man is king.

FROM A DISTANCE HE LOOKED EVEN SMALLER. A man in late middle-age, wrapped in blue polyester, Bill Oncken punched at the air as he made his way down the aisle. He moved half as rapidly as he spoke, spittle spraying on those who thought they had grabbed good getaway seats.

With each stab into the air, he made a point, some more important than others but each stamped with equal ferocity as he punched and spat his way closer to me.

I was enthralled. We were in the presence of a great thinker. Well, at least a clear and solid thinker with ideas so plain that the world had missed them, or dismissed them, until he was forced to fight back with those stubby ever-waving arms.

I have never seen a man perspire so. There, in an over air-conditioned ballroom of the San Antonio Marriott Riverwalk, a man was sweating with more intensity than the brown-skinned city employees laboring in the sweltering south Texas heat just beyond the valet stand.

I

They patched Commerce Street with hot stickiness while Oncken, inside, was paving over old ideas of management with simple yet powerful thoughts that stuck in my mind and wiped across my yellow legal pad.

Oncken sweated through his blue polyester shirt, leaving rings of salt with each wave of effort. A miniature salt flat had formed under each arm. An old-fashioned, even for the times, lavaliere mic dangled from a cord around his neck making an annoying scratch with each step through the audience. Oncken dragged the cord like a ball and chain.

In front of me to the left of the sweating, untouched pitcher of hotel water, a Radio Shack cassette recorder that weighed less than the battery set, wrapped each and every word around the tape spools. There were the words I would take home and listen to again and again until I could do Oncken's bit by heart and mean it.

But the most curious thing the old man said that day was this:

Lesson One   In the land of the blind, the one-eyed man is king.

Such a simple, maybe silly thought. But oh, the power! Like the force of tides or compound interest, there stood little man Oncken in a pool of sweat and spit and ideas with the one idea that has made fortunes, yet was too simple, too easy to reflect on the radar screens.

To borrow a little more from my management hero, Oncken also said, "It's hell working for a nervous boss, especially when you are the one making him nervous!" What Oncken wanted us to understand is that in business and in life, priorities are not always obvious. Sometimes, in Oncken's words, you have to "put the urgent ahead of the important."

That day in San Antonio Oncken added that standing out was a matter of knowing what is urgent and what is merely important. And I can tell you there is only one arbiter of what is urgent—the boss.

George Weyerhauser, the paper magnate, said, "For every problem besetting this company, there will always be a responsible person, and it will never be George Weyerhauser. Now, what can I do for you?"

Do what the boss wants first so you can be around long enough to do what is best for the company.

Here is what is best for you and the company: You have to know exactly who you are and where you are going. As you read on, we will create a road map for discovering and growing your powerful, personal, highly targeted MicroBrand.

In business, the two most important things to know are:

❶ What the customer wants.

❷ What you are going to do about it.

(New scene. Twenty-five years later.)

Now, my hair is silver like Oncken's and I sit with Buns, my wife, partner, and best friend on the entire planet. We are the lone occupants of the Burger Basket. I guess to be certain that I have it correct and that Vicki stamps my frequent customer card I should say we were in Doris's Burger Basket, Highway 27, Center Point, Texas. It's a cold and drizzly Saturday evening. Figuring that we are likely to be the last customers of the day, we prop our feet near the gas burning heater.

"Hello, Mr. Gross."

The voice belonged to a young man with dark eyes and an equally dark countenance. A cold draft helped to announce the newcomer as the wooden door scraped shut too late to keep out the weather.

"Hi! Nice to see you." (I had no idea who he was, but he was happy to see me, which is always a good sign. And, since this happens pretty regularly to me, I gave it my best fake and hoped that he would give up a clue as I struggled to place him—at least in context if not enough to recall his name.)

"I'm reading your book. It's pretty good. I'm about half way through."

From here, it's usually easy. I just ask which book and what he liked about it. I follow up with a little polite conversation, while I struggle to figure from where I might know him.

But he wasn't cutting me any slack.

"You were right," the stranger dove in before I had time to recover.

I wondered what someone in Center Point would be doing reading one of my books. I live here and I love this place, but, well, let's say that I don't have high expectations.

3

"It was a febrile seizure."

Finally, I made the connection. I knew him. I even knew his address. And I remembered holding his infant son.

It had been a hot summer afternoon. The sun had yet to set, but in the modest neighborhood where they lived, the sun was hiding behind the trees that run along the river. Long, cooling shadows laced the small front yard but had yet to begin their work.

Buns and I had been working on dinner, something simple like you always do when the day has been a scorcher. When the pager went off, we pushed the food to the center of the cooking island so as not to tempt the dog.

Buns grabbed the cell phone and had dispatch on the line before I had the 4Runner at the gate. I was knee deep in conversation with the dispatcher before the dust from our road settled on the asphalt of Highway 480. When we are home, I work as a volunteer EMT, where I'm at the bottom of the medical barrel but often the first line of response in nearly four hundred square miles of rural Texas Hill Country.

"Scott Gross, Center Point first responder. I'm en route. What can you tell me?"

"Two-and-a-half-year-old child in seizure. Parents are distraught. Be careful."

When I jerked the SUV to a stop, a worried father (now standing at our table at the Burger Basket and motioning to the waitress that he was here for his carry-out order) was motioning me into the house.

It was a case of febrile seizure. A little oxygen, cool them mechanically, guard the airway, and wait. That's all there is to it. And luckily for me, I had just read about this type of medical emergency in *EMS Magazine* (emsmagazine.com) a couple of days earlier.

Memories came flooding back, and I smiled at the man. "Yeah, I remember. Cute little guy. Looked just like his dad."

The man didn't return the smile. "What you didn't know, Mr. Gross, (I will always be uncomfortable with the Mister) was that when you got there that night, my wife and I had decided to break up. We had been arguing about how to go about it, who gets what, and about our son."

I had nothing to say.

"Well, when you showed up and seemed to love our son absolutely, we were a little embarrassed. We got to thinking that if a total stranger could love our son like that, maybe we should do the same." I waited for him to continue. "So we didn't break up and things are pretty good. I guess I should just say thank you."

Then the smiles came, one from each of us, and they felt great.

Lesson Two **You never know when you are going to touch someone in an important way.**

So. I am about to tell you how you can stand out in a cluttered world. The lessons will be simple, but they will also be powerful. As Obi-Wan Kenobi might say, use these lessons wisely because you never know how they might change your life or even the life of someone you don't yet know.

What Do You Bring to the Party?

You have to have three things to develop a killer brand:

- You must have *something that is unique* or that could be made unique.

- You must be *able to articulate that uniqueness well.*

- You must be *relentless in making multiple, quality impressions.*

> **MicroBranding Point**
> What are you already doing that makes you stand out?
> What skills, talents, or experiences could you put to work to make you stand out? Who are you touching with your brand?

Everybody Has One

Everybody has a brand. They just don't know what to do with it. No matter whether your brand is Wal-Mart; Fred Smith, CEO; Juanita Gomez, director of training; neighbor; honey; or Mom—you have a brand.

Now you're going to learn what to do with it.

It's easy to feel overwhelmed by the big players with big brands and even bigger budgets. But each of us can be king of our own domain once we learn to manage our brand.

As a corporate weenie, I hated seeing new executives being hired from the outside to do things I would end up teaching them to do. I watched them get big stock options and corner offices, while the real work and often the real thinking was being done for them. Was it their fault? No. It was mine. I had the ideas and the talent. I just didn't have the brand.

I remember when a new vice president of marketing was hired. Expensive suits and impressive education. His work was marginal at best. He was a lousy marketer for the company. He nearly killed our brand. But funny thing, he certainly was good at building *his* brand. His personal brand. His MicroBrand.

Now I understand the concept, and in a few hours, you will, too!

MicroBrand
A precisely targeted, highly focused personal or
local brand built through strategic use
of public relations and calculated networking.

A MicroBrand is:

- **Efficient:** Little brand-building efforts spill into nontargeted audiences.

- **Personal:** Likely to involve an individual personality.

- **Local:** Usually restricted geographically or by industry.

It is entirely accurate to say that brands are born, and just as accurate to say that we all have one. If they know your name, you have a brand. It may not be a good one or the one you want, but, by golly, you've got one. The real problem when it comes to the idea of branding is not how to create a brand. The real issue is how to manage one.

Put in more traditional terms, a brand is an idea that you or a product owns in the mind of the market. Whether you want someone to buy your product, your ideas, or even your company, your brand will either help or it will hurt.

Few of us think of ourselves as being branded but we are. In fact, we are multiply-branded. In other words, we don't own the same position in the mind of each of our market members.

One crisp workday we locked the office, let the phones fend for themselves, and headed with the staff to the Burger Basket. There, in front of the forlorn looking former gas station, was the usual line of pickup trucks. Some were new, some were well worn, and all were splattered with the buff-colored mud that means spring is about to come to the Texas Hill Country.

Near the end of the line someone had parked a shiny Nissan sedan. We knew in a heartbeat that a tourist had stumbled onto our lunchtime secret. Inside, amid western hats and gimme caps, mixed with the muddy boots, stained vests, bandanas, over-sized belt buckles, sat two city folk trying to look inconspicuous but failing miserably.

The place was its usual, noisy self, a fact not helped by the fact that nearly everyone walking through the squeaky door knows everyone already seated and must endure a chorus of "Hey, Bubba!"

We sat at the round table just north of the counter and hard next to the deuce occupied by the visitors. I couldn't help but overhear their conversation, which went like this:

"Looks like we're in the center of Podunk!"

"Must be the center of society. It's a happening place!"

If you are wondering if I was offended, I wasn't. Center Point really is Podunk, and we really were at the center of society as far as our society goes. And, by any sensible measure, the Burger Basket would definitely qualify as happening.

"I bet not one of these Bubbas would be comfortable at the Hyatt."

"I doubt they would know which fork to pick up first."

Well, excuuuuse me! Anyone with the sense God gave a goose knows that more than one fork is redundant.

Sitting within spitting distance (and we all are accomplished spitters, thank you) was at least one paramedic, an author, a fellow who flies jets, an aircraft designer, and our neighbor, an international businessman who had flown around the world on the Concorde. Yep, just your average meeting of Bubbas.

On the ride back to the office, I repeated the conversation to Buns.

"I'm surprised you didn't set the record straight," she said.

"I didn't think it mattered. Besides, if I actually impressed them with credentials, they'd want to move here. Better to keep quiet."

"They had you branded!" (And they were right on target because a brand is always in the mind of the market.)

A couple of nights ago, the grandkids who live up the hill showed up at our door. As usual, we got right to work spoiling them. The seven-year-old with the brown eyes goes by the moniker, Big Guy. His shadow of thirty months is known in our house as L'il Princess. Neither has the slightest idea that I've ever written a book, given a keynote speech, or helped with a marketing project. And if you called looking for T. Scott Gross, they wouldn't know who you were talking about.

We are branded Pops and Granny Buns. The sign at the ranch gate might as well read "Pops & Granny Buns. Warm hugs, fun stories, great food!"

We are branded. You are branded. We are all multiply-branded depending to whom you are talking. You might be God's gift to ABC Corporation, but you are just as likely Dad or Mom, Big Sister, Big Brother, or any of a million collections of thoughts placed over time in the mind of your life market.

MicroBranding Point
If they know you at all, you have a brand.

It's Up to You

Individual employees rarely think of themselves as branded. Sign the employment documents, show up for orientation, and wait for the first promotion. This is plain goofy. Normal, but goofy. Helloooo! No one cares about your career until you care about your career. If you are going to be content taking life as it comes, then sit back, relax, and don't complain.

Dads, moms, grandparents, lovers, and friends all have brands but often fail to manage them. Dad, I know you are busy but what have you done to manage your brand with the kids this week—make that this morning? Sweetie, honey, or dear, what have you done with your brand lately? Brought home flowers? Cooked a killer meal? Written "I love you" on the mirror? Trust me. There are others out there with good brands who would love to take your place. Now, move it!

Corporate execs think that managing the brand is something the marketing department does. Give 'em a budget, sweat them through campaign approval, and turn your attention to the really important stuff—like reorganization and right sizing.

Franchisees are the worst. They buy the franchise, put up the sign, attempt to negotiate a lower ad fund rate, and then wait for something to happen. What happens is institutional advertising consisting mostly of discount promotions. There may be direct mail, there could be door hangers, but there won't be much local brand building. Oh, there will also be "bundling," which is a French term for "discount faster."

If It Was Easy...

When our son was twenty, he called the house one evening and said, "Dad! I've decided to move to Kerrville and open my own stereo and alarm store! I think I can do well, and I could live closer to you and Mom."

What followed was a dump of ideas and emotions. I'm his dad but to tell you the truth, I rarely understand everything he tells me. When the Kiddo speaks, I just hang on and try to absorb the flood of information that washes away any other conversation.

I don't remember exactly how the rest of the conversation went but it was something like:

"Well, I'll be home this weekend. Why don't you come up early Saturday and let's check out possible locations," I said.

"I can't wait till Saturday!" (I thought, "this kid is really on fire!") "I'm coming up tonight. I gave my notice today! I have to open in two weeks!"

Well, we found a great location, and I stood back and watched a master at work. The kid never asked for or took so much as a dime from Mom and Dad. But he did call pretty regularly those long two weeks. He didn't ask for advice so much as he seemed to need a friendly ear.

"Dad! You won't believe this! I have to have flood insurance!"

"Dad! I can't understand why the fire marshal has to get in on the act!"

"Dad! This is the stupidest thing ever! They want me to..."

With each outburst, I would just add to his irritation by saying, "Great news, son! If this was easy, everybody would be doing it. There'd be a stereo and alarm shop on every corner."

On more than one occasion, I would be told that he didn't appreciate my sense of humor, but justice was finally served several months after the store opening. Our son quickly established Rod's Stereo Sounds as the place to get good products and great service for a reasonable price. He was so good with customers that the local newspaper sent a reporter and a photographer to do a story that covered nearly a half page and lead with the headline, "Youthful local businessman finds a niche—and fills it."

In the center of the article was a photograph of our son standing in front of what he called his Wall of Sound. But the really cool thing was his quote: " If it was easy to have a business, then everyone would have one."

Yes! There is redemption for Dads who stay on message.

And there will be rewards for you when you follow the steps to MicroBranding. It's simple, just not easy. Remember, easy may not be all that good. After all...

MicroBranding Point
If it was easy, everybody would be doing it.

It's More Local Than You Think

For most businesses, if the world ended more than five miles from their front door, they would never know unless they saw it on the news.

Unless you are in the mail-order business, most of your customers probably come from the neighborhood. Even if you are not in retail, your customers are neighbors at least of a different sort. If you are in the music business, your customers live, work, and buy in that neighborhood loosely defined by your industry. Musicians for some strange reason seem to know other musicians.

I'm more likely to know the names of three other speakers who work in the area of customer service, management, and marketing than I am to name the members of the local school board.

See? Neighborhood is a matter of definition.

And brands are often neighborhood brands many times smaller than Coke, Nike, and GM but still plenty big to run *their* neighborhood. For example, in many parts of the American South, a Dr. Pepper and Moon Pie combo is often a most popular snack.

If you are a smart MicroBrander, you needn't worry about the global competitors. There's plenty of business right in your own neighborhood, and you can own it lock, stock, and barrel!

MicroBranding Point
Define the "neighborhood" for each of your brands.

Let's Get Personal

One problem with brands is that few people realize how personal brands can be. Rare is the individual who understands that self-promotion done ethically is as good and as necessary as any corporate marketing campaign.

It's as simple as asking yourself, "In this group, at this moment, for what do I stand? When my name is called or mentioned, what image is conjured up in the minds of others?"

As a naturally shy person, I secretly wish that my clients didn't have to meet me until after I perform. On the platform, my shyness melts away, but I often wonder how my brand must suffer in the minds of those who deal with me prior to a speaking event.

Brands can be incredibly personal, and most of the time, that's good!

Take, for example, Stew Leonard's Dairy Store made famous by Tom Peters in his book, *In Search of Excellence*. The store and its fame seemed to revolve around Stew himself and now that the torch has been passed, Stew Leonard Jr. is the walking embodiment of the brand.

Perhaps my favorite personal brand is Southwest Airlines (southwest.com). My friends at Southwest blanch at the merest suggestion that SWA is wrapped too tightly around founder and leader Herb Kelleher, but it is. That's not to say that the airline lacks other leadership. There is enough competent leadership at SWA to start a dozen successful airlines and still have talent to burn. But the fact remains that SWA is in many ways Herb's personal brand.

And that's good, so don't panic!

Take the time that another company, this one in the aircraft parts business, adopted the slogan: "Plane Smart." Nice tag and it would have been Plane Smart had it not been for the fact that SWA had dreamed up the tag line "Just Plane Smart." Maybe I have the tag lines reversed, but then, that is exactly the point. Obviously there was going to be some confusion.

Now the good news is these companies were by no means competitors, so it didn't make much difference that they had, through concurrent evolution, landed on near identical slogans. Only the corporate attorneys were near apoplexy. So the legal briefs began to fly, which is when Herb stepped in.

Herb, a well-seasoned senior known for inhaling several packs a day and then clearing his throat at the bar, decided to challenge the young, athletic president of the other company to an arm-wrestling match. Billed as "Malice in Dallas" and held in a filled-to-overflowing Reunion Arena, the two camps met for a showdown. More accurately, a media brawl.

Outfitted in corny costumes and surrounded by a bevy of corporate cheerleaders, the two contestants proceeded to milk the moment for everything it was worth. In the end, everybody won with enough publicity, national and international, to declare the marketing war a victory for all.

Here's the question: How many starch-collared executives would even think of playing a game like this?

When Herb goes, he leaves his personality thoroughly painted on the sides of colorful airplanes and etched deeply into the soul of an entire airline.

Brands are indeed often extremely personal.

Local and Bound to Stay That Way

I remember an interview with a manager of a Home Depot store (homedepot.com). The reporter asked what it was like to be personally responsible for running a multimillion dollar operation owned by such a huge corporation.

The store manager feigned surprise as if hearing for the first time that he had a boss and that he was part of a mega-giant chain. "I'm sorry," he said, acting as if the reporter was sorely misinformed. "This is my store. This is my store to turn into a winner or run completely into the ground. I make the decisions inside these four walls, and I try every day to make good ones because the people in my neighborhood expect me to provide them with the best products and service possible."

The fact is every store is a ma and pa store; somebody's ma or pa is in charge. So no matter what the sign out front may say, there is at least the opportunity for personal branding.

We happened to speak to Grocery Outlet a while ago and in the pre-conference research were surprised to see signs such as "Bob and Carol Allen welcome you to Grocery Outlet." The smart folks know that it is important to help the public match a face to the brand.

If you look at the cover of this book, the subtitle mentions beating your competition. Originally it was planned to read, "Beat the Global Competition," but the publisher was afraid such a subtitle might take emphasis off the key idea that we are building powerful personal or local brands. Fine. But, trust me, a great MicroBrand will beat the big boys, even the ones who play a global game! In your mind, who would be the top competitors, the big dogs, when it comes to global competition?

Does Wal-Mart come to mind?

It did for me when I tossed around titles for the book. To tell you the truth, I really like Wal-Mart and have worked for the company on a number of occasions. I was a little worried that Wal-Mart execs would take one look at the subtitle, figure out I was going to teach folks how to beat them, and that would be the last nice word they would ever have to say about me.

Guess I sold them a little short.

I mentioned the book and its title to one of Wal-Mart's top executives telling him that it is my belief that every store is a ma and pa store since somebody's ma or somebody's pa was in charge regardless of whose name was on the pole sign. His comment? Something to the effect that the concept was right in line with the thinking at corporate.

Wal-Mart understands this concept, and that's one way it beats the little guy. It out-little guys the little guy! What do you think that nice old man or woman greeting customers at the door to Wal-Mart is all about? Mr. Sam understood that it takes even more than low prices to draw and keep customers. Sam knew that, as the company grew, it would be difficult to maintain that small town feeling that brought the company to the party in the first place. So he set out to put a face, a local face, on what would become a global competitor.

Wal-Mart is better at being ma and pa than most ma's and pa's.

Customers are more loyal to a face than a logo. Think Michael Jordan and Nike. Think Suzie Chapstick. Think Karl Malden before you leave home without your traveler's checks.

MicroBranding Point #1
Ma and Pa. Make it your mantra for branding success.

MicroBranding Point #2
Customers want a relationship. Give it to them.

Big Guys Chase Little Guys

When we think big business, what comes to mind? A handful of global brands that we presume are driving the economy? Not so, say the big guys themselves. They may refer to small companies as micro-businesses but together there is nothing micro about them. Small businesses, often run from a spare bedroom, account for 60 percent of America's 5.6 million employers. They may make a small payroll, and there may be times when there is nothing left for payroll at all. But we're talking more than $100 billion in annual spending, and the big boys are out for a piece of the pie.

Staples has announced that it will offer small-business payroll and tax consultant services. The consultants will give advice on payroll and human resources issues. Staple's business services division already offers loans, health insurance, and other services through its affiliates.

Kinko's (kinkos.com) also has small business centered in its sights as it offers more than cheap copies. Got a problem with a presentation? Need a professionally produced sign? Then Kinko's might be the place for you.

UPS (ups.com) has announced plans to buy Mailboxes Etc. This mostly franchised company has nearly 4,500 stores and is one of the best places to spot a UPS truck. The marriage may be a natural for both companies. For the rest of us, just take note that small business isn't really so small!

Even Starbucks (starbucks.com) is getting into the act as it installs high-speed wireless Internet access in all of its North American stores. Why? Because the Internet is where Starbucks customers are going, and Starbucks wants to be there first! Visit any Starbucks, and in addition to fou-fou coffee and tea, you'll see an army of laptop computers just waiting for surfers.

Think Local, Act Local

Brands can be surprisingly local. Speaking to the National Association of College and University Foodservice, we met the good folks with Orion Food Systems (www.orionfoodsys.com), a company that creates branded food court-style operations for educational institutions. Orion's tag line, "Feeding a World in Motion," says it all. It offers ten branded food concepts including Mean Gene's Burgers, Cinnamon Street, and Joey Pagoda Oriental Express.

Orion brands seem to be mostly concentrated in locations served by contract feeders such as colleges and industrial plants. They aren't brands you are likely to see advertised on Super Bowl Sunday. No problem. They are local brands, powerful where they need to be.

> **MicroBranding Point**
> The brand awareness of a MicroBrand is often extremely high close to the target market but falls off precipitously as you move away from ground zero.

There is no point in being famous, or even known, outside of your market. If your spouse loves you, there is no need to flirt. If your boss loves you, there is no need to float your resume. If your customers love you, there is no need to spend a penny outside of your market. Focus, grasshopper, focus.

The difference between a personal brand and a corporate brand is only a matter of control. While a personal brand relies heavily on a single personality, a corporate brand is an aggregate personality. Yes, even corporations have a personality which is nothing more than the sum of personalities involved. For now, if you are building a personal brand, keep in mind that it is impossible to be a truly solo act. Your spouse, your assistant, even the vendors with whom you do business add their personality to your brand.

What You Must Do to Stand Out in Your World

The first thing a MicroBrander must do is decide who not to target. What makes global competitors so difficult to compete with is that they are everywhere. Decide what little tiny piece of the pie you want and target that—and only that.

If you want to be a huge MicroBrand (seems oxymoronic, I know) in, say the dry cleaning business, then decide to be the big guy in your town. Or better yet, do everything it takes to own 100 percent, not of your town, but of your neighborhood.

You can't eat an elephant in one sitting, but you can nibble it to death. Sounds gruesome, sorry. Don't take a big swipe at your Godzilla competitor. Nibble him to death. Take a little piece here, a little piece there. He will be so busy trying to eat the world that he won't miss Manhattan so long as you take it quietly.

The Ultimate MicroBrander

If there is one lesson you must learn early to become a successful MicroBrander, it is this: All business isn't your business. Learning to "just say no" is key to building a killer MicroBrand. When you are starting out, there is usually no business to say no to! This makes being picky doubly difficult. The smart guys figure out from the beginning that focus is the secret.

Just for a moment Southwest Airlines wavered and flew a couple of leased three engine 727s on a few of its longer routes. But Southwest soon remembered that flying a single aircraft type was one of its biggest weapons when it came to controlling costs, reduced training, lower parts inventory, and less down time. That and incredibly short gate times had made Southwest the low cost provider of air travel, a principle that would keep it one or two cents per seat-mile cheaper than the competition. Just enough to stand out.

That's MicroBranding.

Those long-distance routes must look tempting to SWA. It must seem like a natural extension of what SWA already does and an easy way to take advantage of its brand equity. But it's not. And SWA knows that. So the 727s went back to the used jet lot.

The best way to create a brand advantage is to do one thing better than anyone on the planet. To successfully MicroBrand, you must stand out—and the first step to standing out is declaring your market and then sticking to it. In the case of Southwest Airlines, it is short flights, point-to-point.

What is your MicroMarket? What makes you stand out?

Temptation Island

With MicroBranders, the temptation is not on the island; it's off the island. It's logical and natural to think that if one store is good, owning two stores would be twice as good. Logical. Natural. Wrong. That's not to say that small businesses and local brands cannot be expanded. We know that would be a lie.

What is true is this: Expansion is not always profitable. Bigger is not always better. It is better to completely own the island represented by your tightly defined market.

Here's the puzzle: How do you define your island?

Two ways: First, you can dominate a tightly defined market. Second, you can dominate a tightly defined niche within a market.

For example, you could sell all the building materials in a small community. Or you could sell all the specialty hardwoods in a region.

You could be the recognized expert on customer service in the healthcare market or you could be the recognized expert on Positively Outrageous Service. In the first example, you would make it your business to understand customer service in the context of healthcare. In the second example, you would specialize in teaching how to add pizzazz and showmanship to customer service but offer limited industry-specific advice.

> **MicroBranding Point**
> All business isn't good business. Own your island.

Personality Cash

MicroBranding is almost always a matter of personality. You must wrap a personality around your business—preferably yours.

It's easy to think that a personality-based business will be limited in sales potential. Think about A-Rod with the Texas Rangers (rangers.mlb.com) and his gazillion dollar contract. This morning on the front page of *USA Today* (usatoday.com) we read, "Deion makes up his mind." We're talking Deion Sanders, the football, baseball, whatever-he-wants-to-do personality.

Forget about the money for a moment and look at where the money comes from. Right from the beginning, Sanders billed himself as "Prime Time." How's that for a nickname? And it didn't come from the media. It came from Sanders himself, the ultimate MicroBrander.

Sander's incredible physical ability makes him an outstanding pro-athlete on the field. It is his personality and marketing that lets him stand out in the media. Which of those two abilities do you think carry the most weight with the folks signing the checks?

Erik Brady, writing for *USA Today*, couldn't resist mentioning Sander's ability to "entertain and amaze." Sanders has a phrase to describe his MicroBranding efforts. He calls it, "Maximizing my moments." Sanders says that Prime Time was created as a "personal marketing ploy." It made him a star and more dollars than you could count. Sounds like a MicroBrand to me, and we bought it!

MicroBranding Point
How could you become a personality in your business?
How could you give your business personality?

Brand vs. Image

The brand is what your customer thinks. Your image is what the customer sees (or hears or tastes or feels.) The image makes your customer think about the brand.

Take the Nike (nike.com) swoosh. Nike is the brand. The swoosh is the image. When you see the swoosh, you think about the brand. You don't just think the word Nike, you think the *brand* Nike. Get it?

The arches at Mickey D's are the image. McDonald's (mcdonalds.com) is the brand. See the arches and you don't think the word McDonald's—you think Big Mac or whatever is your favorite fast food sandwich.

When our beautiful daughterette says to The Big Guy and L'il Princess, "Do you want to go see Pops and Granny Buns?" I can't imagine those two miniature people mentally spelling out our names. Nope, Pops and Granny Buns are our images. Our brand is something entirely different. My guess (and hope) is that the image conjures up a brand that stands for hugs, stories, and good things to eat.

What brand does your image stir?

The biggest mistake people make when it comes to their branding efforts is the confusion between brand and image. Most folks immediately focus on creating a killer image without giving so much as a thought about the brand itself. This is a classic case of all fluff and no stuff—form without substance.

It is easy to call in a graphics designer to whip up a logo and a killer color scheme. And don't forget that catchy tag line! We recommend something like "Serving the World." It sounds international and leaves you plenty of wiggle room while you decide what the heck it is you sell. "Serving the World" works equally well, or not, for software or soft pretzels; it's beautiful and pathetically worthless.

Unfortunately, image without substance yields a beautiful yet empty brand.

MicroBranding Point
Is your brand as well developed as your image? Does your image accurately reflect the brand you want to build?

■ ■ ■

For the latest tips, news, and worksheets to help
with your MicroBranding efforts, visit www.tscottgross.com
and choose the MicroBranding link.

CHAPTER TWO

From Product to Lovemark

THE PURPOSE OF MICROBRANDING is to transfer ownership from you to the customer. Why? Because customers will never be as loyal to you as they are to themselves. We'll talk more about loyalty elsewhere but for now keep this important point in mind: Satisfied customers are not necessarily loyal customers. They may be happy and yet still be susceptible to a competitor's pitch.

Anybody can create a product; it takes brains to create a brand.

Most of us wander aimlessly through life and business without a brand strategy. We are products in search of a market. If we have or are a good product, and if we get lucky, we do just fine. But there's a better way, and it starts with understanding how a product becomes a lovemark.

We hear men refer to their wives as "my old lady" and cringe. There is a brand effort that is going nowhere. Do you really want to be married to an "old lady"? It doesn't sound like you married well at all. (Then again, your wife didn't get much of a prize either!) Why not turn your relationship from two products in search of shared rent to lovemarks who own a real relationship?

Why not turn your career from a desk in an open-plan office into a career where you can grow and where you are loved? You can but not until you understand the MicroBrand process.

Most people start with a product and assume that because they love it, everybody else will. Not true. When I was starting out in the world of work, I was hired as a field rep for A&W, the root beer people.

One of my franchisees was a little out of control, to say the least. He had more than strayed from the approved menu. Most notably was something listed as "Wild Bill's Burger." I don't remember what all it had on it—mustard, onions, bacon, relish, sauerkraut, and God only knows what else—but it was a meal looking for a Tums. I asked the owner how many of these concoctions he sold and he said, "Lots."

When I actually did the sales analysis, I discovered that the eatery sold exactly one Wild Bill Burger a day—every day that the franchisee, coincidentally named Bill, was on the schedule.

> **MicroBranding Point**
> If you are going to create a product, first ask the market. Otherwise, the product will remain just that, a product. It will never mature into a brand.

Products are owned by you. They exist as inventory on the shelf or unfilled dates on your calendar. Trademarks and patents are for products that have enough uniqueness to be legally defined and protected. But it takes more than a legal definition to declare a brand in more than the barest sense of the definition.

Brands (now things are getting interesting!) are defined by the customer. They exist as a feeling that extends beyond the product itself. The brand experience includes your marketing, customer service, even feelings shared customer to customer.

Trustmarks are brands that have moved well beyond commodity. Trustmarks have earned customer loyalty because they are considered a standard of excellence (i.e., the Good Housekeeping Seal, which is itself a brand).

Lovemarks belong to the customer. Ownership is almost entirely beyond your control. An attempt to change a lovemark will meet stiff customer resistance.

New Coke vs. Classic Coke is a perfect example of what happens when a company messes with a lovemark. The Coke folks couldn't stand that Pepsi consistently beat Coke in blind taste tests. So they trundled off to the lab and reformulated the world's number one brand of cola. But customers, Coke customers, were livid. Coke wasn't simply a matter of taste. It was, or is, to them an experience. Coke is Friday nights at the drive-in, a first kiss, Michael Jackson, or something to wash down baby aspirin when you have a fever. The commercial had it right—Coke, is.

We created Positively Outrageous Service. It began as a book in cardboard boxes that overwhelmed the UPS driver and our ability to put the garden tractor in the workshop. Then something happened. Positively Outrageous Service (positivelyoutrageousservice.com) somehow moved along the continuum and became a brand and then a trustmark.

People told us they had been given the book by their boss, and there were stories about books with highlighted pages and turned down corners. Positively Outrageous Service stories began to circulate that weren't from the book. On the service counters of Southwest Airlines at Phoenix Sky Harbour Airport signs appeared declaring, "Positively Outrageous Service practiced here!"

We received a letter stating that a Canadian company was giving their first POS awards. They didn't ask if they could use POS. Why should they? It's their lovemark defined by them and not me. Of course, I own the trademark but trademarks aren't lovemarks. All they wanted to know in the letter was would I sign the certificates!

MicroBranding Point
Where on the continuum from product to lovemark are each of your brands?

Falling in Love

If you aren't passionate about a brand, why should a customer fall in love with it? Better yet, if you aren't passionate about your brand, why expect an employee to be passionate about it?

I love what Dave Arnott has to say in *The Corporate Cult*. (I don't agree with it, but I admire the thinking.) Arnott says that the key elements of a cult are devotion, charismatic leadership, and separation from the community. He goes on to say that many corporations are little more than cults for profit. (My words not his.)

Okay, Dave, here's my definition of a cult: Any organized body of beliefs or practices. Following that reasoning, we had better watch out for the Boy Scouts, the local Baptist church, maybe even a Jake's Body for Life workout group.

Arnott presents Southwest Airlines as exhibit number one.

Take a closer look, please. First, there is the element of devotion. Talk to SWA employees and it's hard to miss their undying devotion to what is, in their minds, a scrappy, little start-up airline. But so what? It's a fact that people like to be, and want to be, part of something bigger than themselves.

Few of us ever create an organization that is bigger than ourselves. So maybe the next best thing is to be a part of one that has already been created. Why do you think people get so excited about contributing to the United Way through their work? Because while their individual donation may be small, their corporate donation is huge and they are proud to be a part of it.

Charismatic leadership? Well, that pretty much describes Herb Kelleher and a raft of SWA top executives. But what makes for charisma? Is it ritual? Is it spellbinding speaking ability? Well, no, to put it bluntly.

Charisma, at least when it concerns SWA, comes in the form of caring. It's as obvious as the nose on your face that SWA leadership really cares about the people. I have no doubt that they would sacrifice the entire operation to save the people who put their face on cheap, reliable air transportation.

Here's a possible definition of charisma: Caring first.

My favorite Herb Kelleher story also happens to be my favorite Wal-Mart story.

Where is Herb on Black Wednesday, the day before Thanksgiving and the most traveled day in the airline business? He is at some

Southwest Airlines terminal hoisting baggage into and out of SWA's orange 737s.

What can one man (I would describe him as elderly but I think he could whup my butt) do schlepping baggage for an airline with thirty thousand employees? The answer is: plenty. It's not the amount of baggage he moves. This leader is moving an entire airline.

Same story, different logo.

I needed to speak with Tom Coughlin, president of stores for Wal-Mart. It was the day before Thanksgiving and, to be all too candid, I called him not expecting to catch him in but simply to move the monkey from my desk to his. He could call me on the other side of the holiday.

"Sorry, he's not in."

I knew that when I dialed the number. "Oh, I guess he's out getting a head start on turkey and football." Ta da! I was right!

"Oh, no. He's out amongst them."

For non-Southerners, I will translate: He was out in the stores working with his troops. Notice she didn't use the usual retailing euphemism, "hitting the stores." Nope, this guy was out amongst them. Probably intending to join Kelleher for a beer after work!

That's charisma. Caring first.

Ever speak to a Wal-Mart conference? There's nothing like it. I was once invited to speak at 7:30 in the morning. I figured, yeah, right. The place will be a tomb. At 6:30, I walked into the arena in Kansas City hoping beyond hope that at least the audio guy would be there. Was I ever surprised! The arena was packed with 3,500 laughing, cheering Wal-Mart managers singing Wal-Mart songs. (Yes, there are Wal-Mart songs.)

So is this a cult? Not yet. There is still the issue of separation from community.

I suppose if the company dragged you away from family, you could cry foul. On the other hand, what if you loved your work so much that it became like family? In my book, that would beat the daylights out of having a job where you were treated like a stranger rather than a respected member of the group.

I get Arnott's point. But here's the other side of the coin: If you are going to build a brand that customers are passionate about, you had best begin by building a company that your employees love.

> **MicroBranding Point**
> Care first.

Personal vs. Corporate Brands

If there is one point Arnott made, or should have made, it is this:

> **MicroBranding Point**
> Don't confuse your personal brand with your corporate brand.

If the work you do is working you, you'd better get different work. Humans are often defined by the work they do, but they are not the work they do.

If you look into the mirror and see a logo where there should be face, you have carried career too far.

Still, it is good to know that you can, and should, have multiple brands so that you can manage each of your brands to the best advantage.

When you are asked what you do for a living, do you say you are the director of sales or that you are Molly's Dad?

There's a big difference between having a career and having a life. Be sure not to confuse the two. At the end of your life, you will never regret not having passed one more test, not winning one more verdict, or not closing one more deal. You will regret time not spent with a husband, a friend, or a parent.

—Barbara Bush, former first lady at Wake Forest University commencement in Winston-Salem, North Carolina

Sunflower Health Foods

We heard this interesting story about Sunflower Health Foods. Well, it didn't start out as Sunflower Health Foods; it started as a small store simply named, Sunflower Foods. Obviously, a restaurant. In fact, the local authorities even granted it a restaurant license. Problem was, it wasn't a restaurant.

Sales at Sunflower Foods were modest. Nothing spectacular but nothing to be ashamed of either. For many years, the little store helped raise a family paying the bills by pleasing its customers.

When the founders decided it was time to pass the torch, the sons and daughters who came to stock the shelves and ring the register made one small but significant change. They kept the friendly service. They kept the focus on quality at a fair price. But they broadened the sign out front just enough to squeeze the word Health between Sunflower and Foods. And a funny thing happened. Sales blossomed.

No matter what your given name may be or even what clever name you may have given your department, team, or store, there are always unspoken descriptors that your children, lover, boss, or customers fill in mentally. You may be Bette (the nice lady) Price or Grandpa (the guy who takes me fishing) Campbell or Neighborhood (they are never on time) Dry Cleaners.

Now is a good time to think about what it says—and doesn't say—on your sign!

We'll talk more about names and image later!

27

Ten Key Premises of MicroBranding

1. You don't need a globally recognized brand to compete.

2. You don't need leading edge technology or global reputation to create loyal, profitable customers.

3. A MicroBrand is, in many ways, more powerful than a global brand.

4. Building a powerful MicroBrand is easily accomplished on a microbudget.

5. MicroBrands may not always be outstanding, but they always stand out.

6. Building a MicroBrand costs less than you now spend to be mediocre.

7. You already have a brand. You just may not know it.

8. You are multiply-branded, and chances are you are focusing on the wrong one.

9. All brands are MicroBrands.

10. It is much easier to destroy a brand than to build one.

■ ■ ■

For the latest tips, news, and worksheets to help
with your MicroBranding efforts, visit www.tscottgross.com
and choose the MicroBranding link.

CHAPTER THREE

The Brand Advantage

In my whole career, I really believed strongly in three things: the power of a great team, the power of a great brand, and the power of the consumer.

JEANNE JACKSON, CEO WALMART.COM

Customers don't buy products—they buy brands.

Brands Are a Shortcut

HE WAS JUST A LITTLE GUY, AND THE DAY WAS HOT AND HUMID. It must have been a hundred and two outside, and it wasn't what they call a dry heat. It was one of those close as a wet sweatsuit days with nary a breeze to take the edge off.

From the end of the sidewalk that stopped at the edge of the playground at our son's middle school to the bright white door of our house must have seemed like a million miles to a little guy faced with a long, hot walk home from school.

I had made it home early and was sitting at the kitchen table nursing a cold iced tea when the door burst open. My son Rod blew into the room as if the devil himself was in hot pursuit.

His face was beet red. Sweat dripped from his mop of brown hair. His shirt was soaked, and I was certain that some neighborhood bully must have supplied the motivation for what had obviously been a hard run of great distance.

"Son! Is everything okay?"

"Yeah, Dad," he managed breathlessly.

"Then why are you sweating like you haven't got good sense?"

"I ran home from school." By now, he was breathing normally. Not bad for a kid who had just run about a mile and a half on an afternoon that would have sent desert nomads looking for a shady yurt.

"You ran home from school?"

"Yes, sir."

"All the way home?"

"Yes, sir."

"Do you mind if I ask why?"

A look that was far less polite than the preceding "yes, sirs" informed me that the question was not considered to be all that bright.

"Da-aaad, it was too far to walk!"

Too far to walk and not a shortcut or friendly neighbor with a car in sight. Of course! We'll just run home. To all but the terminally parental, it would have been obvious. Walking home would take darned near forever and when you are a kid in a hurry you do what is natural—run home, dummy!

And that is precisely what a brand or MicroBrand is—a shortcut. Brands do part of the work quick and neat and right up front, so you can spend your precious face-time with the customer communicating the rest of the story.

As I write, the NBA is putting on a show from the television across my office. I don't know what the score is. I'm not 100 percent sure who is playing. I just like the sound.

But one thing I do know is: Nike is a sponsor. How do I know this?

Well, I had just glimpsed an incredible ball handling demonstration that lasted, let me guess, sixty seconds.

Higher Price

The highest price ever paid for a New York City apartment (if you can call a 17,000-square-foot penthouse an apartment) was $38 million. Yep, that's million with an "m" and a ton of zeros. A mere $2235 per square foot.

Where was it? Trump World Tower. Tell me that's not the power of a brand!

One of the chief advantages of a great brand is that it allows you to charge a higher price. Notice that unbranded products, called commodities, trade based solely on the basis of supply and demand. Oil, wheat, coal, and natural gas are commodities. So are minimum wage workers. (Now, I am sorry if that strikes you as cold; that's the way it strikes me. But there is a reason for minimum wage, and that is minimum skills.)

If you want your product or service to bring a higher price, you must either make it scarce or exclusive. And, when you think about it, scarce is nothing more than a version of exclusivity.

Here's a quiz:

What costs the same as 112 million ballpark hot dogs?

What bill would a minimum wage earner have to work 23,525 years to pay?

Give up? The answer to both questions is this: The contract Alex Rodriguez, a.k.a. A-Rod, signed to play with the Texas Rangers baseball team. Imagine, $252 million to play baseball!

How does he do it? A MicroBrand!

A-Rod is, at the moment, batting .309. That's nice and certainly better than you or I could do. But is he really worth $252 million? If that's the case, wouldn't someone batting .150 be worth at least half of that? I think not!

Lower Quality

A strong brand takes the emphasis off quality. It is *perceived* quality that really counts; although hard to measure, being "cool" can give a brand a quality pass in the mind of the consumer.

When our son was a teenager, he insisted on buying a pair of Van's canvas shoes. They were loafer style and printed in a black and white checkerboard pattern. All that was missing was a red nose and a tiny car.

He loved those shoes which, to us, seemed to be a real rip-off. And they definitely did not shout quality. A strong brand can get away with that.

> **MicroBranding Point**
> A strong brand takes the emphasis off quality.

Brands Cost Less to Market

When you don't have to devote resources to educating the market, you can spend more reinforcing the brand promise—the market already believes you. You just have to remind them. Reminding costs less than educating because you can do it in less time.

That same line of thinking says that new products that are extensions of established brands are cheaper to introduce because the brand is already built. Given the choice of extending under the brand or starting from scratch, you would almost always be foolish to ignore equity you own in an existing brand.

Who would have thought that in a nation of plenty the one thing we are missing is moistened toilet paper? And guess who is going to spend $40 million to introduce it? Kimberly-Clarke, the folks who bring you Kleenex and Huggies. The new product will come as an extension of the already popular Cottonelle brand.

By the way, if you think $40 million is a pile of dough, just think about the estimated $125 million in sales forecast for the first twelve months. The total category of which Kimberly-Clarke will own 100 percent is thought to be worth $500 million in annual sales once the market matures. Go figure.

CHAPTER FOUR

What Builds Loyalty?

LOYALTY IS DEFINED AS RESISTANCE TO CHANGE. It is better than customer satisfaction because research shows that satisfied customers are not necessarily loyal customers.

According to Thomas Jones and Earl Sasser in a 1995 issue of *Harvard Business Review*, "Any drop from total satisfaction results in a major drop in loyalty." They were introducing the idea that there is a difference between being completely satisfied and merely satisfied.

Looked at in reverse, customers who are completely satisfied are much more likely to repurchase than customers who are simply satisfied. As there are degrees of satisfaction, so are there degrees of loyalty and they vary geometrically not arithmetically. (Little changes in satisfaction make for huge changes in loyalty.)

Loyalty is a major indicator of share of customer. This means that loyal customers give you a larger percentage of their business. Share of customer is important, because in a highly competitive world where everyone is fighting for new customers, you can increase sales simply by doing more business with the customer you already have.

Make customers feel so good they come back twice as often, and you can double frequency and probably sales without adding a single new face.

Satisfying customers is not enough. They must be completely satisfied, wowed, or delighted. Any customer who is merely satisfied is fair game for your competition. Any customer who is only satisfied may have reasons for not being completely satisfied. If you can discover the reasons why the customers of your competitor are not completely satisfied, you have the key to a quick gain in market share.

If you can discover what is keeping *your* customers from being completely satisfied, you have the key to increased customer loyalty and possibly increased share of customer.

How do you find out? Ask!

Do you intend to purchase again soon? Why or why not?

Where else do you buy? Why?

How likely are you to recommend us? Why or why not?

What experiences influenced your decision to purchase from us? The other guy?

Here we are in the lightning round of creating a powerful, personal brand, and it's time for a story.

My good friend John loves his wife Trish just about as much as I love Buns. My guess is that they will be married forever and then some. John and I were trying to figure out what this thing called love is.

They say that love is blind. Maybe so. It's not all that different from products that have moved from trademark to lovemark.

John and I figured that when you love someone you love the entire package. Things we find endearing about our spouses would be downright irritating in someone else. Ain't love brand?

Why does your lover love you? What is the reason for hanging around? Don't know? Better ask!

Dimensions of Loyalty

There are many factors that influence customer loyalty. The goal is to create an "I can't get this anywhere else but here" feeling.

We've named the big ones below, but there are no doubt more. With each dimension, there is a rhetorical question that you should ask.

Product excellence	**Individual employees**
Product leadership	**Value through knowledge**
Operational excellence	**Exclusivity**
Other customers	**Affinity-celebrity**
Cause	**Price**
Government regulations	**Customer intimacy**
Choice-selection	

- **Product excellence:** Is my product better than the competition's product? As perceived by the customer? (The only measure that counts.) As measured qualitatively?

- **Product leadership:** Is my product considered state of the art or fashionable? Is my product "hot"? Do I have the technology locked up or could my competition buy it?

- **Operational excellence:** Is the operation that I wrap around my product better than the competition's? Is service faster, easier, friendlier? Are my bills and order filling more accurate? Are the bathrooms cleaner, the parking more convenient, the telephone answered by a real human? Or does my competition beat us in any category?

- **Other customers:** Is my product cool? Cool in the sense of being used by other people that I know or want to be like. Could the competition easily grab the next fad along with my customers?

- **Cause:** Is my product associated with causes supported by our customers? This is the basis of affinity marketing. "With every use of the credit card, a small donation is made to…" Could my competition out-position me here?

- **Government regulations:** Is the use of my product required by law? If the law changes, you will rapidly discover how deep customer loyalty runs.

- **Choice-selection:** Do I offer better or more choices than my competition? Should I position my company as a specialist?

- **Individual employees:** Would my customers follow their favorite employees if they were to be recruited by the competition? Could my employees become my competition? Can I protect myself?

- **Value through knowledge:** Do I add value through knowledge by training our customers?

- **Exclusivity:** Can my customers get this same product or experience somewhere else?

- **Affinity-celebrity:** Do I make my customers feel special?

- **Price:** Does my price represent a value as defined by the competition and our customers?

- **Customer intimacy:** Do I know my customer better than the competition does?

■ ■ ■

For the latest tips, news, and worksheets to help
with your MicroBranding efforts, visit www.tscottgross.com
and choose the MicroBranding link.

CHAPTER FIVE

Leader of the Brand

Our company has personality.

DO YOU KNOW WHAT AN FBO IS? It stands for Fixed Base Operations (or Operator) and is to private and corporate aircraft as a service station is to automobiles. Except an FBO is often a luxury gas station. Many have conference rooms, most have flight planning rooms, and some even have snooze rooms where weary pilots can wait out a weather system or hang around until the boss is ready to fly home.

There is one particular FBO that to pilots stands for something special, and that's Showalter Flying Service at Orlando Executive Airport. In the aviation community, Showalter is a MicroBrand that really stands out. In fact, Showalter has been featured on the cover of the Land's End corporate catalogue.

We've been to Showalter many times, and no, we weren't attracted by the terminal building that looks so islandy that Jimmy Buffett could call it home. (He is a customer.) And it definitely isn't low prices. There are plenty of options for lower fuel prices. Nope, we are drawn to

Showalter like a moth to an expensive flame, because we're suckers for great service and hungry for Showalter hospitality.

The Showalters—Bob, Kim, and daughter Jenny—are intuitive MicroBranders. We could only define the term. They actually bring it to life.

We'll start by telling you that the Showalters have broken most of the MicroBranding rules. They don't have a mission statement although they say a value statement wouldn't be too tough to come up with. They haven't got a tag line beyond "quality and safety since 1945," which crawls across the bottom of their stationery for no particular reason.

They have tried "many, many times" to come up with the values, mission, and vision statements only to fail each time. Mission statements "always became huge because everyone wanted their mission in that statement and we don't all have the same mission—and that's okay," says Kim Showalter. "They have been wonderful exercises, and we found wonderful thinking came out of it. But we couldn't get them short enough without leaving out something important to someone."

Does that mean they don't have values or mission or vision? Not even. The Showalters know exactly who they are and where they are going. So what if they aren't good at articulating it? They're doing it!

"We hire folks who have similar values so maybe a values statement wouldn't be that difficult," Kim says. "You could say our company has personality. It changes every time someone comes and goes."

If there is something to be learned from the Showalters, it must be this:

■ Your competition may not be obvious.

■ Branding opportunities are everywhere.

■ Loyalty comes from the experience.

Caught in the Middle

Asked who is the competition, Kim said without thinking that "it is not the other fuelers on the field. Pilots may have little choice about where they land, but they have plenty of options when it comes to deciding how much fuel to board."

According to Kim, her competitor "is the FBO they just left and the place they are going to next."

If the crew left an FBO where they have great rapport, chances are they will land on the Showalter ramp with fuel to spare. If the next stop is a favorite, no doubt the crew will plan to make the bulk of their fuel purchases there.

The Showalters wrap so much experience around the visit that the competition doesn't stand a chance. We know! We've been on their ramp many times. Once you are in Showalter hands, you are powerless to say anything other than "top off the tanks."

Opportunity to Burn

Asked about what they do to market the Showalter brand, Kim said, "Five years ago, if you had asked that question, I would have said, nothing. But now, I understand that while we don't do much in the way of formal marketing, we are branding all the time, constantly.

"There are industry functions we are involved with, and, of course, there are the people who come across the ramp. The secret is you have to be prepared.

"Jenny was at the Scheduler's Conference when she met the Land's End people at their booth. They loved our logo shirt, and Jenny said it was one of theirs. That's how we ended up on the cover as well as being in their booth at the National Business Aircraft Association for three years in a row!"

The point is simple. We are surrounded by branding opportunities.

> **MicroBranding Point**
> When opportunity knocks, only the prepared are likely to open the door.

The Showalter Loyalty Experience

Kim was almost stumped when asked about what they did to build loyalty. Then, like most folks who truly understand their business and their brand, she quickly warmed to the subject.

"In addition to everyday good service [I'd say, great service] we give our customers continuity. We have customers who have been coming here for thirty, even forty years. There are familiar faces and experiences to be had here." Makes sense. Some members of the Showalter team are going on twenty years with the company. They are the Showalter brand!

And the Showalters are better than good when it comes to listening to customers. When one customer commented that all he needed was a brass band, he was met by ramp agents using mops and brooms for instruments while performing to the recorded music of a brass band!

Then, of course, there was the customer who, under the special requests section of the fuel order form wrote, "Soul Man" by Sam and Dave. I guess you know how this one turned out.

In my own experience, there was the time we left our dirty plane overnight only to return to discover it washed, waxed, and tied with a huge red bow!

Our favorite was the time we were met by the entire crew. We were marshaled to a special section of the ramp that had been painted with red, white, and blue stars and, upon exiting the plane, serenaded with:

Welcome to Orlando
We sure are glad you're here.
We'd like to sing a song for you
To fill your heart with cheer.
We think of you quite often
You taught us how to play
And now we practice all the time
Get better every day.

Although we're full of history
The building is not old
The trailer cannot represent
The tons of fuel we've sold.

The trailer cannot bring us down.
We'll tell you one more thing.
We'll never be too serious,
Thanks to the Chicken King. (Bow)

Soooooooooooo..............(Swing arms)
One last time we'd like to say
We're really glad you came.
To Scott and Buns, come have some fun
And join us in our games!

— THE SHOWALTER GANG

How's that for MicroBranding!

■ ■ ■

For the latest tips, news, and worksheets to help
with your MicroBranding efforts, visit www.tscottgross.com
and choose the MicroBranding link.

PART II

C H A P T E R   S I X

The Branding Process

Success is a matter of luck. Ask any failure.

EARL WILSON

The Branding Process: Four Giant Steps

IT SEEMS A LITTLE ARTIFICIAL TO CREATE A BRAND FROM SCRATCH, but, in fact, that's the best way to do it. If by simply knowing your name, you can declare a brand, then think about the problem of attempting to recreate an existing brand. Existing brands may come with many good mental associations, but they also carry a lot of baggage.

Have you ever noticed that when young people first leave the nest one of the things they bring with them on their first visit back home is a new name? That's branding or, depending on your relationship, re-branding.

There are four giant steps to creating a brand with about a dozen substeps to make the process complete. (See "The Brand Building Process" at the end of this chapter.) Here is where most people make the fatal mistake. Rather than thinking their brand through from start to finish, they immediately skip to thinking up really cool names and end up with a name more suitable for a rock band than a serious product, service, or career.

Smashing Pumpkins, REO Speedwagon, KISS, and even The Rhythm Ranch Hands are all great names. They are perfect if you are playing Madison Square Garden or a gig at Arkey Blue's Silver Dollar. For the rest of us, well, you just have to go through the steps of getting in focus. You know, actually make a plan! Now there's a novel idea!

> **MicroBranding Point #1**
> The four focusing steps are: Truth or Dare, Value Discovery, Conscious Creation, and Cement Yourself.
>
> **MicroBranding Point #2**
> The *last* MicroBranding step is designing a logo!

If you don't know where you are going, any direction will do. If you are like many, that pretty much describes your career, maybe your relationships, and probably your company or workgroup.

Trust me. A little time spent planning will save a whole lot of time on the road. For most of my career, I have been lucky to have been in the right place at the right time. But now it's time to let old age and stealth beat youth and ambition. Now, I actually plan my moves, and the efficiency of being in focus is incredible.

Eye of the Beholder

The first step to getting in focus is deciding what is important to you. There's a public service announcement running on television these days where a little boy is encouraged to become a doctor. He tells his dad that he would rather be a teacher. His dad says, "But if you are a doctor, you can make lots of money."

The little boy says, "But if there aren't any teachers, there wouldn't be any doctors."

There is an old saying, "Do what you love and the money will follow." Maybe. But it's not likely that a teacher will ever make as much money as a rock star or even a great car salesperson. Maybe a better saying would be, "Do what you love and the money won't matter."

Last summer when the wildfires were raging in the West, I began to feel guilty about being at home watching from the couch. So I called my buddies at the Shasta-Trinity Ranger Unit of the California Department of Forestry and asked if they could use a week of volunteer help. They said yes, so I fueled up the plane and flew to Redding, California.

The first night on duty we were called out for a wildfire of which we made short work and then headed back to the barn. The next morning, I showered and headed for the engine bay where engine 2479 was waiting for morning attention. Alone I started the morning routine of topping off the foam agent, checking the chainsaws for timber and roof work plus the dozen other small details that have to be checked before hitting the streets in earnest.

The morning routine was just that, routine. Eight sets of hands found things to do until there was breakfast: scrambled eggs with peppers, sausage links, waffles with syrup, every cereal known to man including the kids' stuff.

"Check this out!" It was Eric, all freckled and excited, as he read from the front page of the *Record Searchlight*. The article was headlined, "New Book Says Financial Planning Is the Best Job." Eric flipped to the back page of the section and called out the top three jobs over the din of dishes and the competition of a radio playing in the kitchen.

"Number one job is financial planner. Number two is Web site manager, and number three is computer systems. Can you believe this stuff? Worst environment. Guess what? We're number 249! Most stress? We're 249 again! I know who writes this stuff. Someone who doesn't like to work!"

Killer. Here we were camping with our buds, just in from a fast ride in the dark, pumped and primed and ready for the next run. Two minutes from a hot breakfast and some idiot says we have one of the worst jobs on the planet.

"We oughta cut this out. We didn't make the best in any category. That's a joke," said the woman in the captain's uniform who "just loves firefighting."

"Eric! Do they say how they decided on the rankings?"

"Department of Labor data, trade groups, and telephone surveys."

Somewhere in the kitchen a voice said, "If you want to find out how to rank firefighting, maybe they should ask firefighters and leave the financial planners in their windowless cubicles."

> **MicroBranding Point**
> Do what you love and the money won't matter. Better yet, do what you love—and it will show.

Fred Williams, a marketing consultant for Ramsey Resources in St. Louis, loves to tell this story:

"Several years ago I flew to Bangor, Maine, for an interview for the director of photography position with a well-known studio. At the airport, I was told that Mr. Olive, the company president, had been detained and I was to take a cab to the studio and meet him there.

"As I entered the beautifully decorated portrait studio, the receptionist welcomed me and asked me to sit down. A few minutes later a well-dressed family of five walked in. Surprised, the receptionist said, 'Why, Mr. Smith, we had you down for an appointment to be photographed next Saturday. We don't have a photographer on duty today.'

"'But we got up so early, got the children ready, and drove a long way to get here this morning,' Mrs. Smith implored. The embarrassed receptionist turned to me: 'Mr. Williams, would you be able to help us out and photograph these people?'

"I agreed. We entered the photography area, and luckily I was familiar with the camera and lights, all set up and ready to go. Everything went well, although about three-fourths of the way through the session, I noticed someone lurking in a small closet nearby. When I finished, I bid the Smiths good-bye and turned on the room lights. A distinguished-looking little man stepped out of the closet and said, 'I like the way you handle yourself, kid. You've got the job!'

"It was Mr. Olive. Later I learned that the Smith family was really Mr. Olive's daughter, son-in-law, and grandchildren. The entire session had been an elaborate test. Without knowing it, I did a great selling job that day—and I was the product!"

And so we arrive at the first step in the focusing process:

MicroBranding Point
Discover what you love.

If you are serious about your brand, here is where the hard work begins. I'll give you an outline and if you are one to dog-ear book pages, this might be a good place to leave your mark so as the process unfolds you can return to this page and see how we are doing!

THE BRAND BUILDING PROCESS

Truth or Dare
Foundation values: what really matters
Mission: the purpose for which you come to the party
Vision: where you are going
Snapshot: where you are at this instant

Value Discovery
Position: what you want your customer to think about you
Billboard: your brand promise in six words or less

Conscious Creation
B.I.G. Ideas: what will set you apart from the crowd
Image: what the customer sees
Name: we save a critical step for last, where it belongs!

Cement Yourself
Ink & Air
Positively Outrageous Service Marketing

■ ■ ■

For the latest tips, news, and worksheets to help
with your MicroBranding efforts, visit www.tscottgross.com
and choose the MicroBranding link.

CHAPTER SEVEN

Truth or Dare

The purpose of mission, vision, and ownership is to allow the organization to work leaner. Call it enlightenment if you like. The result falls straight to the bottom line."

T. SCOTT GROSS

There is only one valid definition of business purpose: To create a customer.

PETER DRUCKER

At the Foundation

SOMEHOW IN THE MIDST OF BEING POLITICALLY CORRECT we came to the false conclusion that in a diverse society the right thing, the polite thing, even the legally safe thing to do was to leave our personal values at home. Wrong!

Look at the corporations that are doing really well. It's okay if you choose to use some measurement other than pure profitability. There is indeed more to life than the almighty greenback. Even if you wish to be pragmatic, at the heart of the best of the best, you will find a solid foundation of values, more often than not old-fashioned values, that ring of truth, justice, and as Superman would say, "the American Way."

Like it or not, every organization has a foundation of core values. As is true with the corporate personality, corporate values rarely amount to more than the aggregate sum of the personal values of everyone who is part of the enterprise. You may as well include suppliers, shareholders, and even customers.

A corporate personality is the sum of individual personalities. The impact of a leader, who is strong and ever-positive, can still be nullified by a handful of entry-level staff who are just the opposite. The reverse is also true.

So it goes with corporate values. The corporate conscience is nothing more than the collective values of the entire crew. It matters little that the CEO is a person of strength and great character if the remainder of the roster reads like a Prison Times Who's Who.

Actually, the character of the leadership matters a great deal. Organizations inevitably reflect the character of their leadership. As Michael Dukakis said in the 1988 presidential campaign, "A fish rots from its head down."

Putting a more optimistic face on it, the organization looks like the boss. So it's a fair question to ask, "What is the character of the boss?" and "Does the boss bring conscience to work or check it at the door?"

This isn't to say that anyone should take advantage of a leadership position to proselytize. That would be downright unfair and in some cases illegal. But it is to say that managers have a responsibility to bring more than their brains to the office. They should also bring their hearts.

Do organizations that are led from the heart fare better than those that are led by the dollar? Fair question although difficult to answer.

(This chapter is being written at 30,000 feet on an orange Boeing 737 captained, at least figuratively, by a fellow named Herb Kelleher. Herb's Alfred E. Newman face is currently smiling from the cover of *Fortune Magazine*, peering out from a headline that reads, "Is this America's Best CEO?" Stupid question. Of course, he is!)

Herb (and he doesn't do it alone) runs Southwest Airlines. Herb is one of the founders of the nation's sixth largest and only consistently profitable airline. It also may be America's most fun airline. No, it's probably the only fun airline. But then, that's Herb Kelleher, a man who seems to understand what Jim Miller so eloquently said, "When your job is fun, you never have to go to work."

Herb and crew have made Southwest Airlines a fun kind of place. At Southwest, fun is definitely a foundation value.

Every organization has foundation values; they just may be hidden.

How or why was your organization founded? To solve a problem? To give the founder an opportunity to be free from the heavy yoke of big business? To make money or make a difference?

And the biggest question may very well be: Is the organization living up to those values, that original vision?

No matter what were the original values or how noble they may have been, they are meaningless once forgotten. In the best of organizations, it is impossible to escape the foundation values. They are incorporated into nearly every part of corporate life.

In our little restaurant where we learned firsthand the value of values, we had a sign over the dining room door that simply read: "Don't forget to love one another." That unpretentious tag also closed out our radio commercials and frequently found its way to the bottom of employee memos.

It became my habit to verbally and visually remind the crew to love one another, most times when I would leave the store. Sometimes I would hold up two crossed fingers (a little sign my grandmother taught me as her shorthand method for telling me that I was special). Sometimes they would "salute" back, especially if they were too busy to talk. And that's how something as non-businesslike as love found its way into our "corporate culture."

Time Out for a Story

We never were completely sure about this "love one another" stuff. Sure, it seemed to play well, but there were times when as I left the restaurant and turned to remind the crew to love one another, I wasn't quite sure if they really bought into it.

One day a regular customer slid into a chair at my table while I wolfed a quick lunch. It was another of my short "bombing runs" to the restaurant. Sometimes I would run in just to show my support. This was especially common as our other businesses came to demand more and more of my time, which inevitably meant that the restaurant would get the short end of the stick. After all, the place was running smoothly, and the staff didn't need me as much as I needed to be needed.

So, this customer, a regular, a woman for whom we could prepare lunch the instant we spotted her car was crossing the bridge towards our place.

"May I join you?" she asked, after picking up her regular order.

"You already have. How's your day?"

"You know," she continued, ignoring my nothing of a question, "I've finally figured out why I like eating here."

This time she was inviting me to say, "Why?" so I did. "Why's that?"

"These people really love one another."

I made a joke about love being a necessity in such a small workspace, but to tell you the truth, I was mighty glad that it was so darned noticeable.

A few months after we sold the joint, when I was still going through withdrawal, Buns and I were sitting on the tailgate of our pickup, waiting for the local Christmas parade to find its way to us. A small truck pulled to a stop next to us. Out jumped a former employee, Dave Thomas. (Not the Dave Thomas of Wendy's fame but just as important to us.)

"Hi, guys! I want you to see my son," Dave said, proudly unbuckling a small child from his car seat and showing him to us. Naturally, we oohed and ahhhed. The fact of the matter is that we would have done the same thing had he been holding a Pekingese. Dave was sharing something personal and important.

Before we knew it, Dave was back in the truck about to pull into traffic. But what he did next makes our point. Suddenly he stopped, rolled down the window, leaned out, fingers crossed in our "love one another" salute, and said, "Hey, guys. Don't forget to love one another."

I'm not saying that every organization should count love as a key foundation value, but it wouldn't hurt. Actually, it's sufficient to say that your foundation values don't all have to be lifted from an MBA curriculum.

At Southwest Airlines, those folks actually seem to love one another and it doesn't seem to be what you would call a problem. Imagine, an organization where it's perfectly fine, actually encouraged to love one another—and the customers, too!

So how about your organization? Do you love one another? Heck, do you even like one another?

When we finally decided to organize the speaking and consulting business, we decided to formally do all the things we had been doing intuitively. This time, we actually did it on purpose. We created a plan of sorts, like we actually knew what we were doing. And why not? We were starting from scratch like many of today's companies will have to do no matter what year the "Since____" sign reads out front.

We gathered the troops and challenged them to build a company that would make us proud. Each of us had had experiences with organizations, where the foundation values had long since been forgotten. Only this time, we were determined to operate on really important values and not let them be lost in the hurry towards growth and profit. Here are the five foundation values that we chose:

Intelligent risk
Customer first
Love one another
Ownership
Consensus management

■ **Intelligent risk:** We had all seen or been a part of organizations that had turned a corporate back on opportunity simply because it required a little risk. Usually organizations miss opportunities not so much from the fear of losing a few bucks but from the fear of losing face if a failure is born from thinking out of the box. Well, to hell with the box and the risk and the potential for embarrassment. Look instead at the pain brought on by a critical mass of "could-have-beens."

■ **Customer first:** Loving on the customer had brought us to the party in the first place, and we thought that might be a good road on which to continue. Notice, please, that we didn't say, "customers first." We felt like the future of service was pointed in the direction of mass customization where every customer gets exactly what she wants, exactly the way she wants it. So, for us, it's "customer first." One at a time—and we hoped there would be lots of them!

■ **Love one another:** We had all been with organizations where more energy was spent either playing corporate politics (or defending against them) than was spent doing the things that really mattered. Besides, wouldn't it be nice to really enjoy the people on your team? Wouldn't it be great to know that every-one around you actually wanted to make you look good rather than looking for an opportunity to advance at your expense? And wouldn't it be great to work with folks who you would be honored to have as a guest in your home? We thought so and chose "love one another" to help remind us of those ideas as well as the fact that life is indeed short. Why not make the best of it?

■ **Ownership:** Why create an organization where a few get rich by keeping the majority poor? We believe that if we create an opportunity for everyone to be rewarded according to contri-bution, no one will be out looking for greener pastures. We wanted to create a place where it would truly be one-for-all and all-for-one. We're close but still not yet perfect. Still, it sure is nice to hear folks referring to the business as "my company."

■ **Consensus management:** This one is a pure, no-nonsense business decision. From the beginning, we realized that the best way to keep office expenses to a minimum was to keep the office to a minimum. That either means no-growth or work-at-home. You can't have at-home workers who feel no ownership and who need to be managed. So it was "kill all the managers" and hire only people who could and would manage themselves. We also had all felt the sting of autocratic management where good people rarely got better because they were never given a chance to fly on their own. That, we said, wouldn't happen to us.

So we created a real policy. Everyone is included in major decisions. We like the vote to be unanimous. We feel that if an idea isn't strong enough to deserve the unreserved support of the entire group, we may be better off waiting for an idea that does.

A Little Culture

The sum of your corporate values is your corporate culture. Period.

A consultant, who works with corporations on such issues as teamwork and culture, was approached by the CEO of one of her client companies. He said, "I've been hearing a lot about this corporate culture stuff and I was wondering, could you have one for us in time for a four o'clock meeting?"

She smiled and said, "Sir, I believe that you already have one."

And she was right. Like it or not, enlightened or downright medieval, your organization already has a culture. So before we go any further, try this exercise:

In twenty-five words or less, describe your corporate culture.

Values Are Everything

Ask yourself, for what do I want to be famous? How do you want to be known?

And here's the best question of all: For what would I be willing to die?

Big Guy was over the other night because Pops got drafted to help with science projects. We were working on a report about maps and weather. To begin, we walked out into the chilly night and stood facing north, his small hand in mine.

"Look, Big Guy. That's the North Star," I said. "The other stars move during the year, but the North Star stays in its place. If you can find the North Star and have a good chart, you can easily find the other stars and know where you are."

We fished a small compass out of his backpack, twisted the lens of our mini-Maglight, and yep, there it was, just like the universe ordered. It was floating above the horizon brighter than the distant glow of lights that we knew would be Kerrville, Texas.

MicroBranding Point
When you know what is really important, you will always know where you are.

■ ■ ■

For the latest tips, news, and worksheets to help with your MicroBranding efforts, visit www.tscottgross.com and choose the MicroBranding link.

CHAPTER EIGHT

1, 2, 3...Culture!

BY NOW, YOU MAY BE READY FOR A LITTLE HELP. Since recreating a corporate culture is not an instant process, let's go back to those key foundation values. Have you thought about the ones that are most appropriate for you?

Oops! I should have said, "most appropriate for your organization." As long as the toothpaste is out of the tube, if your personal values are not in fairly close harmony to those of your organization, you better put this book on hold while you polish your resume. If there is one sure way to be miserable on the job, it has to be to work where your principles are horribly out of sync with those of the organization.

To help you begin the process of thinking about foundation values, here are a few suggestions:

Honesty	Sharing	Ethical	People first
Trust	Pride	Old-fashioned	Innovation
Fair play	Professionalism	Low price	Aggressive
Casual	Quality	Integrity	Love
Family	Truth	Dependable	Customers first
Ownership	Community	Excellence	Empowered
Consensus	Open	Competitive	Flexibility
Leadership	Value	Responsible	Passion
Teamwork	Freedom	Caring	Intelligent risk

Armed with this list, next question probably is: How do I get started? Glad you asked.

You don't.

For a change in foundation values to take place, all of the key players must be represented, if not included, in the process. This means that a culture change is not something that can be decreed from corporate. Worse, ask the marketing department to whip up a jazzy new slogan, buy a ton of media time, and tell the world about the "All New ABC Group," and stand by for disastrous results.

I can't tell you how many times in a former life we rolled out new programs only to find out that what worked great in the lab and tested well in focus groups was miserably executed in the field. Every time, the problem was simply that there was zero buy-in from the folks who had to execute the plan on a daily basis. All we had accomplished with our scarce marketing budget was to run a few hundred thousand new customers into our stores so that they too could see that we weren't ready.

To get serious about a corporate culture change, you must start at the beginning and include everyone who can make or break the process.

Discovering Foundation Principles

While the trend is toward the "softer" values of ethical, human-centered business practices, criminal enterprise would have core values such as deception, theft, and selfishness.

What are the values of your organization? How are they different from the values that you wish to promote? If political infighting and feather-bedding are your current operating standards, list them and their rules for engagement. Filling in the blanks with warm fuzzy words won't have much, if any, impact on reality.

GUIDELINES FOR CREATING A VALUES STATEMENT

❑ Limit to a few "core" values.

❑ Keep them believable.

❑ Avoid proselytizing.

Remember that corporate values are the combined personal values of each member of the group—like it or not!

Example of a Values Statement

Our values statement is: We believe that the organization should exemplify the values of customer first, ownership, intelligent risk, and loving one another.

Now you try it! What are *your* foundation values?

The Beginning

Now that we've brought it up, just where is the beginning?

A fine gentleman and CEO of a major international corporation read my first book, *Positively Outrageous Service*, and was excited over the concept, deciding in the process that he would make his company a truly POS place to work and with which to do business. Nice thought.

However, he ended up calling my office in a near state of anger, frustrated over the undeniable fact that Positively Outrageous Service is much easier to talk about than to actually do. He had led the charge up the hill towards fun, customer-first service and was bewildered to discover that when he got to the top of the hill and turned to congratulate his troops, he was alone.

The problem was simple. Everyone had heard his call to POS but no one actually believed that: a) he really meant it, and b) it might make a difference for them.

He had failed to sell the concept. In fact, he had figured that since the idea was so simple, so attractive, so obviously the solution to the company ailments that everyone with half a brain would not only follow him up the hill but probably beat him there. Wrong.

The beginning step is this:

MicroBranding Point
Get everyone who has a stake in the process together and begin by asking them to clearly and candidly list the values that are currently shaping decision making.

Be prepared for the brutal truth. You may need to encourage the process by using standard brainstorming techniques that promote getting as many ideas on the board as possible without taking time to argue or be judgmental.

Since this first step can be a bit tough for some folks to swallow, give it time to settle in the minds of those who participated. Go back and ask if anyone would like to amend the results.

It may be that, once this far into the process, you may wish to stop. It's possible that although the results show your company to be far from an enlightened place to work and do business, the personalities involved, including your customer base, think things are just fine the way they are.

One good friend, who is the CEO of a major corporation, shared a somewhat unexpected outcome. As his company got deeper and deeper into its search to define corporate values and culture, it became apparent that not everyone was going to be comfortable with the results. One of the officers eventually stepped forward and tendered his resignation saying, "I agree with what you are trying to do. It's probably even the best thing for the company. But to tell you the truth, all of this customer first and empowerment stuff just isn't me."

Once you have and can deal with an accurate assessment of current corporate values, it's time to get to the fun part of the process, departing from reality long enough to begin thinking about how things would be in the best of all possible worlds.

It's time to begin thinking, perhaps for the first time intentionally, about what values you want to serve as the guiding principles of your company. Remember this must be a corporate effort that includes all of the stakeholders.

MicroBranding Point
The least productive approach to foundation values would be to order up a corporate retreat, negotiate a few rope-and-obstacle courses, and come home with a declaration to force-feed to the troops and hang on the lobby wall.

You'll find yourself with my friend, standing on the hilltop, alone.

Key Market Trends

There is little point in jumping ahead to creating mission statements until you first stop to think about where your enterprise may be heading if you continue on the current course. You may be focused on one direction, but which way is the market heading?

Do you remember arguing over who would get up to change the television channel? If you do, a) you are old, and b) you should hope that your sole source of income is not the sale of channel selector knobs.

The point is that there is no point to creating a mission statement for an organization without a market. What will happen to many of the medical research foundations if they ever find a cure? What will happen to the post office when the information superhighway makes the first-class letter a thing of the past and Federal Express and UPS capture the last of the parcel delivery business?

That's not a swipe at anyone, only a comment that the world is changing and that if you and your organization intend to be there when it's over, you had best begin to think beyond your mission. Mission has to be determined with respect to the market. Otherwise, you are wasting your time.

Here is a list of questions that needs to be explored:

■ Why do people use our product?

■ How could we make this product obsolete?

■ Why do we market to this customer in this way?

■ How is our customer likely to change?

■ What would constitute a breakthrough product or service?

■ What trends are forecast for our industry? What if they come true? What if they come earlier than expected?

■ What other products are a natural for this organization?

■ How would we answer the above questions concerning the individual internal processes in our organization?

■ What is the life expectancy of our product?

■ What position do we own or could we own?

Go ahead! Use your imagination to begin to explore. Play a good game of "What if?"

■ What if our supplier went out of business?

■ What if our costs doubled overnight?

■ What if our product went suddenly out of fashion or was linked to a disease?

■ What if we invented a product to compete with one of ours?

Get the idea? All of the above "what ifs" have happened. Can you think of the products or services that were involved? So why haven't you played "What if?" with your own products and services?

There are some tricks to playing "What if?" that will make the process more fun. Begin by dividing the process into three steps: List, Imagine, Respond.

❶ List everything you can imagine that could impact the situation. List every factor that could even remotely come into play such as people, organizations, things, events, even the weather.

❷ Imagine how each factor or combination of factors would influence your organization if they actually occurred.

❸ Dream up a response-scenario. Try not to let your natural inclination toward either optimism or pessimism shape your response ideas. It's best to try to think of both positive as well as negative outcomes for each of your scenarios.

Let's try an example: Benowix manufactures air fresheners from a type of pine oil found only in the rain forests of Brazil. The oil that is used must be processed in the Benowix plant within four weeks of harvest or it turns rancid. Benowix has been able to charge premium prices due in part to clever marketing that promised that a portion of each sale would be set aside for the preservation of the forests.

List Factors That Can Influence the Situation

■ Weather in the rain forests.

■ Ability to import natural oils from Brazil.

■ Containers for shipping.

■ Shipping rates.

■ Shipping speed.

■ Consumer fascination with rain forests.

■ Price stability.

■ No known artificial substitute.

■ Supply is available year-round.

Imagine How These Factors Could Influence You

■ Public loses interest in rain forests.

■ Brazil demands punitive higher export taxes in response to a U.S. embargo of Brazilian products due to noncooperation on drug smuggling.

■ Value of rain forest wood products soars due to spotted owl problems in the Pacific Northwest. This puts pressure to harvest entire tree.

■ *60 Minutes* reports on the unsuspected health hazards of artificial air fresheners.

■ A major competitor develops an inexpensive artificial substitute.

Responses to New Scenarios

■ Go out of business.

■ Look for an artificial substitute.

■ Consider raising the source trees in south Florida.

■ Purchase own rain forest acreage to guarantee supply.

■ Support key members of Congressional Trade Committee.

■ Diversify line and product type.

■ Consider partnerships with others who promote rain forest products.

These are just a few things and ways that Benowix could list, imagine, and respond to the hypothetical future. There are thousands of other trends that more generally influence the market and the future.

For now, this should give you the idea that the future can turn on a dime. Smart business leaders are always thinking about how such a turn—good, bad, or indifferent—could impact sales, profits, even the whole face of the organization.

There is simply no point in creating a mission statement without at least thinking about what the future may look like without your influence. When you have given yourself permission to list, imagine, and dream up a possible response, you are ready to begin thinking about how you might go about actually shaping the future.

■ ■ ■

For the latest tips, news, and worksheets to help
with your MicroBranding efforts, visit www.tscottgross.com
and choose the MicroBranding link.

C H A P T E R   N I N E

Mission, Vision and Goals

THE MISSION STATEMENT DEFINES THE PURPOSE OF THE ORGANIZATION. It should be written to serve as an internal slogan of purpose, a common goal serving as a center of focus.

CRITERIA FOR MISSION STATEMENT *

❑ Is short and easy to remember.

❑ Is in your face, always top of mind.

❑ Incorporates founding values.

❑ May incorporate key strategy.

❑ Mentions the product and the targeted customer.

❑ Notes the uniqueness of the organization.

*There are no rules that say you must meet all six; some are implied.

Examples of Mission Statements

"Protect and serve."

"Provide affordable family-style entertainment to visitors to Florida."

"Produce world-class transportation options for the discriminating consumer."

"Teach American business how to provide Positively Outrageous Service."

Some organizations begin the foundation values steps by creating the mission statement. We think that is okay but not the best approach. When the mission statement comes first, the values by necessity must come later. Others call the foundation values the "critical success factors." It may be a matter of six of one, but we don't think so.

> **MicroBranding Point**
> Start with your values, take a stand, tell us who you are or at least want to be, and then tell us why the organization was founded.

Whatever you do, draw your line in the sand sometime, somewhere.

Some values-driven organizations even opt to list critical success factors in addition to their foundation values. They look at these factors to be, not supplementary, but explanatory.

Your Mission, Mr. Phelps...

Your mission is to write a mission statement and not one of those goofy things the consultants teach you to write. It should follow the six criteria listed at the beginning of the chapter the most important of which are: short, in your face, and mentions the values.

While staying at a Washington, DC, hotel (a Sheraton, I believe), I asked the door man, "I need help with two things. First, I'd like directions to someplace casual for dinner that's within walking distance, preferably Italian."

"No problem, sir. What's the second item?"

"Well, I was wondering if you happen to have a mission statement for the hotel."

"I'm certain we have one somewhere. If you don't mind stopping by here when you return from dinner, I'll have it for you."

Now you have to admit, whatever their mission statement is, surely this guy was living it. But the funny thing was this: He was standing in front of a huge brass plaque with the mission statement on it! If the nail holding up this monument to consulting fees were to break, this poor fellow would be the first person on the planet to be killed by his mission statement.

MicroBranding Point
Having a mission statement and living it are two distinctly different things.

A mission statement should be short. It should be summarized in less than a dozen words. If yours is one of those two pager deals, trash it. Mission statements should be short enough to get your arms around. They should be something that in a simple phrase answers this important question: For what purpose does this brand exist?

You've seen them. You may even have one. You might even be the person who is guilty of creating one. Give up? Mission statements on wallet cards. Have you ever in your entire life seen an employee reach for his wallet and whip out a mission statement? Me neither! So why waste the card stock?

Mission statements should be in your face. Having a mission statement that never makes it beyond the plaque in the reception area is a waste of walnut, brass, and effort. Put your mission statement on a hat, print it on your name tag, or even write it on your sleeve!

Once the mission statement is done, check it against your values. Better yet, if you haven't given values serious thought, you might want to do so even before you attempt to define the mission.

There are a couple of country songs that are perfect for this moment. One has a verse that warns that unless you stand for something, you'll fall for anything. The other says that some of God's greatest gifts are unanswered prayers. Be certain of your values and never, ever compromise.

If family is important to you, then think before you take a job that has you traveling four nights a week. Let your values run your career and your business.

Some years ago a client called our office saying, "I understand you will be in Atlanta on the 18th. We've decided to hold our meeting on either the 17th or the 19th since you will already be in town."

"Great! I'll be flying commercial and there is a super cheap fare, you'll be paying half of almost nothing!"

"No. We don't want to be billed for airfare since you will already be town."

"I can't do that to the other client; that wouldn't be fair."

"Fine. We'll let you know, then."

The client left a message later that evening on our answering machine that they would "not be requiring my services."

A few days later, the client called again, to say that they had reconsidered and would split the fare.

"I'm sorry," I said at a time when we really could have used the income. "You asked me to do something that just isn't right. I don't think we have a fit here. I'll pass on this one, thanks."

Decide what you value and stick to it.

Multiple Missionality

I know, missionality is not a word. Spell check is reminding me at this very moment, but since part of my personal mission is to have fun, so what if I invent a word or two?

> **MicroBranding Point**
> You have different brands that are your life, so why not have different mission statements?

Are you married? If so, what are you going to do when after the first ten years or so you roll over one morning, see those big brown eyes, and, assuming it's not the German Shepherd, you think to yourself, "Why did I do this?" There, right then and there, would be a great time to have a personal mission statement.

We have three mission statements at our house: a personal mission statement, a professional mission statement, and a corporate mission statement. You should have a mission statement for each of your key brand identities.

I think I read that Stephen Covey spent the better part of six months having family meetings until they finally agreed they had the perfect mission statement for the Covey household. Well, pardon me for being judgmental but does that sound like fun to you? That Covey guy must be a barrel of laughs. Six months!

For you attention-impaired readers may I suggest this? Sit down, whip out a mission statement, get on with life, and—when you think of something better, change it!

In case you are interested, here are our three statements du jour:

■ **Personal:** Have fun and make the world a better place.

■ **Corporate:** Build a business that feels like retirement for us all.

■ **Professional:** Become the number one brand in customer service management.

Now, if you need a few more modifiers, go ahead and add them, just not to the main part of your mission statements.

Our modifiers are:

■ Take fun, challenging projects.

■ Work with honest, enthusiastic clients.

■ Get paid commensurate to our contribution.

■ Don't forget to love one another.

I opened the mail and fished out the latest CD-rom from Jeppeson. It contains all the charts I need to legally and safely fly our plane, Little Girl. The plane is beautiful and is decked out with a fabulous complement of avionics. But I won't so much as taxi across the field without my charts. Funny how few of us wouldn't dream of beginning a complicated project without complete instructions, but we blunder straight into marriage, career, and business without so much as a thought about where we are going and how we will get there. These steps, this "getting on focus" process, are critical!

By the way, before we decided to buy Little Girl, we first wrote a mission statement so that we would end up with an airplane that was mission capable for the type of flying we expected to do. Little Girl is not the fastest or roomiest aircraft on the planet, but it is faster than most, gets incredible fuel economy, and nearly exactly fits our mission profile. And that, to us, makes her perfect.

The Vision: I Can See Clearly

If mission answers the question, "What is my purpose or the purpose of this team or enterprise?" then vision answers the question, "What will this person or product be when it grows up?"

Or better yet, "How will I know when the mission has been accomplished?"

The vision statement is a picture of purpose fulfilled. The vision statement describes the desired future in clear terms, providing focus to the mission.

Without vision, you no doubt will wind up somewhere—you just don't know where.

The vision statement is for you. You can include it in your marketing materials. You can paste it into your business plan. But in the end, the vision is for you. It's there to keep you on track, to keep you focused on your quest for happiness as you define it.

It stands to reason that if you want to get to happiness, you must first decide what happiness is. Make no mistake; mission and vision are primarily for the purpose of ensuring happiness—yours.

Size Matters

For MicroBranders, there is one more important element to a vision statement, and that is a definition of the market you want to own. Key to the idea of MicroBranding is that we don't want to own the world—we just want to own our island.

Decide right up front how big your island is and we're not necessarily talking geography. You may decide to focus on photographers who use flash bulbs or industries with high customer contact or people with one short leg.

> **MicroBranding Point**
> Choose an island where you could achieve all of your goals and then set out to own all of the island. Leave the rest of the world to the other guys. So long as you own your island, there will be plenty to go around.

The vision statement could look like:

We will be number one in name recognition in chemically applied surfaces.

We will be the largest purveyor of Italian specialty products in the Southwest.

Our graduates will be represented in the leadership of a majority of Fortune 500 companies.

We will be the world leader in hair technology.

It is perfectly fine to let loose with a little optimism when you are writing the vision statement. Aim high but not so high that your vision is out of the realm of possibility. What you may not realize is exactly how much really is possible.

Marcia Wieder, author of *Making Your Dreams Come True*, had a modest goal. She wanted to become, we'll use the word "famous," but she may be a bit more modest, as she set out to become known as the leading expert in helping people realize their dreams. Of course, helping others realize their dreams would be the realization of hers.

How do you become famous? Well, you would know if you had seen Marcia on *Oprah, Montel Williams*, and most of the other national talk shows. Get the point? Even if you are a four-foot-something dynamo from San Francisco, you can make your dreams come true. But not unless you dream them first!

Begin by sitting down with the folks you trust and dream about what is or could be possible. Colonel Sanders didn't make his mark until a time in his life when most men are winding down. The same is true for Ray Kroc and a host of other winners. So go ahead! Create a vision and don't be stingy with yourself. You may aim too high and miss. Worse, you could aim too low and hit.

Meigs

Unless you live in Chicago or are one of the few unrepentant geeks flying Flight Simulator software, you have no idea what a Meigs is. Well, a Meigs is a short, stubby airfield clinging to the shore of Lake Michigan at Chicago. Mayor Daly, that's the son of, wants to close Meigs Field. He says it's too much real estate to be tied up by the flying few. Instead, he wants to turn it into a public park.

Yeah, right. I've got a dollar that says it won't be two shakes after the field is gone that Meigs begins to host a gambling operation.

No matter what happens, Meigs will always be special to me. It taught me the power of vision.

When I turned forty, our son gave me a copy of MicroSoft's Flight Simulator program. Maybe it was a hint that I needed to do more guy things, but whatever the motivation, it was a perfect gift. While I was flying in the back of an MD-80, I'd have the old notebook computer lit up and virtually piloting a Cessna 172 into beautiful Meigs Field.

Meigs is the default airport in the program. When you power up, you are sitting in a Cessna high wing 172, engine running, staring right down the center line of Meigs runway 36.

My son bought me the program figuring I would buy the joystick and rudder pedals necessary to actually land that little airplane once you got the darned thing airborne. But I'm cheap and besides there isn't a good way to travel with all the extras, so I would launch that little plane, fly around the Chicago skyline, and then, ninety-nine times out of a hundred, crash back onto Meigs Field.

The saying that practice makes perfect misses the mark. It should have been *perfect* practice makes perfect. So it follows that crashing a 172 repeatedly at Meigs Field cannot help but make one good at—crashing 172s at Meigs Field!

Who would guess that one day, after my practice of crashing hundreds of times, I would actually land a real, not virtual, aircraft at Meigs Field!

There we were. Several thousand feet up and cruising effortlessly just south of Chicago. We followed the coastline of Lake Michigan northbound for ten minutes or so before spotting that all too familiar patch of concrete and fresh mown grass that is Meigs Field. I was about to land my first *real* plane on Meigs.

We listened to the automated weather and decided to land to the south to take advantage of the winds. Tower advised us to join a left downwind and fly parallel to the airstrip from south to north and set up for a landing on runway 18, exactly opposite from how I was used to seeing Meigs.

From downwind I watched the field slide by thinking all the while about the hundreds of times I had mentally made, and failed, this very same landing.

The field looked like it had been designed by MicroSoft—only shorter by a shot. We turned onto our base leg of the pattern and found ourselves looking windscreen to window with the towering skyscrapers of Chicago. If we kept our course, my guess is we would have impacted somewhere about the 40th floor!

I turned final, notified the tower we had done so, and reflected on the irony of this part of the maneuver being called final. A sailboat with a tall mast slid in front of us making for the freedom of the open lake waters; I wished I had taken up sailing.

And then there it was. The shortest runway I had ever seen.

We hit and bounced and then hit and bounced again. At the far end of the runway, which was now looking like the near end of the runway, there was nothing to see except more of Lake Michigan. I stomped on the brakes and waited for an eternity until finally we stopped. Surprise! We had more than half of the runway left. Meigs's unusually wide runway presents an optical illusion that shouts, "short, short, short!"

But there is plenty of runway.

On the ramp, I shut down the engine, secured the controls, and reached deep into my briefcase until I could fish out my copy of Flight Simulator. I tipped the ramp agent a five spot and slipped him a computer program for which I would have no further use.

MicroBranding Point
A clear vision is what holds the dream in place. Start without a vision and your branding efforts will be an eternal surprise.

Goal Card Service:
Goals, Objectives and Strategies

To clear the distinction, the mission statement is not a goal statement.

The mission statement answers the question, "Why was this organization formed?" and the vision statement answers, "How do we want the future to look?"

The goal statement answers a related but still different question, "What steps must we take to achieve our vision?"

Goals should be written, not just for the overall organization but for individual departments and sections. A general rule is that goals should be written at the level of execution.

Effective goals are:

■ Short and clear.

■ In your face.

■ Tied to the mission.

Too many organizations create goals that read like *War and Peace*, too long and cumbersome for mortals to remember or repeat let alone internalize. Human beings need goals that they can get their arms around.

"Uncle Sam Needs You" was a great slogan because it was all normal people needed as both a summary of the situation and a call to action.

And calling people to action is exactly what an effective goal statement must do.

"At Ford, quality is…"

You instinctively filled in the blanks, didn't you? You knew that "At Ford, Quality is Job 1."

If you know Ford's goal statement, why don't you know yours?

Because either you don't have one, the greatest possibility, or you have one but it's too awkward to remember. When asked their company mission, vision, and goal statements, most people just smile at you like a tree full of owls or, if they actually have an answer, they must rummage through their wallet to find the little laminated card that the consultant left with them. (We've done that, too, just in case you assumed that we actually had earned the right to cast the first stone.)

Objectives are the little things that you do every day to get you closer to your goals. We like to say that objectives are the things that you do on a daily basis that make the place better than it was before you got there. And if things aren't better when you leave, why did you show up at all? Do us all a favor and stay home!

There should be performance objectives set at, not for, all levels. And everyone should be required to have a current list of objectives for the day, the week, and the near term. More about this later.

Strategies are quite another animal. Strategies are the little plans or conduct required to achieve the goals. Strategies are such things as:

■ Guarantee quality.

■ Win the Baldrige Award.

■ Participate in industry organizations.

■ Hire the top talent in your industry.

■ Create a world-class retail space.

> **MicroBranding Point**
> Strategy is how we conduct ourselves and our business to enable us to achieve our objectives, which are smaller goals that must be achieved on the way to our larger vision.

Our goals help us realize our mission, our reason for existence. Our vision is our dream of how the world will look when we have achieved our mission.

■ ■ ■

For the latest tips, news, and worksheets to help
with your MicroBranding efforts, visit www.tscottgross.com
and choose the MicroBranding link.

CHAPTER TEN

A Fine Position

Snapshot...Here I Am!

ONCE YOU HAVE THE VALUES, MISSION, AND VISION THOROUGHLY IN HAND, better take a snapshot, a quick picture of where you are right this minute.

> *"A small but growing landscape contractor just beginning to be recognized as a leader in design."*

> *"A unit in a large chain of retailers, we are in the middle of the pack of area retailers. We are known for our children's fashions and could benefit from positive PR."*

> *"A pediatrician new to the area with most new clientele coming from the Yellow Pages. Few of our new patients come from referrals, and fewer still come from the nearby residential development, which is geared for new families. We could benefit from more referrals and a better awareness of our location."*

Why is it important to take a snapshot? Well, few business people can accurately describe their standing in the marketplace. Until you can, your efforts will be unfocused and often off target. Not exactly the hallmark of a MicroBrander.

Not knowing who and where you are can be a killer. You can have the latest technology and the best training, but if you wander off course or worse, get lost and not even know it, you can get killed in a competitive environment.

CFIT

If you are a pilot, you might recognize CFIT as an abbreviation for controlled flight into terrain. It means simply that some hapless pilot flew a perfectly capable airplane straight into the ground, or as is more often the case, the side of a mountain.

How do you do that?

You lose awareness of where you are. As simple and as tragic as that.

In December 1995, an American Airlines crew en route to Cali, Colombia, flew a Boeing 757 into a mountainside a mere one hundred feet short of the nine-thousand-foot peak. All but four of the 163 on board were killed. How did this happen? How did a highly trained crew fly an incredible piece of technology into the ground? The same way otherwise smart people fly perfectly good business models straight into the dumper: They lost track of where they are.

In the case of American Flight 965, two similar navigational aids confused the crew. They ignored numerous cues to discontinue the approach, and, like too many in business, they were in a hurry. The controller had given them a timesaving direct approach, and human nature just wouldn't let them do more than soldier on, even when their intuition was probably screaming "Pull up! Pull up!"

The flight had gone well until a short chain of events, a few simple, perhaps forgivable miscalculations put the outcome in jeopardy without the crew being aware. Finally, small things snowballed into one fireball of twisted aluminum high in the mountains of Colombia.

Flying a business or a brand requires that same pinpoint sense of position as flying an airplane in instrument meteorological conditions. It's not usually one little thing that gets you. It's the combination.

You have to begin with knowing exactly where you are and just as exactly where you are going. Perhaps no lives are directly at risk, but it's for certain that fortunes and livelihoods are. This is precisely why smart business people take the time and effort to think about values, mission, vision, position, and snapshot—to keep themselves from flying straight into a figurative mountainside.

Tighten It Up

There is hardly anything more important to your MicroBranding efforts than settling on a good, no, make that great tag line. A tag line is your position statement brought to life.

In six or seven words, you want to tell what you do, who you do it for, and, if there are words to burn, why you are the best choice. It's hard to imagine that so few words could work so hard, but they can.

There are no wasted words in a great tag line. Every word works and works hard. One trick of the trade is to leave out words that the reader or listener is likely to fill in without thinking.

Another trick is to use words that can be interpreted more than one way. Here's a favorite from Home Hardware in Canada, which has the tag line, "Help is close to home." Just look at that! In one well-built phrase, there are several important messages:

■ Home Hardware is the place to go for help—they are experts.

■ Home Hardware is like being at home.

■ Help will be given freely if you go to Home Hardware.

Here's another great one from Canada's Winners department store: "Winners! It's a new store every day!" You can't improve on this one. Here are my interpretations:

■ There is always something new to see at Winners.

■ You can go to Winners every day and not get bored.

■ Winners is a new store.

■ There are shopping surprises at Winners.

Notice how this one plays along so well with the company name. "Visa: everywhere you want to be." A visa is your permission to travel to exotic locations, and now this Visa is telling you that it will be there no matter where you go. Visa could be talking about geography in the literal sense, but it could just as easily be talking metaphorically. Wherever you go in your career or life, Visa'll be there for you.

You may have to look closely to see the implied suggestion that the other guys—American Express, MasterCard, and Discover—won't be there.

In five killer words, we got the whole enchilada—the who, what, when, and where of Visa. We even got to lean against the competition without so much as mentioning their names.

Looking through the local phone book I see that most businesses do not have tag lines. They are doing little or nothing to help position themselves. Leave it up to the customer, and you get what you deserve.

There are a few bright spots. How about:

Hill Country Mercantile—from rustic to ritzy.

Propane—the driving, cooking, heating, save-you-money clean air fuel. (Whew!)

Omega—local Internet service provider.

Brooks Paving—large or small jobs.

Terminex—no bugs, no hassles. Also—the complete solution from your neighborhood professionals.

Accents—women's "quality" resale fashions.

Back up and take another look at the tag line for Terminex. It's interesting to note that in this case, the company name doesn't tell you much without the tag line. But with it, the name is killer, literally! Terminex. If that doesn't tell you that a whole lot of bugs are going to bite the dust, I can't imagine what would. All by itself there isn't much of a message, when it comes to creepy crawlies.

But "no bugs, no hassles," that's a work of art. In a record short four words, you know there won't be any bugs when the Terminex crew gets done and that they will do all the work. That "no hassles" part of the tag pulls at least half of the weight telling you in two words (two words!)

that Terminex makes doing business with them easy—and that may not be true if you call the other guys!

For some reason, Terminex's marketing guys could not decide on a tag line. So it looks as if they kept the top two contenders, one from the agency and another from the boss. (Well, that's my guess.) Which of the two do you think works harder? My money goes to "no bugs, no hassles." When it comes to bug genocide, that's the way I like it. Kill 'em all and don't bother me with the details.

The longer version doesn't tell us nearly as much as the short one. "The complete solution from your neighborhood professionals." What's that all about? They solve everything? We don't know what it is, but they are professional when it comes to solving whatever it is. They live in your neighborhood, so don't screw up. They're watching!

Sometimes your business name *is* your tag line but notice that the following names are generic, category defining names (which is okay as long as you are alone in an isolated market).

Super Sound Muffler Center

The Vision Source

Kerrville Cancer Center

U-Haul

Off-Road Truck Accessories

Cowboy Steakhouse

The best way to learn about tag lines is to pay attention. As Yogi said, "You can see a lot by looking." Well, here's what to look for: Tag lines that convey lots of message in little space.

Tag lines should, like great brands, serve as mental shortcuts that tell you what the product does, who it does it for, and why it's the best choice.

Keep them to as few words as possible. Use the right words and the reader or viewer will happily fill in the message, often more message than you ever imagined.

Sometimes you don't even need words.

We like to work with Angel Flight, an organization that connects owners of private and corporate aircraft with patients in need of long distance transportation. We fly all sorts of folks. Our most recent passengers were an eight-year-old boy recovering from major soft palate surgery and his mom.

At the FBO (fixed based operator), we fueled the aircraft and greeted our customers, trying as best as our limited Spanish would allow to introduce ourselves and make them feel comfortable. As we walked to the plane, a pilot who had been watching this mini-drama unfold caught Buns' eye. He applauded silently, hands barely touching but hearts fully engaged as he bid us safe journey and good spirits.

More thought needs fewer words.

McDonald's—we love to see you smile.

FedEx—when it absolutely, positively has to be there overnight.

Sprint—pin drop.

Gateway—you have a friend in the country.

Campbell's Soup—soup is good food. (But we all remember—Mmm Mmm Good!)

NBC—America's news leader.

WorldCom—Generation D.

Compaq—innovation technology.

Chicken Soup—for the soul.

Montana—big sky country.

Southwest Airlines—freedom to fly.

Ernst & Young—from thought to finish.

Parliament—out of the clear blue (cigarettes in a blue package).

Barnes & Noble—books as far as the mind can reach.

CNN Headline New—the get-to-the-point network.

Staples—the office super store.

La Frontera—Mex-Mex food.

Notice that one of the tag lines above is not a phrase. It's an image. Sprint tells you everything you need to know about its service without so much as a single word. Its technology is so good you can hear a pin drop.

And check out CNN, the get-to-the-point network. That's not the most romantic tag line nor does it grab you emotionally. But then, CNN is not the network you watch for romance or emotion. CNN gives you all the gotta-have-news in thirty minutes—and then it gives you the same news again. CNN doesn't expect you to make an evening of it. So its reporters get to the point. Great tag line!

A great tag line mentions the unique selling proposition (USP). In a few words, it lets the customer know precisely why this brand is the brand of choice.

"We love to see you smile" is a great tag line, but could it be better? Look at La Frontera and the tag line, "Mex-Mex food." In three words, you know what makes La Frontera unique.

Down the street, owning an entirely different position in the same market, is the decidedly California Chevy's where the USP is "Fresh Mex Food."

While you are in the kitchen whipping up a fresh tag line for your brand, remember to think like a customer. Remember, the position statement tells what *you* want the market to think, but it's not necessarily a reflection of reality, the real position that you own. You could try to shape the market with your tag line but why not let the market do the shaping, especially if it is already heading in your direction?

Kitchen Aid did just that when it created a new campaign for its counter-top appliance division. Research showed that consumers weren't interested in simply having another appliance. Their interest was the food. The appliance was only a means to an end. Sort of puts things in a different perspective, doesn't it?

One print Kitchen Aid ad featured lemon souffle pancakes—food! Smaller images of the appliances used to prepare the dish seemed to be almost incidental—exactly how consumers think! A Web site was also listed inviting the reader to click for the recipe. Did it work? The company reported double digit growth in the first six months.

Who's on First?

There is one critical thing to know about position: Whoever grabs a position first pretty much owns it forever. It is difficult to steal a position owned by someone else, but get this: You don't have to be first to own the position.

Puzzled? I'll explain.

Say that you own an independent building supply center in a small town. Based on feedback from the contractors who do business with you, you think free delivery would be a significant competitive advantage. So you go for it.

Scenario one. You begin to offer free delivery and you invest in a campaign to let the market know. You even adopt as your slogan, "We Really Deliver—And It's Free!" In a matter of months, the world as you know it grants you the position of free delivery.

Since positioning is always against someone or something, you might improve on the slogan by saying, "The Store that Delivers—Free!" This implies that the other stores don't deliver.

Your campaign is a success, and your competition notices. What can they do? You own the position. The best they could do would be, "We Deliver—Too!" Not good.

Your competition will have to come up with a different niche, unless you made a mistake and never grabbed it in the first place.

That leads us to scenario two. You offer free delivery but don't aggressively capture the position. You deliver but don't tell the market. Now your competitor sees your success and goes for the position with the slogan, "Number One in Free Delivery." Now who owns delivery?

The first to grab a position owns it.

MicroBranding Point
Position is in the mind of the collective market. Reality hardly counts.

Position vs. Positioning

A statement describing how you want your brand to be positioned in the mind of the customer is your position statement. Take your time; be as wordy as you need to be. Just think it through carefully.

Beware: If the gap between your position statement and your position is too great, your customers won't make the leap. If you discover that where you are is too far from where you think you'd like to go, go somewhere else! While it may be unreasonable to think your brand could represent the world's greatest, it may also be unnecessary. Just be the best in your tightly defined micro-market. Strive for that, and the customer is likely to follow, if not actually help!

A position is always compared to or against other brands. It might read as simply as: "Positively Outrageous Service will become the number one brand of customer service management. It will be recognized as the name to call when meeting planners want a humorous yet information packed presentation at conferences of all kinds. POS will be first in the minds of managers and corporate trainers when thinking about their service training needs. It will be regarded more highly than service."

MicroBranding Point #1
The position statement describes the position you want to own.

MicroBranding Point #2
Positioning describes the mental real estate you actually hold.

This is an example of positioning: "Many meeting planners and corporate execs are aware of Positively Outrageous Service. It enjoys a modicum of national recognition but would benefit from additional media exposure, positioned against speakers who use PowerPoint."

Whatever you do, stand for one thing and one thing only that will help you stand out in the market. Focus. In this one instance, it is best to narrow your position.

Make certain that the one thing that makes you stand out is also a competitive advantage.

> **MicroBranding Point**
> Advantage is always defined by the customer.

The "Other" Position

It's easy to forget that a MicroBrand applies just as easily to a personal relationship as it does to relationships with customers. It even applies to relationships we have with peers and employers. Take a moment to ask (and answer) these important questions:

- What position do you own with your spouse? Is it the one you want?

- If you have children, where do you stand with them? Do you need to adjust?

- How would your peers define your position with them?

- What position do you own with the boss? Is it a position that builds a career?

In each of the above, keep in mind that the position you actually own is not likely to mirror the position you want to own. Worse than having a gap between your personal position statement and your position is not knowing the what and why of the difference. As in all things, marketing progress begins when you ask.

That Killer *You* — Positioning Your Personal Brand

Here's the deal. If you want to stand out, it would be helpful if you or your product didn't look or act like every other similar offering on the market. As a speaker who works in the area of customer service management, why would anyone pay big bucks to fly my backside halfway across the continent if all I delivered was what any junior college professor could do given a couple of hours to prepare? They wouldn't.

But if they want Positively Outrageous Service, well, there's only one place in the whole wide world that you can get the genuine Mr. POS himself. Right here.

I was way ahead of schedule one wintry day at Chicago's Midway Airport so I sprang for a *USA Today* and took a chance on surviving breakfast. At the cash register, an older woman who was obviously a supervisor was huddled with two young women in the uniform of the snack shop.

"Okay, who called this meeting and why wasn't I invited?" I jumped feet first into the conversation with a smile.

"Oh, we were just having a little life lesson..."

"Let me guess. You can't figure out why you have to work such crummy hours for next to nothing." The looks told me I was right on target. The supervisor smiled and stepped back leaving the heavy lifting to me.

"Well, here's the deal. If you want to make more money, you have to be able to do something that not just anyone can do. If you want to drop out of school, that's a great idea so long as you don't mind driving an old car and getting paid dirt for the privilege of working these godawful hours."

The supervisor gave the girls an I-told-you-so look and said, "Amazing! Just when I needed somebody's dad, one appeared." As she walked off, she turned once more to the girls and capped the conversation saying, "See?"

Tom What's-His-Name

Okay, it was Tom Peters, the *In Search of Excellence* guy who said something to the effect that your "career should be a steady diet of interesting, challenging, provocative projects." Good idea.

Here's a better one: Put yourself someplace lucky.

Say you're sixteen and looking for a job. What do you really want? A car with an awesome stereo and cool tires and rims. That's normal, and so it is also normal that you will walk down the street until you get to the first fast food joint with a help wanted sign. Bingo, a career!

Careers are almost a form of religion. Ask your parents why they are Baptist or Catholic or Unitarian and they will hem and haw while they are trying to figure that out for themselves. The truth is a whole lot of Methodists had Methodist parents, and the same is true for the rest of them.

Now, ask your dad why he chose his career and somewhere in the story you will hear how he had this part-time job or a friend of a friend or some other goofy introduction that somehow caused him to be delivering mail for the next thirty years.

> **MicroBranding Point #1**
> When it comes to careers, there are no small decisions.
>
> **MicroBranding Point #2**
> If you have to work somewhere, put yourself someplace where you are likely to meet people who can help you or teach you or both.

I started my working life standing on an egg crate washing dishes at a Frisch's Big Boy Restaurant in Dayton, Ohio. Good, honest work. And, surprise, surprise! I ended up spending the next thirty-three years in the restaurant business. What would have happened if my dad had been a doctor or knew a doctor and I had wound up washing dishes or doing clean up in a hospital?

If you have to work somewhere, why not give it some thought? Put yourself where you might have a chance to learn something interesting. Put yourself where you will be in contact with people who are going places. If you want to be an interesting person, it helps to hang out with interesting people.

A Little Culture, Please

I saw a guy in the grocery the other day with a tattoo that said, "Selena Forever." Here was a guy who had marked his body for life in memory of a deceased Tejano musician. Would you do that?

While walking the streets of a trendy Atlanta neighborhood, we saw a little boy, about age four, with an earring? Would you do that?

While eating at a nearby greasy spoon, we watched a mother and grandmother light up in front of their eight-year-old daughter/granddaughter. Would you do that?

While working with the Phoenix Fire Department, we were called to a multiple-casualty scene. The incident commander assigned our company to a fourteen-year-old boy who had been severely injured. There were four medics in our group. Two took waist up, two waist down. I got the right leg.

I took my bandage shears and started up the leg of his jeans so I could perform my part of the assessment and treatment. Imagine my horror when I cut to the crotch of his pants only to see his left knee! It took me a moment to figure that it was the sag look. His knee was in the right place. It was his pants that were, according to my culture, too low!

Culture has a huge influence on how our products and services are perceived. Here in south Texas, it's easy to find fresh tortillas in the grocery. It's part of our culture. And isn't it interesting that you don't have to be Hispanic to consider tortillas a part of your culture?

Your job is to discover how culture is impacting how your brand message is being received.

Culture Counts

In 1970, 78 percent of the U.S. population returned their census forms. By 1990, returns barely reached 65 percent, and forecasters were predicting that without drastic intervention, the best that could be expected in the 2000 census would be a paltry 55 percent. So for the first time in history, the U.S. Census Bureau launched a paid advertising campaign.

The problem was that busy people didn't understand why the census was important. To many Americans, the census was a useless interruption, another form of government intrusion. You could say that the census was poorly positioned.

A tag line for the campaign was created: "This is your future. Don't leave it blank." But here is where the genius comes in, and here is the lesson for MicroBranders. A different tag line, call it positioning, was created for different target markets.

For example, blacks are known for their strong sense of identity to the group. Their tag line was, "This is our future. Don't leave it blank." Native Americans are likely to think in terms of heritage both in the sense of history and history to be. Their tag line was,

"Generations are counting on this. Don't leave it blank."

When you think about positioning your brand, don't think so much about the mental space you want to fill. Think about the mental space available!

■ ■ ■

For the latest tips, news, and worksheets to help
with your MicroBranding efforts, visit www.tscottgross.com
and choose the MicroBranding link.

CHAPTER ELEVEN

Conscious Creation

Creating the B.I.G. Idea
(Brand Identity Genius)

HOW MANY B.I.G. IDEAS DO YOU NEED? One will do just nicely. We had a neighbor who retired early because he decided that there was a market for glow-in-the-dark condoms. Someone invented the clapper, and I actually know someone who has one. She uses it to turn on her Christmas tree lights and avoids having to crawl under the tree. Unfortunately, her poodle has learned that a loud bark is good for holiday entertainment!

While there are some ideas that are truly revolutionary, most B.I.G. ideas are simply evolutionary, a step further along an already beaten path. Tom Monahans didn't invent pizza delivery. He invented thirty minutes or free pizza delivery.

Herb Kelleher didn't invent air travel, but he added the innovation of point-to-point service at a time when the trend was taking the other guys, along with their reluctant passengers, to hub and spoke terminals.

This morning after sweating in our home gym we tossed diet to the winds and drove to the Donut Palace. Donut Palace didn't invent donuts or donut holes, but it is known far and wide for giving a couple of donut holes along with your order. How big of an idea do you really need? The Donut Palace was loaded!

Sometimes You Just Get Lucky— Developing the Killer App

The B.I.G. idea that got us started is Positively Outrageous Service. POS, as we call it around the office, was part perspiration, a touch of inspiration, and a hefty dose of plain old luck.

Here's the thing about getting lucky. It helps to pay attention. I like the definition that says luck is when preparation meets opportunity. When opportunity finally knocks, it helps if you, a) have the key to the door, and b) are listening!

I was in San Francisco speaking to a group of movie theater operators when I received a phone call from a woman starting a speakers bureau.

"What are you doing in San Francisco?"

"I'm speaking to movie theater operators."

"What about?"

"Customer service and," I added on a whim, "showmanship. I'm probably the only guy in America who speaks on showmanship."

Now, I don't know if she was impressed, but I was! I heard a knock at the door. It was opportunity. I grabbed one of the tiny pencils operators of cheap hotels steal from miniature golf courses and wrote s-h-o-w-m-a-n-s-h-i-p on the pad by the phone. "Hmmm, the only guy speaking on showmanship. That ought to be good for something," I thought.

"What do you call your presentation?"

Actually, I hadn't given it a name. Customer Service, I supposed. "Outrageous Service," I said!

"Can you write that up? I have a client who is going to love that!"

A couple of days later I was noodling the first draft of the keynote, "Outrageous Service," on a yellow pad from a perch on a stool in our kitchen when the phone rang. It was an old friend from Arby's.

"I want you to come and speak to us on customer service. What do you have?"

"Funny you should ask. I am just now writing up something I call Outrageous Service."

"That sounds perfect. Do that."

"Don't you want to know what it's about?"

"I like the name. Just do that."

Hanging up the phone, I said to Buns, "I think this is our home run idea. People seem to love this title!"

The Arby's presentation went well and turned into a few additional presentations. I was right; people loved the title and the material that went with it. But here is the thing about titles; they open the door to the material. Hide the best material or product behind a poor title, and it will remain hidden. Names and titles are the critical opening step when it comes to discovering your B. I.G. idea.

In a few short months, we once again lucked out and found ourselves with a contract to write a book. Remember, at this time the title was *Outrageous Service*, and that's where we ran into our first opportunity to blow it big time.

We were just beginning the manuscript, still feeling our way around the concept, when the publisher called.

"We had our sales meeting today. Everyone loves the idea of the book, but we're not too crazy about the title."

Uh, oh! Trouble.

"We think Outrageous Service is too negative. People might think it's a book about bad service, and we want a book about good service. So we want to change the name."

First-time author meets publisher who is holding the keys to the kingdom.

"What do you have in mind?"

"We want to call it, *How to Give Really Good Service*."

Oh. My. God. I'm dead meat.

"Outrageous is a really important word. Can I call you tomorrow with a suggestion?" I asked.

"Tomorrow. But then we have to go to catalogue if we intend to get this book out in the spring."

Walking the dog that afternoon, I recounted the conversation with Buns.

"The publisher doesn't like the title *Outrageous Service*. Says it's too negative."

"Well then," Buns replied, "why don't we just call it *Positively Outrageous Service?*"

Go figure. Simple. A B.I.G. idea was born.

If you weren't born smart, no matter. It truly is better to be lucky than good, and you will get a whole lot luckier if you will work hard and listen intently.

A FEW OF THE BIGGEST B.I.G. IDEAS

Progressive Insurance—mobile claims service
Southwest Airlines—point-to-point air service
Starbucks—coffee as an experience
Amazon.com—retailing on the Internet
MicroSoft— graphic user interface
FedEx—overnight delivery service via a hub
Napster—music theft over the Internet
Sesame Street—television as teacher
Weather Channel—24-hour weather
Dell— factory-direct computers

And here's a *little* B.I.G. idea. Research showed that heavy users of Kool-Aid like to do more than simply add water to the powdery product. They like to customize it. Now who'da thought "customized Kool-Aid?" Apparently customers!

Research also showed that the less-than-heavy users of Kool-Aid are more likely to do their socializing out of the house.

How do you put those two ideas together? An ad campaign that featured friends and family in a social setting talking about how they like to customize their Kool-Aid.

For the MicroBrander, there is one powerful lesson. Listen to your customers. They might give you B.I.G. ideas!

To create your B.I.G. idea, you might want to start with a little idea or maybe just an old idea. There really aren't as many new ideas as there are variations on a theme. Engineers call the process parallel analysis.

The idea is to find dissimilar industries with problems that are similar to yours. See how they solved the problem or at least how they view the problem. Chances are there will be a new idea (to you) that you can adapt or adopt for your situation.

For example, when we ran our fried chicken franchise, we noticed the airlines and their customer loyalty programs, called frequent flyer programs. We started a Frequent Fryer program. Okay, so that wasn't a big B.I.G. idea, but you get the point: parallel analysis.

Here are four more interesting ideas to start the thinking:

■ Avoid Michael Jackson Change.

■ Add complexity to make things simple.

■ Remember that incompetence foils innovation.

■ Give customers an experience—they want one.

Mr. Jackson

I don't really know a thing about Michael Jackson, but I like to tease that while each of his surgeries made sense, when you put them all on one face, you end up with Latoya.

What I mean is that change for the sake of change can have drastically unintended consequences. Any one change might, by itself, make perfectly good sense. But a whole series of changes considered and made individually might combine for a totally unintended and possible unwanted result!

When you are creating your B.I.G. idea, make sure that you think about the context in which your B.I.G. idea will be put to use.

K.I.C.K.

People like to say, KISS—keep it simple, stupid. They have it all wrong. Here's why. It's possible to make things simpler by first increasing complexity. I say, KICK—keep it complicated, kid!

There is more to efficiency than can be measured with a stopwatch. Efficiency has to take into account all of the costs in addition to the expense of time. Sometimes we fail to consider the expense of morale. Sometimes we fail to account for the toll extracted when intelligent human beings, instead of being challenged to think, are denied the opportunity to think and are saddled with boring, repetitious tasks that numb the brain and stifle the chance of future innovative thinking.

Look at modern food service. We know one almost client in the food business that decided to cut costs by moving the production of its killer dinner rolls from fresh-baked in the units to commissary-supplied as a bake-off product. Now, with no mixing or proofing in-store, bakers simply popped pre-baked rolls into the oven just long enough for them to brown. The end product was almost as good and considerably more consistent.

Too bad.

Management followed one stunt with another substituting pre-baked pies for fresh-baked. Again, almost as good.

Thrilled with fractional cents of lowered costs, management went on a hunt in search of other items that could be out-sourced and still be almost as good, considerably more consistent, and, of course, even less expensive.

They did this until once proud in-store cooks and bakers lost the thrill of creating wonderful, delicious meals with local variations. The chain was soon not even almost as good as it had been, and customers and employees soon found other places to work and eat.

Incompetence Foils Innovation

While researching a book on adventure in the workplace, I learned an interesting lesson. Competence holds fear at bay. When people are confident in their training and skills, they are more likely to act positively under stressful conditions.

I first got a look at this concept in action late one night when, as a volunteer EMT, I was called to the scene of a stabbing. Dispatch had warned that the scene was potentially dangerous even going so far as to suggest that the perpetrator might still be present. We were instructed to get close to the scene and wait until the sheriff's deputy had reduced the potential for violence. At least, that was the plan.

As luck would have it, we rounded the dark corner looking for the address and suddenly found ourselves smack dab in the middle of a whole host of those folks you talk about when you say, "I wouldn't want to meet him in a dark alley."

Well, we were in the dark alley and that mythical fellow was right there with his equally threatening friends.

I was looking for the sheriff when Buns said, "He twitched! He's alive!"

Swell.

So out I bailed, trauma kit in hand, and started to work the victim.

I started chest compressions while attempting to bag him. As fast as I pumped the heart, blood spurted from everywhere. I was breathing for this guy, and he was staring back with eyes that would not see. A voice somewhere near my right ear shouted, "Don't let him die, dude!"

My first thought was that these folks weren't so bad after all. My second thought was, "I am the only one standing between him and a murder rap. No wonder he wants me to save this character."

I lived but the patient did not. Later, back home in my own safe bed, Buns's hand found mine and she asked, "Were you afraid?"

Yeah. Of course, I was afraid. But fear wasn't first. It was second. My training came first, and it stayed first until we had hosed the blood out of the back of the ambulance. Then I was afraid.

Why don't people take chances at work? Because they don't have enough confidence in themselves and their training to take a chance. It takes an enormously competent organization to take intelligent risk. It is from intelligent risk that innovation comes.

No employee ever gets up in the morning and says, "I can't wait to go to work! I am such a goof."

This may seem out of place, but you cannot build a MicroBrand without careful hiring and even more careful training. Why?

> **MicroBranding Point**
> Incompetence kills innovation. MicroBrands are built on standing out. Standing out begs for innovative thinking.

Customers Want an Experience

If you are looking for a B.I.G. idea but don't think you are ready to invent a new source of energy or an exotic new technology, then look for new ways to present a familiar product. Customers today want more than stuff; they want an experience.

Go find the latest Land's End catalogue, and you will find a story. Dig up the Lillian Vernon catalog, and there will be a story. It will be her story because as she says, "Customers want to know about me and my life. We have even branded my pet, a Maltese named Mopsey. Mopsey has become a favorite among our customers and even gets fan mail."

Do you want to correspond with Lillian Vernon's dog? Whatever the answer, the point is simple: Customers want stories. Customers want an experience.

We met an interesting fellow in northern Wisconsin who had just spent nearly two years renovating a huge old Victorian mansion with the intention of operating it as a bed and breakfast.

"Is it historic?"

"No, just old."

"Does it have a ghost?"

"No. Just a big, old, and now beautiful house."

"Get a ghost."

Get a ghost, get a story, entertain. Deliver an experience!

Thinking B.I.G.

Your B.I.G. idea (that's Brand Identity Genius, in case you have forgotten) is going to take a bit of creative thinking. Here are a few suggestions.

First, the process should be methodical. Some of us get lucky. The rest of us have to think!

Your B.I.G. goals should be to:

- **Go where the competition isn't.** Standing out is just as often a matter of doing something different as it is doing something differently. The first people to offer pizza delivery were doing something different. The first to offer it in thirty minutes or it would be free were doing it differently.

■ **Think of what would wow the market, not merely satisfy.**
Offering long-distance cell phone service at the same price per
minute as local service was a wow. Notice that what wows today
may be merely the first effort to raise the bar. Today's wow will
be tomorrow's expectation. Raise the bar and then get ready to
raise it again.

■ **Put conventional thinking in collision mode.** B.I.G. ideas
often come when two ordinary ideas are smooshed together or
when a usual idea is placed in an unusual situation. Haggling
over price is unheard of in a restaurant but common in an auto
dealership. Think differently and you've got Saturn with fixed,
menu pricing.

Beer bars and Laundromats are nothing new, but an
enterprising thinker in Atlanta put them together. In Dallas,
that same thinking resulted in a movie theater with food service
at your seat. Two ordinary ideas collide to create something
extraordinary.

■ **Opposites attract.** While Southwest Airlines has created an
all-time winner with no frills, one-class service, Midwest
Airlines has taken the opposite approach touting an all-first
class airline. Southwest costs less. Midwest costs more. Both are
B.I.G. ideas.

■ **Be trendy.** Pay attention to the trends, and see how you might
get ahead of them. And what are some of the trends of the
moment? Consumers are taking control of their shopping
experiences, often trading experience for a lower price and just
as often deciding to pay more when it really matters to them.
While 84 percent say they would change brand of hotel for a
comparable brand at a lower price, nearly the same percentage
will pay extra to wear a shirt with Tommy plastered across the
chest.

New minority and immigrant groups are showing up in urban areas. In some cities, nearly every cabbie is Nigerian. Can you figure how to take advantage of that?

Nearly 50 percent of all marriages end in divorce, and a huge percentage of children are born out of wedlock. What kind of services will these families need?

Energy costs are skyrocketing. What does this mean in terms of transportation, home heating, and cooling, even entertainment and healthcare?

■ **Conjugate.** Find something your market already values and then conjugate it by making it bigger, smaller, faster, lighter. You get the idea.

Be the Best Brand for the World

For many MicroBranders, being the best in the world may be a bit of a stretch so why not be the best for the world? There is no law that says who you are and what you do have to be mutually exclusive. Nor is there a law that says work cannot be fun and enriching. You have to set up the game so that when you do what you love the money follows.

There are plenty of brands that either started or evolved into altruistic business models. The Body Shop and Ben & Jerry's are two that come to mind. As for a personal brand, you may not be the world's best Dad but there is still room to be the best Dad *your* kids could have.

It's All Emotional

Customers live in an emotional world. Even those who buy on price and price alone are probably doing so not out of love of money but out of the emotional experience of getting a great deal.

Engage customers emotionally. Pay attention to the experience you wrap around the transaction.

> **MicroBranding Point**
> Brands are emotional statements.

Cool?

Looking cool or sounding cool is not enough to sustain a brand. But brands that *are* cool can last forever so long as the definition of cool doesn't change. And cool is defined by the market. What's cool? Whatever the market says it is. How do you make something cool? You pay attention to the entire experience of buying, owning, and using the product.

■ ■ ■

For the latest tips, news, and worksheets to help
with your MicroBranding efforts, visit www.tscottgross.com
and choose the MicroBranding link.

CHAPTER TWELVE

Image Is Everything

Anybody who is any good is different from anybody else.

FELIX FRANKFURTER

**There really is a way to sell your product without selling
your soul...but first you have to sell yourself.**

IF THERE IS ONE THING TO REMEMBER WHEN IT COMES TO IMAGE, IT IS THIS: Image is what
makes the customer think of the brand, and it is far more than a mere
logo.

Image is personal as well as corporate. A logo is not important to a
MicroBrander, because MicroBranders build brand awareness through
clever public relations and strategic networking. MicroBranders do little
or no image marketing and, therefore, have little need for a jazzy logo.

Logo is last when it comes to creating a MicroBrand.

For MicroBranders, there is often little difference between personal and corporate image. Powerful MicroBrands are often personal brands. (Think Tiger Woods.)

Do this: Conduct an image audit.

Keep in mind that every contact influences image. Remember that your perception and the customer's perception are often going to be different.

This past weekend our Big Guy showed up to spend the night with Pops and Granny Buns. He announced that he would like to sleep on the couch in the "storytelling room." We didn't know we had a storytelling room. We thought it was the den.

Everything your customer can see, smell, taste, hear, touch, and emotionally experience is part of your image. Good and bad are of no matter. Only congruency counts. Does what the customer experiences at each opportunity of contact seem to be congruent with the brand promise?

Hot Belly

When I checked into the Don Cesar, a package was waiting in the room. My client, East Pasco Medical Center (EPMC), had left a welcome note and a beautiful blue chambray shirt. I often wear the logo shirt of clients while on the job. It seems to make it easier for me to become part of the group.

The event went well, and, in a hurry to catch an early flight, I headed to the airport still wearing the EPMC shirt.

Several hours and a couple of thousand miles later, Buns picked me up at San Antonio International and we literally headed for the hills northwest of town. Just as we expected the big city traffic to thin, we encountered an accident.

The accident couldn't have been more than a couple of minutes old. Traffic had started to pile up, the gawkers and the hurried in conflict as they pulled around a pickup twisted and lying on its side. A harried sheriff's deputy was directing traffic, unsure what to do about the three bodies lying in the roadway.

Buns grabbed a pair of latex gloves and waved them out the passenger window as a sign that we had good reason to push our way through.

(When I am home, I serve as a volunteer medic covering an area of, I guess, nearly four hundred square miles of rural central Texas. By the way, does this in any way affect my brand as far as you are concerned?)

I grabbed the trauma kit and headed for the victims, confident that Buns would handle our SUV and be there if I needed help.

We had, in the parlance of the street medic, three hot bellies: internal injuries and almost always serious. We'd be needing a chopper, maybe two. I shouted to the deputy to make the call, while I completed three rapid assessments and began to fit C-collars. It was summer, hotter than hell, and the sweat was already soaking that nice blue shirt.

"I'm a doctor, too!" I looked up to see a young man in a T-shirt and shorts racing to assist. "I'm a doctor at Lackland. How can I help?"

"Finish up with the C-collar on that guy over there and then start a detailed assessment. Help yourself to the trauma bag. Got gloves in the open pocket, and there's a an extra set of ears in the middle compartment if you don't mind checking breath sounds."

Additional emergency personnel began arriving, including a woman who assumed the role of incident commander, marshalling assets and communicating with the two inbound helicopters.

When the paramedics arrived, they rushed to my side asking, "What would you like us to do?"

"Get vitals on the remaining patient. Help the doc over there with packaging his patient and let's get them all on backboards and ready to fly. I guess you could start your IVs now since the flyboys (helicopter paramedics) won't want them without a line started."

The scene unfolded according to plan, and in a matter of moments, we had three customers packaged and loaded for the quick and necessary trip to the trauma center.

The IC thanked me for my help and offered to resupply my kit from one of the ambulances.

Back in the SUV, Buns asked how it had gone.

"Fine. But it was the weirdest thing. Everyone kept asking me what to do, like I would know what to do. Most of them were paramedics. I even had a doc on scene, although he needed a bit of instruction on how to apply the collar. Maybe he was a podiatrist. Still, it was amazing to have them all asking me what to do. I guess that's what I get for being first on scene."

"No," Buns said. "That's what you get for being fifty, looking distinguished, and wearing a crisply pressed shirt that just happens to say East Pasco Medical Center. They all thought you were a doctor. As far as they knew, it was your scene."

So how do you make every scene your scene? Well, you can start by looking the part. Remember, a brand is a single idea that you own in the mind of your customer, whether she is lining up at the cash register or lying in the middle of the road. The idea you own is greatly influenced by appearance.

More on Appearance

Yesterday I picked up the local paper and this headline caught my eye, "Clothes encounters of the thug kind." Columnist Leonard Pitts of the *Miami Herald* was writing about the clothes that young people wear today. He made the point that, like it or not, people do judge a book by its cover. And in many cases, he said, you really *can* judge a book by its cover—how we dress says plenty about our "mind-set and sense of self."

Pitts seems to think that adults have a responsibility to provide a bit of guidance saying that, "What you show the world, how you allow yourself to be perceived, will have profound implications for the way people treat you." And I'll add, "the way people pay you."

Get it? When you are building a brand, take into account customer expectations. If the customer expects a certain look to be congruent with your expertise and price, you'd better figure what that look is and make a serious decision.

The Brand Obligation

Understand that brands create obligation. Once you have set up an expectation, it is brand suicide not to meet it.

Gotta be brand congruent. There is another lesson. Don't try to be something you are not. And yet another lesson. Don't try to go where the troops aren't about to follow.

It's better to make a modest offer you can keep than drive everyone up a wall with an offer that isn't going to happen. In one of my favorite stores, I couldn't believe the sign we saw yesterday: "If I fail to greet you and thank you with a smile, call my manager."

Oh. My. Gawd!

Sometimes I like to kid with customers who call our office and comment on the friendliness of the crew and how easy we are to do business with. I like to tell them that in my next life I am going to write a book titled, *How to Give Pretty Good Service Occasionally*. It would sure take off a lot of pressure with trying to be brand congruent!

> **MicroBranding Point**
> Better to make a modest promise that you can keep than an outrageous promise that leads to certain disappointment.

People, Products, and Pricing

One of the surest killers of a great brand is incongruent pricing. Too low is worse than too high. It is better to start with a little higher price and add value to justify it than to start too low and plant the seed of poor quality in the mind of the customer. It goes back to the idea of exclusivity.

A too low price often denotes commodity, and surprisingly, it becomes an invitation to haggle for an even lower price.

Perhaps the only thing worse than a price that is too low is one smack dab in the middle. The deadly middle tells the world that you are nothing special. Good perhaps but not great, and that is certainly no way to build a killer MicroBrand. At least prices that are too low can create a sense of loyalty among the bottom feeding bargain hunters.

Beware that we are not suggesting high price and questionable value. Remember that the entire package that represents your brand must be congruent. If you are higher priced, make certain that the entire experience reflects the price. Better said would be to make certain your people, product, packaging, place, and price all look like they belong to the same brand.

If you are going to play the "low cost provider" game, then make the rest of the experience congruent. Look at Sam's and Costco. They don't offer much help. You have to scrounge for a box to pack your purchases. But they let you in on the secret and make schlepping through a warehouse part of the fun.

Story Time

Remember that a brand is a shortcut. Show the logo, read off the tag line, do whatever it takes to trigger the brand memory, and along with it comes a story, sometimes more than one.

Truly loyal customers have and tell stories about their favorite brands.

Did I ever tell you about the time I went to Boyd's Camera in San Antonio, and Harry Boyd put a new camera on sale just for me? They were trying to help out after my old camera had been stolen.

Say, did you hear about the time I went to Cowboy Steakhouse and brought my own chicken because the restaurant was out and nobody makes chicken quite like Cowboy Steakhouse?

A friend in the Boston area sent us an article from the *Boston Globe* Sunday edition. The article featured Chuck Batchman of New England Spas and Sunrooms and his rendition of Positively Outrageous Service. A customer asked Chuck for a special spa installation. She wanted a one-day installation, so she could surprise her husband with a new spa in the backyard when he came home from work.

Now, this is a tough request under normal conditions, and we're talking New England in the snow. Up the ante by the fact that the tight quarters required the use of a crane. And, oh, yes, don't forget to mention that the ground was frozen solid.

But Batchman came through. And notice what it got him—front page of the *Globe's* Sunday Living section! How much would you have paid for that placement assuming you could have gotten it?

Those are all stories. They are the kinds of stories you want your customers to tell about you and your product.

Here's the good news. They are already telling stories about you.

Here's the other news. The stories your customers are telling may not be the kind you want others to hear. No matter what, stories are being told. They are all shaping the brand.

Rebel Alliance

At the too old age of forty-nine, I went off to California to research a book on high performance teams and wound up as one of the oldest graduates from the fire academy run by the California Department of Forestry. The young guys in my class nearly killed me, but somehow I made the cut and found myself assigned to the Shasta-Trinity Ranger Unit in Redding, California, at the height of fire season.

The powers-that-be made certain that the old guy got bunk space with the crew of engine 2479, a hulk of red steel and well-kept chrome that had seen even more fires than the grizzled captain who ran the show. Captain Tim Thompson is a bear of a man who knows the power of branding, although I have a dollar that says he couldn't define brand if you sat him on a dictionary.

No problem. You don't have to define branding to be good at it, and Tim is a natural. There isn't anyone on his crew who doesn't feel special, make that honored, to have earned or lucked into a spot on 2479. I, babe in the proverbial woods, didn't realize I was working with an elite unit.

It turns out that, like any team, high performance folks don't just automatically accept a new player. They may be friendly from the get-go, but in the end, they want to see a little performance before considering you one of the crew. So it wasn't until the third day and the umpteenth fire and medical run that Squeeb, the crew chief and about twenty years my junior, pulled me aside and said, "Do you know about the Alliance?"

"No, never heard of it. Should I?"

"A lot of people know. It's kind of a legend. Let me show you." Squeeb pulled his wildland helmet from the open cab of 2479 and tossed it to me. "Check out the emblem on the front."

I pulled up my goggles and saw a scratched black symbol that looked like it had been cut out of electrical tape. It was shaped sort of like the fire axe symbol often associated with firefighting but it was different.

"Did you see *Star Wars*?"

"Sure."

"The Rebel Alliance, the good guys, had a symbol kind of like that. We're the rebel alliance in this part of the world, and most of the firefighters know it. Now you're one. People know that when we're on scene, we're going to get the job done no matter what. I guess you could say we're famous because when guys see the symbol, they often say, 'Oh, we've heard about you.'"

A brand. A story.

> **MicroBranding Point**
> The stories told about a brand define the brand as much for those who own it as for those who want to own it, the customers.

Customers, bosses, we all want to be part of something that is bigger than ourselves. That's why employees get so hummed up over the annual United Way campaign, because while individually their contribution may not be much, together they can make a big difference.

Stories, true or implied, help explain why normal human beings are willing to pay for the privilege of advertising their favorite brand. Recently, the legendary race car driver Dale Earnhardt was killed in a NASCAR crash. Guess what happened to the sale of memorabilia with Earnhardt's number three on it?

Culture on a Napkin

Think of the great brands, and there will be a story.

FedEx comes complete with the story of how Fred Smith was given a low grade in college for a paper that later served as the business model for Federal Express. Longaberger Baskets in Dresden, Ohio, is a story of entrepreneurial tenacity and social responsibility that comes complete with its own small town and story line that does more than serve as a modern day morality lesson; it enhances the value of the handmade baskets that are now world famous.

Several years ago I was invited to attend a celebration of Southwest Airlines' 25th anniversary. And what did I keep? A stand-up display that tells the "tale of two men, one airline, and a cocktail napkin," the story of the founding of Southwest Airlines.

Great brands come complete with great stories. Great brands *are* great stories.

Smart MicroBranders capture great stories, (I suspect sometimes they make them up) and then make certain that they are told and retold.

MicroBranding Point
What is your story? Are you telling it?

■ ■ ■

For the latest tips, news, and worksheets to help
with your MicroBranding efforts, visit www.tscottgross.com
and choose the MicroBranding link.

CHAPTER THIRTEEN

Name That Brand!

Anna Fanna Bobanna

IT WAS CALLED "THE NAME GAME." Do you remember it? Brander brander bobander fee, fi momander…brander!

It was a silly song, but judging by the names that people choose for their brands, you can hardly blame MoTown when it gets a little goofy. But you can blame business professionals who mess up the most elementary, and we should say, critical step in building a MicroBrand.

What kind of a name do you want for your MicroBrand? A name consumers will remember. (Puff Daddy is now available. If P. Diddy was under consideration, it is now taken.)

How your name is remembered is almost as important as being remembered at all.

Thinking and reading about the science of naming, it comes to one key point:

MicroBranding Point
Generic names encourage generic business.

Everything else is subordinate to this rule. The subordinate rules are:

■ Choose a name that works hard.

■ Use an ordinary name out of context.

■ Choose a name that is culturally appropriate.

■ Be careful when choosing names that have multiple meanings.

■ Your name is a good name, especially when you are the product.

■ Avoid monograms.

■ Let the name leverage the brand promise.

Generic Names

Give your brand a name that also describes the category, and you will have a difficult time building a killer brand. Can you be successful? Absolutely! But will you lead the pack? Probably not.

If you are selling an undifferentiated product (why would you do that?), then generic names are less of a liability but they are never a plus. Think of the rush to grab category names as URLs. There is eToy, Beds.com, batteries.com, grocery.com. Do you remember any of them? A category name is pretty much the kiss of death.

Have you heard of a store named Rooms 2 Go? How about The Room Store? On the face of it, both of those chains are well named. Their names pretty much tell what they do or at least hint at it. They don't have a lot of need for a tag line since their names pretty much *are* tag lines.

But, in fact, neither store is well named. Generic names encourage generic business. Watch television in Dallas, one market where both stores compete head-to-head, and you are likely to see a commercial for one subtly reminding you not to get confused by the other. Bad names. Too generic.

Now, Fred's Rooms to Go, or Marty's Room Store...those would be an improvement.

Do you remember Polo or Ralph Lauren? Ralph gets the nod, am I right?

The world's greatest brand names are proper names. There is Albertson's Supermarkets, American Airlines, Coca-Cola, Dell Computer, Cisco, Sysco, Proctor and Gamble, Kellogg's, Nokia, and Jewell. None of those are category names. Is Toys R Us an exception, or does it in some way fit the rule? My guess is that the toy retailer gets a Get out of Jail card for being first in the category, and therefore, its name is, to the category, a proper name of sorts. Still, Toys R Us is skating on pretty thin ice in the name business.

Stop-N-Go...good

7-11...good

Circle K...good

Mini-Mart...not good

Check out the four names above. Can you tell me why the first three are good names and the fourth could use some work? The first three are proper names. The last describes a category.

Could Stop-N-Go ever be considered a proper name? Yes, it can and is! It has the added benefit of being its own tag line. When you say, let's head down to the Stop-N-Go, you know exactly where you are going and you have a pretty good idea of what you can expect from the experience. Try that with the name Mini-Mart and you could wind up at Mini-Mart or at Stop-N-Go, 7-11, or even Circle K because in the mind of the consumer, "Mini-Mart" is a category.

Look at these three:

- **KFC:** a monogram created by the customer. This is a good name that allows the company to stray from bone-in chicken and even distances it from that evil word in modern marketing—fried!

- **Outback:** a good proper name that hints at the kind of experience you can expect.

■ **Waffle House:** not good after 10 a.m. Now, I love the Waffle House. Friendly as a neighbor, as comfortable as an old shoe. No doubt it keeps plenty of heart surgeons in business. But Waffle House? Great name before ten in the morning. After that? Miserable. The same was true for International House of Pancakes, but now you can IHOP during any time of the day.

To cement the point, the reason proper names work best is that human beings, or at least Western-thinking human beings, are wired to believe that a proper name is the first *responsible* identifier. For example, when the folks at the ranch next door pay us a visit, I doubt that they think, "Let's call the neighbors, Scott & Melanie." More likely they think, "I wonder what Scott and Melanie, our neighbors, are up to?"

A few years ago I had a wonderful corporate client, Grocery Outlet. I didn't give much thought to the company's name until I walked into one of its stores and saw, "Fred and Eileen welcome you to Grocery Outlet." Perfect recovery.

Work Hard

Your brand name should, in many but not every case, work hard. Here's a hard-working name that could have been better: National Tire and Battery. It tells that the company is national in scope and that it sells tires and batteries. I think it would have been better had it also been associated with a great proper name brand. Unfortunately, NTB is owned by Sears, which does not have a great name in auto repair so a proper name was left off.

Category

Customers don't buy companies; they buy brands. But the funny thing is customers don't get nearly as excited about new brands as they do new categories. The best a new brand in an old category can do is grab a share of the limelight, while in many cases an all-new category can steal the entire show.

While you are inventing a new brand, think about inventing a whole new category.

Take a lesson from the big boys: All competition is not bad. Here's what the big brands have learned: Instead of competing for space for your product, help the customer manage the entire category. Show her how your product fits with the others in the same category. Understand that when the entire category does well, your product (or service) also does well.

Promote the category rather than yourself.

What does this mean to a MicroBrand? Simple, be a team player not a lone ranger. Be willing and smart enough to promote your market, not just yourself.

For example, we are about to speak to a group of merchants in a lovely area of the upper Midwest. For years, the area has been in decline and the merchants have been fighting one another for every last tourist dollar. Huge mistake.

Instead, they should be doing category management. They should promote the entire area as a desirable destination. They should cooperate with other merchants and even nearby towns. They should create packages and cross-promotions, and in the end, the area will grow and everybody will win.

The lesson is simple but not intuitive: Don't fight other brands. Fight other categories.

Customers don't care about new brands. They don't care that you have opened the Scott's Motor Inn in East Podunk. But they do care about new categories. This means that while you have little chance convincing them to visit your hotel, they might well be interested in visiting East Podunk, a new category. Sell the category, and they will buy the brand.

Last point, let them know that you are the leader of the category. Sell them on visiting East Podunk and then remind them that you are the best brand in the category (hotels in East Podunk).

Out of Context

Closest to our heart has to be the name Positively Outrageous Service. Outrageous in this case is used in a surprising way. It is one of those words that can be interpreted as good or awful. The common understanding is that something outrageous is usually not good at all, while the slang use of the word is right up there with cool, hot, and tuff.

Death by Chocolate also comes to mind. Got any ideas of your own?

Culturally Appropriate

A client called the other day in a panic. He was charged with translating our audience resource materials from our southern version of English to French. "Is there another way you can say, 'love on your customers?' It doesn't translate well into French." Well, I would have thought French would be perfect for loving on customers!

If you have a name that is difficult to spell or pronounce or if it may seem foreign to the culture, it might not be the best name for your brand.

Multiple Meanings

Here's an example: My name. Gross.

I used this to my advantage in college where I could rush an already full class and set the professor up for a play on my name. "Hi, I'm Gross. I'd like to be in your class." About half the time they would take the bait, say something juvenile at my expense, and let me in the class.

For some businesses, using my surname all by itself would be suicide. Gross Weight Loss Center. Gross Bait Shop. Gross Waste Haulers. But in Kerrville, Texas, I would consider opening Rod's Honda, which would be our son's killer MicroBrand married to a wonderful mega-brand.

When You Are the Product

Choose your own name when you are the product. T. Scott Gross & Company works just fine for our company. As they say in our office, "Disney has Mickey; we have Scott." Folks who speak for a living are essentially selling their personalities, so using your name as the name of the company makes sense.

Would you rather do business with F. Lee Bailey or Advantage Legal Services? Get it? So long as it is not difficult to pronounce or spell or is otherwise offensive, give your brand a personal name.

Even if you don't have a name on the sign, there is one on the business. We like to fuel our small airplane at Lunken Field in Cincinnati. The FBO we use is named Million Air (a great name by the way. It's as if someone said, "I wonder how a millionaire would expect to be treated" and then set about creating a business wrapped around that model). As good as Million Air is, when we are planning our flight, we often find ourselves saying, "Let's stop and see Sharon in Cincinnati." Sharon is the service manager at Million Air, and it is *her* place, no matter what it says on the sign.

Avoid Monograms

Think about it. Is GE a monogram? Is IBM? Not even! We all know that GE stands for General Electric and IBM for International Business Machines. According to conventional wisdom, even their original names would have been marginal. They didn't start out as monograms. They evolved into monograms that aren't really monograms at all; they're just shortcuts to names we already know. But then they have the advantage of years of efforts backed by maybe billions of dollars of marketing. Can you do that? If not, then avoid giving your brand a monogram for a name.

The same is true for International House of Pancakes (IHOP). Had the restaurant adopted the name IHOP from the beginning, no telling how long it would have taken to develop brand awareness. (What's an IHOP?) But this name, like GE and IBM before it, came from the market. IHOP was smart enough to follow along.

Brand Promise Leverage

In some rare cases, you can let the brand name leverage the brand promise. Terminex. There are two great word blocks at work here. Term as in terminal and ex as in exterminate. Looked at backwards, you have the basis for the entire word which is also the promise— exterminate. Add in the tag line, "no bugs, no hassles," and you have a powerful brand name and tag.

It Ain't Rock 'n Roll

Too often we get caught up in what brands mean to us and forget the customer. Too many brand names would work swell for a high school garage band. Smashing Pumpkins, Nine Inch Nails, you've got the picture. When you're naming your product, think about the customer!

Own a Single Word

More than anything else you want to own a word in the mind of the consumer, and, remember, we only care about the consumers on your marketing island. Someone on another island can own the same word—and you don't care.

We own the word Outrageous when it comes to customer service as in Positively Outrageous Service. We don't care what happens to the word off our island, which happens to be the island of customer service training. We've seen Outrageous Cleaners, as well as Outrageous as a brand of evening wear. We've even seen it as a keyword linked to an Internet porn site. We don't care.

You should care about owning, in the mind of the consumer, one word. One, single word. Now, once you own it, you may have to fight to keep it. (There's a thought that brings tears to my eyes. Pass me a Kleenex. Sorry, I meant, tissue. No, I really want a Kleenex. Thank you.)

Logo

You are on your way when a customer sees your logo and thinks your brand. That said, the most important part of the logo is not the logo. It's the brand.

MicroBranding Point
The logo, or image, is what the customer sees. The brand is what the customer thinks.

The biggest mistake in branding is that entrepreneurs get all excited and start by developing cool logos and stationery. Cool but totally worthless.

Always the right place to start with logo development is brand development. If you haven't worked through the values, mission, and vision process, you aren't anywhere near being ready for image. The reason is a matter of congruency. Everything about your brand needs to be congruent. If not, you are going to be caught in a branding lie that will put everything you do in question.

Maybe you've heard the analogy of the coffee stains on the fold-down airline tray. I don't know where the story came from but the idea is this: If the passenger sees coffee stains on the fold-down tray, what will he construe about engine maintenance?

> **MicroBranding Point**
> MicroBranders would be better off saving the logo development for last. You may never need one.

Throwed Roll

I'm writing this from a 16th floor hotel room overlooking the deep blue waters of Puget Sound in Seattle. The talk of the town and certainly the talk of the conventioneers I will be addressing tomorrow is the fabled Pike Street Market, where the staff are famous for tossing fresh fish and repartee with abandon much to the delight of the astonished customers.

One look at an airborne mackerel, and you know you aren't in Missouri. Sykeston, Missouri, to be exact. You see, in Sykeston, there's another place famous for throwing food. To the locals, it's known as the Lambert Café (I don't recall café actually having a little thingee over the "e"), Home of the Throwed Roll.

I don't know the whole story. Apparently one day an impatient Lambert Café customer couldn't wait for busy Mr. Lambert to deliver a hot, fresh dinner roll. Maybe he said, "Aw, Ed, just throw me one." Or, maybe he didn't. However it happened, a food service legend began with the launch and presumed successful landing of a home-baked, hot-from-the-oven dinner roll.

Want to taste a legend? Better get there early, because by noon the possibility of immediate seating has flown out the window along with the first hot roll of the day.

And God Created...

The franchise agreement for a restaurant we owned required us to serve all of the company menu items. No more, no less.

One that I just couldn't see was fried okra. I couldn't figure why anyone in his right mind would want to eat that stuff. It was, for me, proof that God has a sense of humor. I imagined that after God made oysters, He thought to Himself, "That's pretty interesting. I wonder what would happen if I made that as a vegetable?"

And so there was fried okra. And it was good, but not to everybody.

What's the point? It doesn't matter whether you like it, only that it will sell.

If the customer likes it, it is good.

This morning our son was venting about the stupid new styles that are attracting today's young kids. He made a big point that he was not about to buy that "junk" for our grandson should he ever get the notion to be interested in clothes.

Too cool. This from the same kid who wore black-and-white-checked Van's tennis shoes and parachute pants. This from the kid who makes a rather nice living putting fifteen hundred dollar stereos into fifty dollar cars.

If the customer likes it, it is cool.

Qualifier or Eliminator?

Sometimes it's just as important to know what the customer doesn't like. Look at your product offering as consisting of qualifiers and eliminators.

Qualifiers represent the minimum you must offer just to be considered as an option. For example, clean restrooms won't get you selected if you are in the restaurant business, but dirty restrooms will get you eliminated.

Or here's an interesting restaurant example. If you could only offer two pies, which two would you offer: apple, cherry, or pecan? Well, research shows that most people who eat cherry will also eat apple. But most people who eat apple will not eat cherry. To the majority of pie eaters (they prefer apple), offering cherry is not seen as another choice. Offer cherry along with apple and all you are likely to do is split the sales two ways. But offering pecan pie is likely to result in additional sales.

When I was young and ignorant, I knew tons of cute, slightly off-color stories. Maybe it was the times or maybe my age. Now and then I would tell a story and notice someone wince. My prescription for them was to get a life. You know, get over it.

Perhaps we have all grown up or I'm just hanging with a better crowd. One day many years ago, I was listening to a Zig Ziglar audio tape, and I heard Zig say that when it comes to hiring speakers, many meeting planners will not hire a speaker who is known for off-color humor. He went on to say that in reverse, there are few meeting planners who actually seek out speakers who tell dirty stories.

Duh! I may be slow, but I'm not stupid. That day marked the first day of my all new repertoire.

It's always amusing to speak to large corporate audiences and see who smokes and who doesn't. My guess is that no one was ever hired because he smoked. I can tell you quite a few have been eliminated because they did. Chances are, they didn't even know what counted them out.

When a large corporate group takes a break from a meeting, watch who smokes. I guarantee you that it is the entry-level folks who race outside to light one up. Why they don't notice that none or few of the brass join them is beyond me. Maybe they think the big boys are just being snobbish. But the facts seem to be this: The higher you look in the corporate hierarchy, the fewer smokers you will see. Get the message?

The same is almost true for alcohol. I have a personal rule never to drink with clients. Make mine club soda. Double the lime if it's a wild night!

I once was invited to speak to an association of lounge and bar owners. It was Las Vegas, the Mirage, if I remember correctly. On the trip over, Buns and I remarked that we hadn't been in a bar in so long, that maybe we should find a nice local place and treat ourselves occasionally by slipping out for a margarita and an order of nachos.

At ten in the morning, my client's group took a break. It was, believe it or not, for a liquor tasting. Yep, ten in the morning and these folks were sipping scotch on the rocks.

When the meeting restarted, I was amazed to see the room had been divided into smoking and non, and that, by far the smoking side had the most people. They filed in one after the other holding their cigarettes and lighters; most even carried their own ashtrays. It looked almost ritualistic. The audience puffed, while I choked my way through the longest hour on record.

The meeting planner had said that the industry was facing declining sales and couldn't figure out why. Well, take a deep breath, sports fans. Most Yuppies don't smoke, and they're the ones who have the money to buy the drinks with the umbrellas.

Anything can be an eliminator.

■ ■ ■

For the latest tips, news, and worksheets to help
with your MicroBranding efforts, visit www.tscottgross.com
and choose the MicroBranding link.

CHAPTER FOURTEEN

Building the Brand

The Congruent Napkin

SOUTHWEST AIRLINES PORTRAYS ITSELF as the scrappy little start-up airline from Texas… aw, shucks. It is scrappy and it is from Texas, but it is hardly little. Southwest has one of the largest and newest fleets in the world. It is profitable and built to stay that way, thanks in part to its absolute certainty as to who it is and what it is in business to accomplish.

Once I received a birthday napkin from Southwest. Right, a napkin not a card. The legend of Southwest is that it originated as an idea scribbled on a napkin. The idea was to create a low cost, point-to-point airline and, oh yes! an airline where cheap would become a mantra and where the customers would be let in on the plan.

I remember the days when Southwest flight attendants wore hot pants and go-go boots. I also remember when customers (they call them customers not passengers) waiting to board a flight would be herded down the jet way even before the arriving flight had landed. Customers would often begin mooing in mock revolt at being treated like cattle.

I remember that. But I don't remember Southwest Airlines reporting a money-losing year. Ever.

Part of that success is its dedication to the brand and being steadfast when it comes to staying congruent.

On the outside of the envelope containing my birthday napkin was printed, "Our company started thirty years ago as an idea on a napkin."

On the napkin the message continued in a font resembling handwriting, "We hope your birthday turns out just as BIG! Happy birthday from your friends at Southwest Airlines."

Cool!

> **MicroBranding Point**
> Your brand is a promise. Your brand is a story. Never vary from either.

The Brand Commitment

Your MicroBrand will attract customers that share your values, and it is important to publicly support the causes and ideals that you share with your market.

> **MicroBranding Point**
> Brand values naturally lead to a brand commitment.

If you find yourself attracting customers with whom you have little or nothing in common, the problem is not with the customers. There is something wrong with your message.

We all have causes that we could support. The truth is there is no way we could support every cause we believe in. So as long as you cannot say yes to everything, why not try to find out what causes are the hottest button for your market and support those?

Just so you know, the number one value, worldwide, is protecting the family. Number two is honesty, with health and fitness coming in as number three. Worldwide! What does that tell us? It's not that hard to find values that you can easily and honestly share with your market. There is no need to tweak a customer's nose by flaunting a value not shared. Look for common ground and openly support that position.

When you choose a cause to support, it might be a good idea to wrap your brand around a branded cause. Ronald McDonald House, Habitat for Humanity, and the American Cancer Foundation are all examples of strong brands that will boost your brand while you are doing good things you should be doing anyway.

Link yourself to socially responsible causes that are logical for the industry you are in. A homebuilder is a natural for a drive to build a Battered Women's Shelter. A dry cleaner is made-to-order as the honcho for a clothing drive. Get the idea?

Keep in mind that there are many locally branded public service opportunities. Often these MicroBrands are stronger than their nationally known counterparts. (See? Anyone can get in on the MicroBranding act!)

Whatever you do, be consistent over time. Pick your associations and stick with them, as like all good public relations, it takes many multiple impressions to add up to one lasting impression.

The advantage of a MicroBrander is that we are dealing with markets that not only are focused by need; they will naturally self-select according to shared values. For example we are known for Positively Outrageous Service. Companies that aren't absolutely on fire for customer service aren't going to call a guy who espouses Positively Outrageous Service. They're going to call the PowerPoint speaker who offers "Concepts of Service for a New Century." But while I try not to yawn, that customer will be thrilled for having hired the other guy.

MicroBranding Point
Discover what your customer values. Make common values known. Self-select.

■ ■ ■

For the latest tips, news, and worksheets to help
with your MicroBranding efforts, visit www.tscottgross.com
and choose the MicroBranding link.

PART III

CHAPTER FIFTEEN

Signature Showmanship

*Showmanship? This is like a spelling bee. I should spell it
and use it in a sentence? Well, showmanship is the ability
to bring to life, and bring life to, the show.*

BOBBI CANDLER, SINGER/ACTRESS

CRASH! CLUNK! THERE ISN'T AN ELEGANT THING ABOUT THE SOUND OF A COWBELL. And in the quiet almost sedate surroundings of beautiful Old San Francisco Restaurant, the noise seems even more out of place. Yet, it has been precisely this out-of-the-ordinary sound, plus a world-class dining experience, that has made the Old San Francisco Restaurants favored haunts for discriminating diners throughout Texas.

The cowbell marks the ascent of an attractive, young woman who is buckled safely into a red velvet swing arching its way over the bar. Much as the swing has been suspended over the bar, diners have suspended their conversation mid-sentence as they watch the hourly performance at the front of the dining room.

It would be a mistake to imagine that the success of the Old San

Francisco group was solely due to the gimmicky performance of a pretty girl in a red velvet swing. But it is the swinging that customers can talk about for days after the memory of their meal has faded.

The swing. Who would have thought to put a swing over the bar? Who would have thought to create a lavish routine that has a young woman swaying from one side of the restaurant to the other, climaxing in an arch so high that she can ring a cowbell hung at either end of her route? The bells hang from the ceiling. (Also on the ceiling are the marks of a few missed attempts as well.)

When customers bring friends and visiting relatives to Old San Francisco, it is because they have in mind a special treat. They tell their guests about the food, but most save the girl in the red velvet swing as a surprise.

Surprise!

Surprise is the first element of industrial-strength showmanship. If you want to develop "signature showmanship," then surprise is the first element to consider. Surprise makes ordinary events special.

A cupcake isn't likely to create a lot of excitement. But deliver it with a lighted candle while singing "Happy Birthday," and you've got yourself the makings of a real surprise that turns the ordinary into a show.

Years ago while working my way through college as a Denny's cook, I used to enjoy surprising my customers with messages written in strips of sliced cheese melted across the top of their cheese omelets. Simple messages like "Vote" on Election Day or just a short, yellow "Hello!" for customers who hadn't been in recently always got a laugh.

Once I even put my phone number on the omelet I thought had been ordered by an attractive woman. How was I to guess that she had ordered for her macho-looking boyfriend while he was looking for a parking place?

The fresh-baked cookies that we sometimes slipped onto the trays of diners at our restaurant took on an added value, because they were unexpected. Anything ordinary has the potential of becoming special if it is presented as a surprise. I can't resist mentioning the restaurants that cut off the neckties of guests who do not know their "no tie" rule.

What makes it fun is the fact that the guest doesn't expect to have his tie attacked; he is surprised. Not to mention, of course, mad as hell!

Theme

If you are looking to develop signature showmanship, it might be a good idea to consider your theme—or not. If your business has a logo, tag line, or décor theme, there may be a natural opportunity for showmanship. The folks at Menke Manufacturing, makers of duck tape, have an open book when it comes to opportunities for showmanship. When they have a great quarter in terms of sales and profits, they invite their best vendors and suppliers to join them for a group race to jump, clothes and all, into their duck pond. They are quick—or should we say "quack?"—to tell you that things aren't all that they are quacked up to be, and a jillion other puns that just naturally follow a product called duck tape.

Following your theme, tag line, or logo may be the most obvious way to create signature showmanship. Then again, the obvious may not be what you want. Think about the girl in the swing at Old San Francisco. She may match the theme, but really, when would you ever expect something like that? She fits the theme only because she dresses like a hostess in an 1890s saloon, the theme of the restaurant. Swinging would be a surprise no matter what the theme of the restaurant.

Do–able

Whatever you consider for your signature showmanship, it must be something that you can do. Better add the idea of repeatability to the list. Whatever you choose, make certain that you can do it again and again for years to come. Choose flame-swallowing as your signature showmanship, and you'll have to live with the fact that flame-swallowers are not found on every corner.

Smart folks go with things that are fun by nature and that require little more in terms of talent and props than a sense of adventure. Remember, signature showmanship does not need to be an elaborate production. It can be something as simple as a funny business card, an engaging story, or a simple bar-quality stunt. It only needs to be different, and slightly out of context, to WOW.

There are dentists who visit schools dressed like the tooth fairy, nurses who tell funny bedtime stories, truckers who delight in giving perfect strangers a piece of sugar candy, and traffic cops who execute stunning ballet moves while directing you through the intersection. Nothing expensive. Nothing difficult. The emphasis is on different, unexpected, and just plain fun.

Macaroni Grill near my home is one of my favorites because I enjoy the sense of showmanship that makes every visit more than a meal. It is an experience. When we called for permission to shoot a segment for a satellite network on showmanship, not only did the folks at Macaroni say yes, they asked us to wait until Friday night.

All right, folks, what's wrong with that picture?

Nobody in their right mind requests that a video crew wait until the busiest night of the week to drag through the dining room with lights, cables, equipment, and a small army of techies.

Then again, who said that they are in their right mind at Macaroni?

They are crazy. Crazy, as in "Come on Friday; that's when we schedule our hammiest hams and when the crowd is most in the mood to play." Also they are crazy, as in "Well, let's take another million to the bank!"

But the point we need to mention here is that the fun at Macaroni includes Italian opera, beautifully performed tableside. The risk and effort is in the need to recruit talented opera stars to work as servers.

Can't you imagine the classified ad? "Wanted. Waitpersons. Must be able to sing in Italian."

Better to stick to signature showmanship that is a bit less ambitious. While it's not likely that your average customer will either appreciate opera or be able to sing along, they can both appreciate and join in something more common. There's the choice. Something tending toward the common or the truly knock-your-socks-off unique.

Nontopical

Choose a signature showmanship that is not likely to go out of style before word gets around that you are doing it. Or pick something that is so far out of style that it has become nostalgic.

Hooters restaurant is a great place for a Philly cheese steak and an ice-cold brewski. It's also a great place to brush up on your Hula-Hoop ability. While you are waiting, the hostess at Hooters is likely to entertain you by challenging you to a round of Hula-Hooping. Now, when was the last time that you dragged out the old hoop and hula'd to your heart's content? Been awhile, hasn't it? And that, of course, is the point. Hooters picked up on a bit of showmanship that was so far out, it's in!

Nordstrom has taken the higher road. Walk into a Nordstrom department store, and you are likely to be greeted by the delightfully soothing sounds of a grand piano. Not of the recorded variety, either. A real, honest-to-goodness, grand piano whose ivories are being tickled by someone for whom the term, "piano player" just does not apply. Say "pianist," please.

Elegant or mondo-bizzaro, choose a signature showmanship that is not going to be rethought two weeks after you finally master the routine.

Careful About Core Values

Our banker friends are always cautious about Positively Outrageous Service. And it is fair that they would be careful about organized silliness in a financial institution. There isn't anyone who would like to have fun while doing business more than I. But when it comes to handling my money, even I, the clown prince of industrial foolishness, am willing to sacrifice entertainment for accuracy.

The point is simple.

> **MicroBranding Point**
> Choosing a signature showmanship style must take into account the nature of the business itself.

A mortuary that sponsors casket races can count on plenty of free media attention but not many customers when it comes to icing a favorite Uncle Fred. Medical professionals can and do benefit from a little applied showmanship. But when it comes to their particular area of medical art, they need to be as serious as a heart attack.

Still, those who can successfully push the limits, and perhaps poke a little fun at themselves or their professions, have an opportunity to score big with the public.

Linda Wilkinson, of the Dane County Credit Union, is one such person. Her claim to industrial-strength showmanship may be found in a box of bright red, foam clown noses that she keeps stowed in her desk drawer.

Linda saves the clown noses for those touchy situations when a credit union member shows up with a cranky kid in tow. Rather than allow the disruptive little darling to tear the building to its foundation, Linda offers a clown nose to keep the little reprobate entertained. You don't expect to receive a clown nose at your credit union, and that is what makes it such a special treat. (A clown nose would not seem out of place in an attorney's office. Neither would leather underwear.)

Let Me Choose

Bill Behling, the master showman for PFM, the college contract feeders, believes in the idea of vicarious participation. Whether from sheer practicality or simply because not every customer will want to play, Behling says that you can leverage your corporate fun simply by performing your showmanship in the presence of a crowd, even though perhaps only a single customer or guest can participate directly.

> **MicroBranding Point #1**
> Industrial-strength showmanship should never make the customer uncomfortable.
>
> **MicroBranding Point #2**
> Industrial-strength showmanship should allow the customer to choose whether or not to participate.

Flying into San Francisco aboard Southwest, we were treated to the usual/unusual entertainment that has become legendary among folks lucky enough to be served by the Southwest route system. The flight attendants announced a scavenger hunt, and the prize was something I don't remember, but it wasn't likely much more than a double ration of the famous Southwest breakfast peanuts. (Southwest is not known for food service. Its philosophy is that if you are after a good meal, you should stop at Denny's. If you want to fly from point A to point B and you want a wide choice of flights at low, low prices, then Southwest might be a better choice than Denny's.)

Frequent Southwest flyers joke about the availability of breakfast peanuts, lunch peanuts, or the ever-popular dinner peanuts! Then they laugh about the money they are saving by not trying to buy dinner at 35,000 feet.

The flight attendants must have been up half the night dreaming up their list of oddball items that were soon the object of an intense plane-wide search. We looked for a sock with a hole in it, a compromising photograph, foreign currency (easy), and even a small bottle of shampoo. The passengers were having a great time. Even the few conservative souls who were much too self-important to participate personally occasionally gave a look over their reading glasses—and one was even caught smiling.

But the point is important. No one was forced to play, and even those that did not, participated in their own way.

No Extra Charge

Showmanship that you have to pay for quickly loses its shine. It is much better if it is perceived as an extra, an unexpected goodie that was tossed in as both a surprise and an added value.

Another favorite game that they play on Southwest is "guess the combined age of your flight attendants." There's nothing more amusing than to watch three flight attendants parade through the cabin trying to look as young as possible. The prize is always something inconsequential. It is the playing of the game that is the fun. Talk about cheap entertainment!

The following story is to remind you that even if you don't feel a need to develop a signature style of showmanship, perhaps being known for a variety of surprises is just as good. A sense of humor and the willingness to take a risk is all that's required.

Doodee

Showmanship can result from the smallest inspiration. The secret is to learn to be open to possibilities. A chance remark, a dream, the odd juxtaposition of words in ordinary conversation. Anything and darned-near-everything can set off the creative mind. After all, a surprise is nothing more than the result of our insistence on viewing the world as a predictable place only to discover that somehow our predictions, our expectations, have been thwarted.

Jill Hicks is one of those easy-to-meet people who doesn't mind sitting on the front row of a seminar. She shows up ready to learn and hoping to play. She laughs easily, probably because she is able to find humor under every rock or turn in the conversation.

While managing her family's theater in tiny Florence, Oregon, Hicks spent a lazy afternoon previewing the film *Caddy Shack* on the day it was to open. In the movie, there is a swimming pool scene in which a Baby Ruth candy bar gets away from some kids and ends up floating in the pool—repulsed swimmers quickly empty the pool when one of the kids surfaces beside the candy bar and screams "Doodee!"

That's rude and crude but, you have to admit, funny as the dickens. Most of us have a touch of sixth-grade scatological humor left in us, and this pretty much fills the bill. Well, the scene struck a twisted chord with Hicks who realized that she had a full box of Baby Ruths in stock at the concession stand. Perfect ammunition to set up a prank that would be the talk of Florence for years.

Before she climbed the long staircase to start the film, Hicks handed a Baby Ruth to each patron in the auditorium. She said not a word to spoil the joke, and since this was the premiere night for the film in Florence, no one was likely to anticipate the surprise. The audience was abuzz over the unexpected free candy as the film finally began to roll.

Caddy Shack, as a movie, is full of sight gags and surprises but none quite as hilarious as the looks on the candy bar munchers when the swimmer on the screen surfaces and clears the pool. He, with the help of Jill Hicks who was grinning from the back of the house, grossed out an entire auditorium by yelling "Doodee!"

What have you done lately to yell "Doodee" to your customers?

Don't get hung up on the scatology. Think instead how fun a little showmanship would be to your customers and employees alike.

Parallel Analysis

Good ideas for corporate fun, like good ideas for marketing and new products, don't have to come from the same industry. In fact, it is a fun exercise to look at other nonsimilar industries to see how they have handled similar problems or taken advantage of similar opportunities.

Looking for a good time? Then observe what others outside your industry are doing to play with their customers and think about how those ideas might be adapted to your special needs. Don't be afraid to let your imagination and your research wander.

A few years ago, we looked at Fiesta Texas, a San Antonio amusement park, in search of ideas for showmanship in the casual dining segment of the restaurant industry. Much to our surprise, we discovered that the acting skills required of Fiesta Texas' "Streetmosphere" performers were directly applicable to restaurant operations where they are serious about serving fun along with dinner.

What wasn't much of a surprise was the discovery that a few miles west along the freeway, Phillip Romano had beat us to the punch. He had the foresight to arrange for a university professor to present acting lessons to his waitstaff as part of the pre-opening training for his Macaroni Grill.

Tom Peters and Robert H. Waterman wrote about the world's greatest idea scroungers in their book *In Search of Excellence*. Stew Leonard, owner-operator of what is billed as the world's largest dairy store, was reported to conduct intensive searches on a daily basis for new ideas. Leonard's policy is to require each of his top managers to find at least one good, new idea every day.

Leonard and his managers frequently pile into the "Idea" van and drive off in search of their next big idea. They have no problem borrowing any idea, so long at it is a good one that can be used as is or adjusted to fit the Stew Leonard operation.

Stories such as these make for interesting legend, but as any successful person will agree, it is easier to talk-the-talk than to walk-the-talk. I found out that the Leonard family is exactly as advertised, when

I happened to share a lunch table with Stew Leonard, Jr.

During the conversation, I mentioned our Southern Fried Sundays, a weekly event where we barricaded the parking lot and set out hay bale benches so that we could treat our customers to a free evening of country western music. Ah, now that was unusual, and if Stew Leonard's is anything at all, it's unusual.

Stew Junior perked up and leaned forward so as not to miss a word. Then he reached into his jacket pocket and retrieved a small notebook. He scribbled a few words, asked again the name of the promotion, and followed with a few questions about procedure. Then he smiled. He had his idea for the day.

The message is simple: Good ideas don't have to come from you. They don't have to come from an industry guru. Good ideas can come from anywhere if you will only open your eyes—your mind—and look.

Stick to a Theme—or Not!

Consider adopting a theme for your operation or at least your signature showmanship. Then carry the theme throughout—or not. Restaurants are famous for following a theme, but there is definitely no law governing this area. So why can't a theme be useful in other areas, and why must a theme "fit" naturally?

For example, a new hardware store could easily follow the theme of a turn-of-the-century, old-fashioned general store. That theme would be a natural. But why must a theme be obvious? A men's clothing store wouldn't suffer from the adoption of a railroad theme to make the décor more interesting. Even a dry cleaner could choose to adopt an Old West theme.

The Yacht Club Resort at Disney World has successfully adopted a nautical theme based on the days of traveling aboard luxury steamships. This is a tightly focused theme, but there are others who follow theme along more general lines.

The shops in the Pittsburgh Station Square follow the general theme of railroading but don't hesitate to stray if they happen to run across a piece of memorabilia that is interesting, even if it doesn't fit the theme exactly.

Speaking of railroads, treat yourself to a visit to the Crowne Plaza in downtown Indianapolis. The historical district surrounding the old railroad terminal has become a tourist mecca. Parked regally in the lobby of the Crowne Plaza is an impressive array of refurbished Pullman sleepers that are available for overnight guests. The crowning touch: Delightful statuary depicting scenes from the days of the railroad heydey. A businessman in bronze waits patiently for a train that he will never board. A woman carries a baby who will never leave her arms, and small children marvel at a train that will carry them only in the realm of the imagined.

The works are so lifelike that it is difficult to resist the temptation to ask the time or comment on the weather. No doubt more than one overindulgent conventioneer has made the mistake of engaging in innocent chitchat to bronze ears from a century nearly forgotten.

The Crowne Plaza has used a theme to enchant the jaded traveler and offer an environment that is both entertaining and educational.

Some cities have made themes the lifeblood of thriving tourist trade.

Old Williamsburg, Virginia; Fredericksburg, Texas; and New Orleans, Louisiana, with its intriguing French Quarter alive with visitors nearly twenty-four hours a day, each of these areas tenaciously protects the integrity of its historical themes, knowing full well that it is the theme itself that draws tourists by the thousands.

Disney is the master practitioner of theme. Inside a Disney park, visitors find one interesting theme after another curiously juxtaposed in a patchwork quilt of sights and sounds. What makes Disney such a worthy example is the attention it pays to even the smallest detail. Whether it is a park bench or wall clock, the trim around a shop window or the hardware on a door, Disney remains faithful to every important detail.

Better still is its insistence that each and every employee behaves as an actor on a stage. The stage may be as large-as-life and the audience may be closer than any on Broadway, but it is still an acting job for each employee.

They are hired by the casting office and report to wardrobe for their costumes. And that, more than any detail, is what allows Disney to put the New Orleans area right next to Frontier Land without so much as scratching the thin veneer of make-believe or without allowing an ugly flood of reality to spill into the fun.

Wherever a theme is used successfully, it is because of attention to detail, remaining true to the theme, and insisting that each employee adopt a character, not just a position on the schedule.

Décor is an important part of any theme, too. It is the visual cue that primes the customer's expectation.

Play It to the Hilt

If you ride into town on the theme bandwagon, plan on playing it to the hilt. If you have decided to operate under the theme of an old-fashioned hardware store, do it completely. You'll need hardwood floors and nails sold in kegs. You'll need to provide snap brim caps for your employees and carry at least some merchandise that, even though you don't expect it to ever sell, will add to the décor. In fact, some merchandise should not be carried as inventory, but instead should be written off as décor.

Theme works best when it captures the imagination of your customers. Actually, a theme carried to its extreme approaches theater. A theme played well actually engages the customer.

A perfect example of theme-as-theater is the development of theme restaurants that present the guest with an evening of dining in an oversized medieval castle. Such operations exist in major tourist cities, such as Orlando, Dallas, and Las Vegas.

Once beyond the imposing façade, the customer becomes court supplicant and is treated to an evening of daring horsemanship and skill, as knights joust in the arena below, vying for the attention of any and every fair, and not-so-fair, damsel in the house.

One fun part of the theme: Dinner is served with not a single piece of silverware in sight. Customers dig into their meals with both hands, exhibiting table manners that would get them into trouble at home and thrown out of most self-respecting restaurants. The joke is that here you have a restaurant that has made the lack of amenity part of the service. The price actually goes up as the service goes down. What a neat joke that people will pay to be inconvenienced as long as it is in keeping with the theme!

> **MicroBranding Point**
> Whatever your theme, play it to the hilt.

In Mexico, we were invited to take a short dinner cruise to a nearby island. The theme was roughly stated as an evening of rowdiness aboard an anything-goes pirate ship. Our hosts made announcements as though they were speaking to their fellow swabbies, and the crowning touch was the pantaloons that each of the tourist-cum-pirates was invited to wear. The concept was good. If the passengers had looked anything like the attractive models featured in the brochure, and had they really worn the pantaloons and tops with the daring side splits as had the models, it could have been an awesome evening. They weren't; they didn't; it wasn't.

> **MicroBranding Point**
> Play the theme, but be certain that it matches your product and your customers.

Consider Group Showmanship

Not far from our home is an anomaly. Actually, it is a small town. What makes it so special? The retail sales in this small town of 8,900 friendly folks are nearly eight times greater than what would be expected for a town of this size. Perhaps that is why the people of Fredericksburg, Texas, are so friendly. They're making money in buckets.

The reason for their good fortune? They have agreed, as a group, to play the same theme. Fredericksburg has a wonderful historical district. To violate the integrity of its old German-Texas theme would be the death of the town. Tourists travel for miles to sample the art, handicrafts, and German-style food and baked goods featured in the quaint shops that line an always-crowded, never-hurried Main Street. Add a plastic fast-food operation, throw in a gas station convenience store, and stir in a steel-and-glass office building, and in less than the time that it would take to say the words "ghost town," you would have one.

Fredericksburg, Texas, exists simply because of a theme that group consensus and city ordinance has declared will be the order of business. No one would claim that the food, art, and general merchandise offered by the casual, accommodating merchants of Fredericksburg are all that special. The presentation makes the difference. These savvy merchants have learned to sell both the sizzle and the steak. The sizzle allows them to sell at a premium.

The merchants of Fredericksburg may complain about the high rent in the historic district, but they know that it is exactly this access to civic décor that puts strudel on the table.

How could you work with other nearby businesses to create a group theme? It doesn't have to be an historical theme. It could be something as simple as baskets of flowers hanging from the lightposts that line the street in front of your business.

Check out Tacoma, Washington. Tacoma is a small town that would otherwise be remarkably unremarkable, if it were not for the gorgeous hanging baskets of flowers that add color to every corner.

Check out Victoria, British Columbia. In addition to horse-drawn carriages, you'll see another theme that revolves around breathtaking landscape and lovingly restored architectural delights.

Or visit Mill Valley, California. A hidden valley across the bay from San Francisco, Mill Valley is home to an eclectic mix of shops that, either by design or pure dumb luck, mesh comfortably in a neighborhood where doors are propped open, music is a hallmark of nearly every shop, and steel and glass are noticeable only by their absence.

What could you do to rally merchants in your neighborhood? Whatever it may be, try to march, not in lockstep but at least in homage, to the same drummer. Imagine the impact you could have on a shopping, dining, even service experience.

■ ■ ■

For the latest tips, news, and worksheets to help
with your MicroBranding efforts, visit www.tscottgross.com
and choose the MicroBranding link.

CHAPTER SIXTEEN

Retail Theater

IT'S NOT THE PRODUCT THAT MATTERS. That's not to say that issues of design and quality are not important. It's only to make the point that a great retailer, one with a bit of imagination and the guts to take an intelligent risk, will be successful no matter what the product is.

If there is anything to be learned from the best of the best, it is probably this short list of key principles:

- Listen to the customer.

- Dare to be different.

- Take good ideas and run.

- Be absolutely committed to being the best.

These characteristics will be required for anyone who wants to be more than a "me, too," or worse, an "alsoran."

Beyond paying close attention to the operating values of other successful operators, it will be doubly important to keep a steady eye on the operating values of today's consumer. Quality and value will no longer be worth any more than entry into the game.

There may have been a time when such values as "clean," "safe," and perhaps the idea of "value-priced" were considered to be competitive advantages. This is no longer true. The consistency brought to the marketplace by franchising and chains has made what used to be significant points of difference no more than the price of admission in a game where possessing such values does little more than keep you from being eliminated from consideration.

Meeting the minimum expectation is no longer equivalent to leading the pack. Today's consumers are too sophisticated and spoiled by equally sophisticated retailers, service providers, and even slicker media campaigns.

The winners in the shakeout among retailers will be those who keep in mind the three "E's" of Success: Entertainment, Education, and Environment. These watchwords capture today's consumer, who is increasingly looking for value in the purchase experience that transcends the product itself.

If there is a fourth "E," it is the small-case "e" as in e-commerce.

Magnificent, Miracle Merchandising Mile

Take a walk along Chicago's Miracle Mile, the stretch of high-priced real estate that stretches along Michigan Avenue, north of the loop, and you will see America's most innovative retailers showing off their products in an orgy of razzle dazzle that would have made P.T. Barnum proud.

If you really do walk this street and dare to wander into the highest profile show-offs, you won't be by yourself. The customer traffic in the busiest of stores will easily rival that of the mega-sized discount stores that today mark the borders of any self-respecting suburb.

The three anchors of this frenzy of merchandising are the Sony Gallery, Nike town, and FAO Schwarz. And maybe Crate & Barrel would make a worthy fourth, based strictly on its drop dead, stunning exterior presentation.

More, More!

Everywhere retailers are coming to the conclusion that consumers want more than product in a box. In a world where shopping time comes at a premium, consumers are asking for an opportunity to combine shopping and recreation. They are willing to pay for the pleasure. Our job is to come through when they ask themselves, "Is it worth it?"

In Minneapolis, developers have built a shopping experience so-big, so-grand that it has become a travel destination. Who would think that a shopping mall could ever become a vacation mecca?

The Mall of the Americas has become just that. Every day, tour operators deposit thousands of bus-riding tourists at the entrance. Hours later, shoppers will drag back onto the bus, totally awed and absolutely exhausted.

Jammed with a representative of nearly every retailer in America plus scores of independents, the Mall of the Americas can't truly be appreciated in a single visit. But you could spend all day and never have to worry about things to see and do. In the central court, you can ride a roller coaster. If you get dizzy you can visit a doctor. Feeling better? Then head for one of dozens of restaurants and eateries.

What many Americans have to come to dread, a trip to the mall, has now become an eagerly anticipated event.

Feel Me, Touch Me

The rock opera *Tommy* said it all. We all want to be touched. We all want to participate and be a part of the fun. That is the lesson of the retailers' delight playing daily at a "retail theater near you!"

Positively Outrageous Service

Product quality is no longer a point of difference. Sure, there are exceptions to the fact. For most goods, quality isn't an issue. Do you remember when "made in Japan" meant something was cheap, shoddy? Now "made in Japan" has become a sign of quality.

"Made in China" has replaced "made in Japan" as a sign of slipshod manufacturing. No, I take that back. Boeing and most of the other quality manufacturers have plants in China. Is it Korea? Maybe North but certainly not South Korea.

I have in my file a brochure for a model of the Big Boy Locomotive last built in 1944. It is $1/32$ scale and accurate to the last gorgeous detail. The next time I find myself with a spare $11,250 (plus shipping), that bad boy will come to live in my office. Where do they manufacture this work of mechanical art? Germany? Switzerland? How about the Samhongsa Company in South Korea?

Nope, quality isn't going to set you apart.

Is it price? I don't think so. Why? Because, particularly with our new ability to price shop on the Internet price, isn't going to be much of a factor—all prices will be close to the margin for commodity items.

What's left? Brand. Service. Experience.

Put them all together and what you have is what I call Positively Outrageous Service. POS is a matter of surprising and delighting customers by wrapping an experience around the transaction.

Check out the most successful catalogue retailers. What do they do that allows them to charge an above average price for otherwise average merchandise? They include an experience.

Remember J. Peterman? Think of Land's End. How about L.L. Bean? We're talking charging a premium for products, and yes, quality comes with the package. But what really counts big with the consumer is the experience that is wrapped around the product and the transaction.

All of the upscale catalogues feature stories. Some about the products; some about the experience of owning them.

From Levenger with a photo of an antique biplane on the cover: "One accomplished poet we know likes to compose his stanzas outdoors, on misty mornings or in softly falling rain." (They are selling all-weather pencils.)

From Galls selling police, EMS, and firefighter gear comes this line, "Touch it and you'll know this is not your ordinary duty gear. It's softer and more flexible so you can wear it in comfort each day. But don't be fooled; this gear is tough." Just what you want in a belt holder for your Mace!

I found this on a turned-down page of Bun's Plow and Hearth catalogue: "Our Love Seat Glider's relaxing motion gently takes you back to the simpler times, and gives you all the fun of a swing without having to hang it." (Guess we're getting a glider.)

The current Land's End features a story titled, "Muffy Rides Again." You look.

Victoria's Secret doesn't seem to include written stories, but any reader with half an imagination will, no doubt, fill in their own stories.

"Island time. Buffett's music playing in the distance. Not a thought about the office, your kids, or the school board meeting next week. You'll feel your worries slip away as you..." What are they selling? Darvon? Nope, Tidewater stretch denim shorts. Forty-eight bucks from Sportif USA. Comes complete with an island experience provided you shave your legs first.

Smart marketers understand that the sizzle has become more important than the steak, and they are wrapping an experience around everything from fried onions (Bloomin Onion, Outback Steak House) to small, inexpensive automobiles (Saturn).

MicroBranding Point
Since consumers pay with money, time, and feelings, better deliver an experience that delivers all three.

Now the magic fourth "e": e-commerce. While there is no law of marketing that says you must use e-commerce to sell, use the Web to complete the customer experience. Your Web site should be a place to serve, sell gently to those who are ready, and act as a repository of your brand story. Also it must be a place where customers and potential customers can work on their relationship with you, your product, and the market.

POS Defined

What is Positively Outrageous Service?

- ■ It's random and unexpected.

- ■ It's out of proportion to the circumstance.

- ■ It invites the customer to play (or be otherwise involved).

- ■ It creates compelling, positive word of mouth.

Random and Unexpected

The important point about Positively Outrageous Service is that it is not something you do for every customer every time. It is not something that you can take out of a box and apply to every situation. POS is of the moment and from the heart.

Like customer service in general, Positively Outrageous Service is manufactured on-the-spot, one customer at a time. If you plaster a huge banner over your door proclaiming, "We're going to give you Positively Outrageous Service," you have missed the point entirely. POS, to be POS, must be random and unexpected.

Out of Proportion to the Circumstance

Like the theater and circus that it is, Positively Outrageous Service often relies on exaggeration to make customers say, Wow!

When you want to wow a customer and are short on ideas, try doing something ordinary in an extraordinary way. Do a common thing—big!

How about the time we ate at the Cowboy Steakhouse in Kerrville, Texas, when I asked for a glass of water "the size of a house" and was served a brandy snifter of water that must have held a gallon. I laughed, the people at nearby tables laughed, and we all talk about the incident to this day.

And here's the good part. Once you have received POS, it creates a halo effect around subsequent transactions. That time at the Cowboy I had been served by Nancy. Now, we always make a point of sitting in Nancy's section. This is the only time I will sit in a smoking section. Why? Because either Nancy gives us great service or at least I think it is great service.

From a recent e-mail comes this great story of POS from Jeff Bloniasz: "I had just finished a tour of the Big Dig in Boston with two of my team members who do the same job as I do. One of them has a large customer working in the largest construction project being undertaken in Boston. After our tour, I asked the two if they would prefer fresh seafood from the pier or fresh pasta from the Old North End (Boston's little Italy). They chose the latter.

"I suggested a place where I had eaten previously, La Summa. We found parking after about twenty-five minutes of looking. The North End is narrow roads, not comfortable with today's traffic demands. We parked and walked ¼ mile to the restaurant. The door was unlocked, but when we poked our heads in, a polite young lady stated that they were closed. I saddened quickly and stated that I had spent the last forty-five minutes telling my two guests about the pasta and sauce of La Summa.

"Her response was 'Come on in.'

"Mr. Gross, I must tell you that with the limited crew, they seated us, 'No problem.' Asked the chef if he would cook for us, 'No problem.' They served us bread with the best seasoned olive oil, fresh-made Caesar salads (made the old-fashioned Italian way), and probably the best gnocchi and pasta sauce we have ever had.

"The young lady, Lori, was the owner's daughter. Her mom, helping in the kitchen, Barbara, came and sat with us, talking as we dined. She then gave us a tour of the restaurant and kitchen, treating us like we were the first customers she ever served. We thanked them all, including the chefs and left with a good feeling in our stomachs, but a GREAT feeling in our hearts. Someone had outrageously treated us special. I will not eat anywhere else in the North End ever again."

Invite the Customer to Play

POS invites the customer to play or be otherwise highly involved. It touches customers on a personal level. It invites them to play or in some fashion participate in the experience. Now, here's an interesting side benefit of POS. When you give POS in a public manner, other customers will vicariously participate.

Have you ever been to a magic show where the magician asks for a volunteer from the audience? What do most people do? Besides the one or two extraverts who are shouting, "Me! Me! Me!", the rest of the audience is doing what my magician friends call the "Incredible Disappearing Audience" trick. They look at their lap.

"Well, he can't see me. I'm looking at my lap."

That's okay. You can't bring everyone on stage in person, but you can sure drag them up vicariously. When you saw Fred in half, you are in a sense cutting the entire audience in half. They are watching and thinking, "Wow, that could have been me!"

When you give POS, try to do it in a public manner so that more than one person can benefit.

Create Positive Word of Mouth

Positively Outrageous Service is the service story you can't wait to tell. When you have been wowed, there is no doubt that you are going to tell everyone.

Notice please that the definition of Positively Outrageous Service, the best service you have ever received, is also the definition of plain, old, outrageously awful service. How could the definition of the best service also be the definition of the worst service? Part of it is a matter of expectation.

Service that would make you rave about McDonald's might not even raise an eyebrow if you were dining at Ruth's Chris Steakhouse. Expectation.

POS is the act of stepping beyond the brand promise.

Under promise. Over deliver. That's Positively Outrageous Service.

Horsing Around with Your Brand

A brand is an idea. This idea includes everything—the product and every experience that you can wrap around that product.

Stuart rode into work with this tale about buying a horse for his daughter Katy: Stu was looking for a gentle horse sometimes referred to as a "trail ride horse." Now, Miss Katy is all of eleven so a horse with a few manners was just what the cowboy ordered.

Someone at the feed store suggested that Stu contact a horse trader in nearby Waring, Texas. (If you want to know, Waring is about half way between Comfort and Welfare, which if you think about it pretty much describes us all!)

When it comes to dealing with the good ole boys, you never know just what to expect. Stu figured he'd see some good horses, but he never imagined he would run into a world-class MicroBrander.

When Miss Katy slid out of Stu's dust-covered pickup, she was ready to shop. More than a dozen pairs of huge brown eyes peered at her as their owners stepped cautiously toward the fence, tails swishing rhythmically in the late afternoon sun. Miss Katy was instantly smitten by a tall brown horse already reaching across the fence rail and headed off to stake her claim.

"Whoa, little lady," said a bubba-bellied rancher poking his head from the barn. "That one's a mite rowdy for a new rider. Do you like any of my other girls? How about this one?" The trader put his denim-covered arms around an older mare that was also among the first to tag the fence rail and pulled her face-to-face with Katy Bug.

"She's real gentle and just your size. She's also one my own kids like to ride so I know you two would be great friends." He spit a brown bullet aimed perfectly at the base of a fence post.

It didn't take much misdirection to sell a horse already nuzzling the Divine Miss Katy.

Hooking his miniature cowboy boots over the bottom rail and watching intently was younger brother Tyler, the original Big T.

Well, Stu negotiated a few bucks off an already fair price (you have to do that; it's just the way of things) and allowed that it would be several days before he could manage to pick up the new member of the family.

"No, problem. I'll be happy to drop her by first thing tomorrow. It doesn't seem right to keep a young lady waiting." Turning to Miss Katy he added, "And it doesn't seem right to send you off with a horse and no bridle. Step into the tack room and pick out a new bridle for your new horse."

Big T was feeling decidedly left out.

"And for you, cowboy, I have just the thing."

Fishing into a box lifted from a high wooden shelf, the trader found a package that jingled. Two blue eyes watched the mystery unravel as a pair of shiny new spurs were placed in his hand.

"You can't ride your sister's horse without these, cowboy." The trader adjusted them expertly and put them on Big T's dusty boots.

Now here's the deal. Big T wanted to wear those spurs to school. More importantly, because of this MicroBranding horse trader, he said, "Dad? Can I sell my motorcycle? I think I'd like to get a horse."

After the Party

There is no more powerful marketing than positive word of mouth. The goal of a MicroBrander is to entice customers to talk about the brand after the party.

How do you do this? You have to stand out. You have to do something beyond the expected. The good news is that this is neither difficult nor expensive. All that is required is a touch of imagination and perhaps a pinch of daring.

Some years ago, we bought a new Ford Explorer. Why? A friend recommended it. He even told us what dealer we should buy from.

We called the dealer, were impressed by the sales guy we talked to, and pretty much made the deal over the telephone. This wasn't our first new vehicle, but we were still plenty excited when we pulled onto the lot. Steve, the sales guy, met us at the door wearing a white western hat. (This dealership billed itself as being "the good guys in the white hats." In cowboy movies, the good guys where white hats; the bad guys, well, you remember!)

Steve showed us the vehicle starting with the engine. Hey, I knew it would have one so what was the big deal? When we finally got to the rear of the Explorer, Steve lifted the hatch and began fishing around in a small compartment on the left side saying, "In here is the jack, the jack stand, instructions, and everything you need to change a tire should you ever have a flat." He pulled out something that at first I didn't recognize. "And these, Mr. Gross, will make sure you don't get dirty in case you have to change a tire on the way to an important meeting." He was holding what had instantly become the most important feature on a fairly expensive vehicle, a pair of cheap, cotton work gloves.

When I got home did I talk about the engine? Did I mention the drive train or the towing package? Nope. Showed half the neighborhood a cheap pair of cotton gloves.

> **MicroBranding Point**
> Your mission is to think about what you can do to create positive, compelling word of mouth.

The Apostles

Executive Jet in Columbus, Ohio, calls our office every now and then to order a couple of hundred books. I don't know where the company was introduced to *Positively Outrageous Service*, but I do know that its people are apostles, true believers that practice and promote POS.

If you are going to wow a customer, who should it be? One that is already an apostle is the best choice. Why? Because you know they are going to talk about you. In marketing, there is a saying that it is easier to peak the peaks than it is to raise the valleys. It is also true that it is easier to impress folks who are already impressed than it is to create new converts.

You shouldn't go looking for converts.

You should focus on the apostles. Love on the apostles. Let the apostles bring in the new converts.

■ ■ ■

For the latest tips, news, and worksheets to help
with your MicroBranding efforts, visit www.tscottgross.com
and choose the MicroBranding link.

CHAPTER SEVENTEEN

Cement Yourself

The right to be heard does not automatically include the right to be taken seriously.

HUBERT HUMPHREY

Ink and Air

IN AN OVER-MARKETED, HIGHLY COMPETITIVE AGE, GETTING NOTICED ISN'T EASY. We are drowning in a sea of messages yet gasping for attention. That's the bad news. The good news is most of us compete on a personal or local level. Still, breaking through the clutter is tough.

MicroBranders break through clutter not with the brute strength of dollars spent foolishly but through clever public relations and strategic networking—or as we call it, ink and air.

Clutter

University of California Berkeley researchers Peter Lyman and Hal Varian say that people in the world generate two exabytes of information each year. That's 2,000,000,000,000,000,000 bytes, to be not precise at all. But it amounts to roughly 250 megabytes for you and the same amount for me. In simple language, 250 megabytes is simply "too much."

If we reached for the floppy disks to save all this information, we would be reaching pretty high as the stack would be two million miles high or as Ralph Cramden might have said to Alice, "to the moooon!"

No wonder that in this over-messaged environment, 84 percent of Americans say that television is boring. You're going to have to work hard to catch *their* attention.

So how *do* you break through the noise so you can be heard?

If you have a new brand or even a brand that is undeveloped, there is good news and bad news. First the bad news. Advertising won't work. Besides, it's expensive. Here's the good news. PR will do the trick—and it's nearly free!

Read on. We'll show you!

Push-Pull Marketing

There are two fundamentally different approaches to marketing—and only one works. You can *push* people to you, or you can *pull* them to you. Push marketing is not much different than herding cats. Possible but, gee, it takes a lot of effort.

There are two words in marketing that by themselves are dangerous. Together they are explosive. The first is "discount." The second is "coupon." As a bonus, we throw in the word "bundle," which is French for discount a lot of stuff at the same time.

There is something natural about push marketing. We figure that if we offer someone a hot enough deal, they won't be able to resist. But deep discounts are exactly what won't work for two reasons: First, if the discount truly is deep, you won't be able to maintain a profitable margin. And second, the discounted price educates the customer to a new perceived value for the product.

Early in our married life, we ate out once or twice a week and almost always at a discount. One midweek night Buns asked if I wanted to go out and I suggested Sizzler Family Steakhouse. "Oh, not tonight," was her immediate reply, "tomorrow is when they run their specials." We had been trained to eat at the Sizzler but only on deal!

When we ran our fried chicken restaurant, we were amazed to learn that many customers only came in when we ran a margin-killing coupon. At other times, we could drive past our competition and see those same customers in their drive-through using their coupon.

We decided to let the competition have all the low-margin customers.

One Sunday I walked into our restaurant and noticed a line of folks all waiting for the next batch of chicken to come up. They were happy. Someone had given them courtesy drinks, and things were going just fine when a newly arrived customer approached the counter waving a deep discount coupon that he had brought from nearby San Antonio.

It was a coupon for a large order discounted to a low profit price of $4.99. My guess is that the customers waiting so patiently were good for nearly $100 in sales when first one, then another asked what was the $4.99 special. In an instant, almost all of them changed their orders, and we had managed to turn a hundred dollars into fifty. "We lose a dollar on every sale, but we make up for it in volume." Duh!

A favorite association client asked members what was the worst $500 they had ever spent on marketing. The responses were all examples of the kind of push marketing we should know better than to do. There was advertising on the back of cash register receipts. There were Welcome Wagon promotions, ads on prescription bags, even Web sites that came complete with the promise of a listing on major search engines.

Curiously, the only one reported to have worked was a direct mail campaign to five hundred top customers offering a selection of coupons. In this case, not one coupon was redeemed, but sales jumped considerably. So if not the coupon, what did the job? Being in the face of the top five hundred customers—pull marketing not push advertising.

MicroBranding Point
The MicroBrander approach to marketing is to let the market come to you.

You can't afford to drive sales to your door if you have little or no brand awareness. Lack of awareness is almost always a result not of being too small a fish but of swimming in a pond that is way too big. That's okay. The very essence of MicroBranding is that we want only to be a big player in a small area.

One of the early things you must do is define your market. Then, don't do any marketing that is not precisely on target. Leave the image marketing to the big boys. MicroBranders know the who, what, when, where, why, and how of their target market.

Begin by listing the parameters that apply to you and your product. You and your market are defined by price, location, interests, sex, age, life-style—the possibilities are endless:

Professional women who live in the Midwest and own 401Ks.

Water ski enthusiasts who prefer to rent boats rather than own them.

Small-town retailers with five or more employees.

Healthcare providers competing with HMOs.

Men nearing retirement age who live in the Ozarks.

MicroBranding Point #1
Until you tightly define the market, you cannot efficiently build your MicroBrand.

MicroBranding Point #2
Once the market is targeted, it is time to hit it again and again with clever public relations.

PR

There is one point to public relations: Positive publicity that is free. It's as simple as that.

That was the good news. Here's the bad. Getting great PR is difficult. It requires effort, imagination, timing, persistence, technique, and effort. (I know, I wrote effort twice but I want you to get the idea that the PR machine isn't something that works on battery. It's tough.)

Just for fun, we'll look at technique first.

Great PR needs four things:

■ A ticking clock.

■ An innovative hook.

■ A What's-In-It-For-Me.

■ And finally, a sedative.

Time Bomb

The secret to getting response to your PR is timeliness. Tell me what is in the news, and I'll tell you what makes reporters sweat. They don't create the news; they follow it. The news takes control of the media, which is always looking for news. So whatever you do, make your PR efforts tie into the news.

If it's a magazine about houseboats, make your PR relate to houseboats and you're likely to have your story printed. If the hot news is wild fire in the Midwest, a release that relates to fires, firefighters, or victims of fire is likely to get noticed. Oh, yes, did I mention that above all, PR must be honest? Give 'em a great story but don't stretch the truth. Just gently hype it.

Let's look at the three top stories in the U.S. as this is written: The Bush budget, NBA playoffs, and here's a local issue, water rights. Does this mean you have to have a story that relates to these items exactly to be noticed? Not at all. Just tie them loosely.

For a musical instrument store: *"Bush Budget May Boost Bands."* *This could be a story of how a local store owner hopes that lower tax rates will result in more donations to local school bands. He may note that band participation has been severely limited by lack of instruments.*

For a car dealership: *"Local Man Scores Points With NBA!" Follow this with a story about how a car dealership is offering a $1000 donation in the name of car buyers who can match the free throw percentage of the favorite NBA team.*

For a plumbing service: *"Plumber Flushed in Water Fight."* The *story reports how a local plumber has gone to bat for water rights in the area by running for a seat on the water commission.*

Get the idea? Use your imagination and tie to what is in the news. All you have to do is get close.

Innovation

There is one giant obstacle to innovation. It isn't a lack of ideas; it is fear. People don't do, or sometimes even think of, things worthy of media notice for one reason—they think people will laugh at them. Great!

> **MicroBranding Point**
> Humor is a key element of great publicity.

It takes a ton of chutzpah to dream up really great publicity hooks. Imagine walking in to your boss and saying, "Boss! I've got a great idea for generating tons of free, positive publicity. Let's float a giant target in the ocean near New Zealand with our logo on it. Then, if a falling space station drops out of the sky and hits the target, we'll give everyone a free taco. What do you think?"

Well, what do you think? Would you have tried it? That's exactly what some genius at Taco Bell did when the Soviet Space Station Mir was about to de-orbit and crash to the earth. I saw at least three prime time mentions of the offer on NBC, and I imagine there were countless others.

The MIR stunt was exactly the kind of thinking I would expect from a MicroBrander, yet here it was coming from a global competitor. Taco Bell is a part of TriCon, whose other two players are Pizza Hut and KFC. Imagine that! A big player dabbling in what my friends Marc and Jeff Slutsky call Streetfighter Marketing.

Betting on a falling space station is exactly the kind of thinking you expect from an entrepreneur with empty pockets but not from a big budget player like the Bell.

Maybe this should be a warning. It looks like the big guys are learning to think small.

I had to know more about the MIR stunt, so I did what all good MicroBranders do, I asked.

Rarely do you hear enthusiasm from a corporate weenie. They have their rules, their cubicles, and their 401K plans. Okay, so I'm not always right. The Taco Bell folks are absolutely on fire over their MIR success. At least that is the impression that I got from talking to Carol Anawati, a member of the team.

It turns out that CEO Emil Brolick actually suggested the creation of what he calls the Buzz Marketing Team. The idea is to think out of the box, think like money was an issue, and take advantage of topical events to break through the clutter. Brolick had heard that other companies were doing grassroots marketing, and he wanted to take a shot.

The Buzz Marketing Team is made up of creative people from corporate. I thought it was odd that there are no operations folks and that the franchise community is not represented at all. I have a dollar that says that will eventually change. Why? Because a) there are lots of ideas out in the field and Brolick probably is too smart a guy to pass them up, and, b) now that the team has had a huge success, everyone will want to play.

Remember, it takes courage to think outside the box. Nontraditional thinking is by nature risky business. Only competent organizations will risk the unusual.

The Buzz Marketing Team was set up to meet every two weeks, but now that the MIR success is written into their logbook, the powers that be have decided that a weekly meeting makes more sense—and probably a pile of dollars!

The details of the MIR stunt are fairly simple: Float a huge target in the Pacific Ocean just off Sydney, Australia, in the general area where the aging Soviet MIR space station is forecast to fall to earth. Offer everyone in the United States a free taco if the ship or any part of it hits the target.

How do you begin to think up an idea like this?

We've long said that the best marketing ideas come when you put two or more ordinary ideas on a collision course. The director of merchandising and member of the team had heard on the radio that the MIR was about to de-orbit and that it was the largest man-made object to ever hit the earth. Russian scientists would have to perform a tricky maneuver to ensure that the station hit the ocean rather than a populated land mass. It was an event that the usual group of negative Luddites had billed as having apocalyptic potential.

The much publicized event was too tempting for a creative marketing mind: "Hey, why not put up a big target and let them try to hit it?"

Ideas already on the table included a suggestion to springboard on an earlier campaign that pondered whether a burrito should be zesty or not zesty. So originally the stunt involved letting the falling satellite determine zesty or not. Unfortunately, it wasn't all that likely that the station or even pieces of it would hit anything other than empty ocean.

First run of the idea involved putting the target on a building. That one was quickly abandoned although most of us could nominate a suitable building without much thought. Since the Russians were targeting the ocean, it only made sense to put the target there. And because it wasn't likely the target would be hit, the deal was changed to give a free taco to everyone in the United States if it was.

So an Australian firm was hired, a target was created and floated, insurance was purchased, and contingency plans were made. The Australian Coast Guard got involved as did a shipping company that had to be hired to monitor the target area.

Plans were made to print coupons that the public could pick up at a Taco Bell good for a free taco on staggered dates—should the Mir hit the target. These guys thought of everything including the incredible impact the promotion would have at store level in the event the company had to make good on a free taco for the entire U.S.

How much did it cost? Well, Taco Bell wouldn't say other than it was about what it would have cost for a full page color ad in the *Los Angeles Times*. (We're talking in the neighborhood of $60-80K.)

Who cares what it cost? We want to know what they got! How about an estimated 120 million impressions! The readership of the Southern

California edition of the Sunday *LA Times* is just over 4 million. In the simplest terms Taco Bell enjoyed a leverage on its efforts that was at least thirty times greater than traditional advertising. At least. But we think it was a lot more.

Would you notice a one-time full page ad in your local paper? Maybe, maybe not. But if you saw the president of Taco Bell on the *Today Show* complete with footage of a target floating in the Pacific, my dollar says you would notice and probably even talk about it!

Not bad for Taco Bell's first attempt at Buzz Marketing!

The Hook

> *REVEALED: The Best Street In Toronto*
> *—Globe and Mail*

All great PR begins with an innovative, call it outrageous, hook. You have to say something that grabs attention, and the best way to do that is to say something that seems barely plausible. The reader or listener should have a "no way!" reaction.

And the hook must be true. Oh, you can stretch the truth a bit and there is always that matter of opinion to fall back on, but in whole, your hook has to be truth if not quite believable.

In the example above from the *Globe and Mail* in Canada, the writer promises to let you in on a secret. Notice, the word *revealed*. That word alone promotes a sense of mystery and promises that you are about to come in to a bit of insider's knowledge. Of course, the best street in Toronto is a matter of opinion but too late! You've already read the headline and maybe the entire article. (In case you want to know, it's Charles Street West.)

Check out the press releases in this chapter and see if you can spot the hook. Actually, I like to use a double headline, sort of a one-two punch. My theory is that if the first one doesn't get them, the second one will.

For Immediate Release

For More Information
Contact: Melanie at 800-635-7524
Buns@hctc.net

Everybody Has One

… a brand, that is! If they know your name, you have a brand. Whether you are a teacher or lover, a mayor or a department head, you have a brand that needs to be managed if you want to get the most out of love and labor.

Do they call you Grandpa or Colonel? Either way, you could benefit from the secrets the big boys use to manage global brands. And, if you own a local store, why not use the secrets of MicroBranding to beat the global competition? You might even create such a powerful presence that the big box discounters will run from you!

MicroBranding: Build a Powerful Brand & Beat Your Competition was written by a little guy for all the little guys (and gals) who are having trouble standing out in a world long on message and short on meaning.

Isn't it about time we all got a brand?

They just don't know what to do with it!

T. Scott Gross, best known as the creator of Positively Outrageous Service, is back, and this time he's going to show us all how to stand out—without being outstanding. The same techniques that global competitors use to win the hearts and minds of customers everywhere can be yours for the asking.

Scott will show you:

- Seven ways to stand out anywhere.
- How to put the good old boy network to work for you.
- Three secrets of getting your name in print.
- How to use marketing principles to get your life back on track.

If you know Scott, you know you're in for a fun interview. He'll treat you to his usual raft of great stories, while he teaches you how to make a buck by making a difference.

Call for an interview or go to T. Scott Gross's Web site at www.tscottgross.com.

# # #

For Immediate Release

For More Information
Contact: Melanie at 800-635-7524
Buns@hctc.net

Texas Businessman Says, Employees Should Be Branded!

If that sounds a little harsh, maybe you should read on. T. Scott Gross may be the world's expert when it comes to helping individuals, organizations, even entire cities stand out in a world that is cluttered with competing messages.

How do you survive as the owner of a small business when the big box discounters surround you? How can you move your career forward when there are younger, brighter new employees being hired every day and gunning for your raise or your promotion—if not for your job?

T. Scott Gross says the answer is *MicroBranding*. Gross says that you can brand-manage your life and your business in a way that helps you stand out, even if you're not exactly outstanding.

Gross can show anyone how to create and promote a personal, local brand. Gross says you should be branded and...

So should your preacher and your mayor!

T. Scott Gross is the author of *MicroBranding: Build a Powerful Brand & Beat Your Competition.* He is best known as the author of the management classic, *Positively Outrageous Service.* This is the guy who teaches the big guys like Ford and Southwest Airlines how to use humor and surprise to capture customers. And now he shows us how to use the secrets of brand management personally.

This is the one interview you won't want to end!

# # #

WIIFM

If there is a single greatest branding mantra, it has to be the old standby, WIIFM: what's in it for me. When faced with a mountain of press releases, the reporter is often moaning out loud, "Why should I print this garbage?" In other words, he is asking, what's in it for me?

Reporters, like the rest of us, will take the easy way out—every time. If the story you want them to promote for you is going to take a lot of work on their part, the only answer you could reasonably expect is: NEXT! In newsrooms large and small, there is one piece of equipment that goes right next to the fax machine; it's the trash can. Most press releases never make it beyond the trash can.

If the story you want them to run is of little interest to their audience, again, you will hear them mutter under their breath as you make your contribution to the recycling bin.

E-mail is not even that glamorous. Like the rest of us, reporters and editors read their e-mail with one finger on the delete key. Fail to impress in the first three seconds and another electron stream bites the dust.

Media people are good people, and they want to help. But they aren't going to run your story just because you are nice or your cause is good. And they aren't going to run your story if they think their editor is going to say, "Why in the name of good sense are you doing this story?"

You have to make it easy. And you definitely have to answer the question of what's in it for me and what's in it for the audience.

You as the Expert

If your press release makes it past the first two hurdles, there is one key question that will be asked: What gives you the right to speak on this topic or for this group?

No matter what the subject, give yourself a title. Author, explorer, spokesperson, VP of public affairs, any of those will do so long as it is appropriate to the story.

Call Me

There is only one goal for a press release. You want editors and reporters to pick up the phone and call for more information. Here is where so many folks lose their momentum. It makes no sense to drive reporters to telephone a number answered by voice messaging.

Like the press release, the phone call is one more step in the decision process. Just because a reporter calls, it does not mean he or she is going to do a story. In most cases, the phone call is a form of audition and if you think you can run a reporter through six levels of voice messaging, you have another thing coming. They just aren't going to do it.

Make it easy. Make it fun. Make it valuable to the audience.

When the reporter calls, be ready. You have maybe thirty seconds to sell your story and yourself as the spokesperson. If you have a great story but come across like a wet blanket—fageddaboudit.

Be cheerful and upbeat without being gushy. Have your facts close at hand and be ready to back them up if you are asked a follow-up question. Remember, if you are talking to radio or TV people, they are auditioning you as a potential guest—so be up, speak in sound bites of thirty seconds or less, and give the reporter a chance to ask follow-up questions.

The goal of the follow-up call is to get the reporter to ask for additional information. You have, as a fisherman would say, set the hook.

The hook got them to call. The call sets the hook. Next, send them the bait.

There is one sure-fire way to get media attention. It is so powerful I have been saving it for last. Surveys. Surveys are killer when it comes to attracting the media. They love claims like "24 percent of American workers report that they are chronically angry at work" or "one in four doctors admit flirting with patients." (Those are made up so no quoting!)

Just this morning I picked up *USA Today* and staring at me was the better part of a full page dedicated to Mellody Hobson, president of Ariel Mutual Funds. How did Ms. Hobson earn such attention? A survey!

Ms. Hobson is on a mission to increase African-American investing, and her survey on her target market's investing habits bought her and her company more quality free press than you could buy with a bucket of bucks.

What kind of survey could land you a full page in *USA Today*? (And if it did, what would it be worth to your career or business?)

Almost There

The bait that you want reporters to run with is a press kit that provides them with all the additional material they need to write or run your story.

The press kit should include examples of other media hits, a list of FAQ (frequently asked questions) and their answers, and a complete story. You will be amazed at how often a story will run almost exactly as you hand it to them.

On the next page is an example of FAQs for a book I wrote on personal negotiating. Notice that I provide my introduction. Also notice that at the end I insert a question about how to get the book. In hundreds of interviews, I have never *not* been asked that question!

Paying for It

There are two ways to build a brand: the traditional way and the MicroBrander's way. One costs a pile of money. The other is free, just not easy.

Networking and public relations may be the only way for a MicroBrander to break through the clutter. So many big buck companies are clogging the airwaves with relentless discounting messages that humor and creativity may be the remaining technique for reaching your audience. It also requires a huge dose of persistence.

> **MicroBranding Point**
> For networking and public relations to be effective, they must be continuous.

What you save in hard costs will be paid for in effort. But an impression made via personal marketing will last considerably longer than the coupon for discounted bananas in the weekly grocery circular.

How to Get What You Want from Almost Anybody

Introduction: "T. Scott Gross is best known as the creator of Positively Outrageous Service, an idea that he teaches to corporations so that they can give great service. But Gross is also good at *getting* great service, so we've invited him to share his secrets for handling rude clerks, pushy salespeople, and store policies that just don't make any sense!"

1. How did you get into this business of customer service?

2. What is Positively Outrageous Service?

3. What's the craziest thing you've ever done when it comes to service?

4. Does service always have to be bizarre to be considered Positively Outrageous Service?

5. Who would you say are the best companies when it comes to great customer service?

6. You have four key tips for getting great service. What are they?

7. What if your tips don't get the job done? Is there a way to complain that actually gets results?

8. Not all customers are going to use your advice. Some are going to be pretty rude and aggressive. Any tips for the working stiff who just wants to get through the holiday season?

9. It's not easy being a boss these days. What advice do you have for the boss who may be short of help and under pressure to produce?

10. If I'm a boss and I want to know more about customer service, how do I contact you? (Now follows a tasteful but shameless pitch. It won't hurt, and it will be over before you feel it—promise!)

To contact T. Scott Gross:
800-635-7524
www.tscottgross.com
www.positivelyoutrageousservice.com

Targeted, Timed, and Tenacious

One press release means nothing.

Like any other form of marketing, press releases need multiple repetitions to break through the clutter. One press release will get results but not half as much as two. Four releases will get you more than twice the responses of two. Why? Because it takes awhile to break through the clutter.

All good MicroBranders should have a media schedule.

Timing is another issue. Print media such as magazines need at least ninety days lead time. Again, keep in mind WIIFM. Target the magazine, and better yet, target the issue. Go to the publication's Web site where you will learn what is the theme of each issue. Target the issue. If you think your story is strong enough and the exposure is good enough, consider changing your schedule to match theirs.

Other media need less of a lead time but must still be targeted. For example, you may want to target a particular radio show rather than a radio station. Or target a particular column or section rather than just the newspaper.

When you target precisely you let the editors know that you have done your homework and that you think there is a fit. This gives them confidence that you know what you are doing and aren't just trying to squeeze them for a free mention of any kind.

You should never seek media for a one-time mention. Better to miss an opportunity than to force a poor fit. When you act like a professional, you have the chance of developing a long-term relationship in which they will, from time to time, actually seek you for an opinion since in their minds you are the recognized expert.

When you are not the right fit, say so! There is no better way to develop trust with the media than to say when you are not the expert they need. Better yet, suggest who is the right contact and you will be regarded as a trusted resource.

Networking: The Power of Influence

Forget the organizational chart. Networking is the source of influence.

In a recent episode of *Friends*, Rachel was having a networking crisis at work. Her boss was a smoker who frequently left Rachel behind in the office while she went outside to smoke with a coworker. Outside in the haze of smoke a lot of key decisions were made. As a nonsmoker, Rachel was left out of the loop.

Silly story? Goofy premise? Yes, on both accounts. But does it happen? Every day.

The fact is people like to hang out with people who are like themselves. A friend of ours has a son who had a terrible school year because he got caught up with the "Skaters." His complaint was that after being labeled a Skater, he was unable to connect with the kids with whom he really identified. They shunned him and he felt left out.

Never mind what a Skater is or a Goth, Kicker, Druggie, Jock, Cheerleader, or Prep. Just know that the network you are in determines the information you receive.

If there is one piece of career or branding advice I would want you to remember, it is this: Put yourself where you can network to your advantage. If the folks in the network where you want to be are golfers, better learn the game. If they are drinkers, then be prepared to play their game or find another game to play.

The Best Network Position

There are two key network positions. They correspond roughly to long-term play and short-term advantage. They are takers and connectors.

If you only want one quick connection out of a network, then find out who can facilitate the connection, make it, and leave.

If you want to truly tap into the power of the network then become a connector. The connector focuses on helping others and is seen as the "go to guy," the one who knows everyone and can connect anyone. The go to guy, the connector, is ultimately regarded as the most powerful person to know.

When I had a real job, the president of our company was a poor networker. He hated conflict and wasn't exactly what you would call a people person. So he hired a presidential liaison, someone who was charged with handling the bulk of the president's communication with the rest of the organization.

Who was soon seen as the most powerful person on or off the organization chart? The presidential liaison. Why? Because he had the power to connect—or not.

You don't need a title to play the role of connector. And you don't need permission!

Networking for Fun and Profit

Sorry, I couldn't resist the cheesy title to this section. It's just that too many people have the idea that networking is nothing more than a fancy name for brown-nosing. It isn't.

But there is an unseemly side to networking so we may as well be honest and talk about it.

Is there such a thing as a good-old-boy network? No doubt about it. It's probably age-ist and no-doubt sexist, but it's there nonetheless.

Is there a good-old-girl network? Take it to the bank.

How about the Hispanic Chamber of Commerce? If being Hispanic is the standard for membership, how could you call it anything but racist?

Prisons are full of gangs based on race or color. Got any idea why?

Then there are the Young Republicans, as opposed to what, the Old Republicans? There are the Royal Ambassadors at the local Baptist Church and don't forget the quilting club, the Sweet Adelines, and even Alcoholics Anonymous.

One day while shopping for a camera, the clerk leaned over the counter and in a conspiratorial tone said, "Haven't we met?"

"I don't think so, but maybe."

"I believe I know you from 'the program'."

I don't think so but why disabuse him of the notion if working with a fellow traveler made him feel more comfortable?

If you are reading this and if you are normal, you are already trying to figure my age, race, sex, religion, and politics. You want to know if I am like you—or not.

Face it. We like to do business with people whom we are comfortable around. And even though for the right amount of money most would cut a deal with the devil, all in all, we want to be around folks like us (whoever "us" is.)

Just to prove the point, I caught a news report yesterday that said a college marketing student had sold his soul on e-Bay. I believe it went for $400.

I think we all have a responsibility to fight inequity wherever it rears its ugly head. But while we are fighting, it wouldn't hurt to be practical. Recognize that if you aren't in the group, you're going to have to work harder to get what you want.

Start by being aware that you may have a disadvantage and then work to overcome it by doing whatever is possible, practical, and doesn't involve soul selling.

When I began my work career I was, no surprise, one of the youngest executives in our company. Twenty-five and full of enthusiasm and undeveloped talent, I couldn't wait to show my stuff. I thought the old folks in the office were nice but awfully stuffy in their expensive suits and blue-hair cars. Our chairman drove a navy blue Cadillac with gold trim and wide white sidewall tires. Yuck! To me it looked like a pimpmobile.

On the weekends, the old folks headed for the country club, while I scooped up the family in the pop-top Volkswagen camper and boogied to the coast.

I, on the other hand, rode a candy-apple red Honda motorcycle to work. Two reasons. First, we had sold my car so I could invest in a rental house. Second, I loved motorcycles. I also hated suits so off to work I would ride every morning with my suit coat rolled into a backpack. Rain or shine, burning hot or icy cold, I rode that motorcycle eight miles to work often arriving too cold to unwrap my frozen fingers from the handle grips. Sometimes I would show up soaked from unexpected rain showers.

Stupid.

Not riding a motorcycle. Stupid because riding a motorcycle kept me from looking like the other executives whose cars lined the reserved spaces near the front door. And stupid for not dressing in the conservative suits favored by the executive suite crowd. And double stupid for racing home to wife and kiddo instead of stopping at least for a quick one at the local pub with the boys and girls who made the big bucks.

Okay, I wouldn't really do it all differently if I had it to do again. But for certain I wouldn't park a fire red Honda motorcycle next to a latte-colored Mercedes.

Do you think I fit? How much did riding a motorcycle cost me, really? What would it have been worth to me to invest in a decent suit?

Would a membership to the club have paid off? The truth is, I didn't look or act like the brass I was working for. Had it not been for good ideas and execution on my part, I doubt I would have lasted six months. But, oh, could I have improved my lot had I just been more careful not to make folks uncomfortable.

That said, how in the world do you network without being a brown-noser?

Ask the Expert

Good science is repeatable. If you have a theory that works once and if it's a good one, it will work again. If I run the experiment and it is based on good science, I will get the same result as when you run the experiment.

So I like rules. I like to break things into simple steps that anyone can follow to get great results. That is what trainers do: Remove mystery. So that was the goal when I started thinking about networking. Look closely at the mechanics of networking to see if there are a few simple rules or steps that would help anyone become a better networker.

We once had a video editor who gave notice so she could pursue a career in journalism. She didn't ask for my advice but I gave it to her anyway saying, before you pay too much attention to a professor, ask him how many books he has written and how many of those were actually sold. If the answer is millions, pay close attention. If he has only studied journalism but never actually made a good living in the field, run!

So, in chapters 18 and 19, I bring you two interviews with the sharpest networkers I know.

■ ■ ■

For the latest tips, news, and worksheets to help
with your MicroBranding efforts, visit www.tscottgross.com
and choose the MicroBranding link.

CHAPTER EIGHTEEN

Road Running

FRED VANG SINGLE-HANDEDLY SELLS MORE CARS THAN MANY DEALERSHIPS. He does it without running a single ad. He is never on the radio. Fred has no inventory. He rarely has to leave the comfort of La Casita, a small but comfortable office apartment tucked a few steps behind his gorgeous home in Santa Fe, New Mexico.

Fred's customers come to him.

Fred is the world's greatest networker.

Fred *knows* more people than could be listed in a good-sized phone book. I don't mean he has their name and address or that he has met them casually. Fred *knows* people. He knows what makes them tick.

If Fred has read a book, chances are he *knows* the author. I don't mean able to recite the name; I mean Fred knows the author and the author knows Fred.

If Fred takes you to a restaurant, he knows the owner—and probably the chef and definitely the waiter and no doubt the bus boy as well.

When Fred drives a car, he knows it, too. He knows the chief engineer, the director of marketing, and the guy who prepped it at the dealership.

Fred knows world class musicians, actors, inventors, and moguls of industry. He *knows* people, and that is the heart of his networking abilities.

Ask Fred (fredvang@earthlink.net) if networking is a talent or if it can be learned and he says, "Both! I think it's a discipline. You have to be consistent, and you have to know what to be consistent with."

Here is a guy who learned networking early and made it a lifelong endeavor. Networking isn't something Fred does on cue. It's his life. Cars have been Fred's life and love forever.

As a college student selling cars to pay the bills, Fred remembers the day a large group of brown-skinned young men poured out of a car that had pulled up in front of the dealership. (The custom in car dealerships is for the salespeople to sign in as they arrive for work. First in becomes first up and gets the first customer through the door.)

On this morning the grizzled first up salesman announced that he would pass on the strangers now approaching the door. Second up took a pass, and number three likewise made himself unavailable. The assumption was that they were young, of color, and worse, carried purses. That could only mean that they were too poor to buy and gay to boot.

Fred was excited, not turned off, as first up snarled, "Go ahead, college boy."

Fred began by asking where they were from. The Philippines. To Fred that was an invitation to discover something new and meet new friends. He took the group into the dealership and pulled out his atlas (hard to believe someone would make an atlas part of his standard work gear but you'd have to know Fred).

It turned out that the young men were all cousins of high-ranking Filipino politicians. Fred discovered that the young men were homesick while in the U.S. attending college.

"Who does the cooking?" The boys pointed to a dour-faced cousin and indicated that while he was the best in the group, they hadn't had a decent home-cooked meal in quite awhile.

Fred called home to his wife Martha, and the troop piled back into their car in reverse order and headed to a home-cooked meal. At dinner, a guest asked Fred if he had any hobbies and discovered that Fred collected license plates from around the world. A quick phone call to the family driver in Manila produced a package that arrived two weeks later containing a freshly minted license plate from each province of the island country.

Eighteen new cars later, Fred and Martha were guests at the new family home in Pebble Beach where all of the cars Fred had sold were lined along the drive for a picture commemorating their good fortune in meeting the Vang family.

Networking pays.

There is a side bar to this story. The day after meeting the Filipinos, a neighbor mentioned to Fred that someone in the neighborhood drove a BMW and that Fred ought to meet him. Standing in the middle of the road, Fred flagged down the driver and invited him over for barbecue.

It turned out this fellow was also a Filipino, a supporter of the Opposition Party. No problem for Fred who now figures this chance introduction was good for exactly twenty-five new cars sold by—Fred!

I asked Fred if networking was always a conscious act. "Martha says, "Fred, you never stop!"" But I wondered if it was always a good and ethical act. "You are building your relationships, and you have a sale in mind from the beginning. Everyone has needs, and they might as well be satisfied by someone who knows them better than anybody else!"

Sometimes Fred doesn't network; he connects. Our standing routine is we fly to Santa Fe for lunch, and Fred supplies an interesting lunch or dinner guest. We have met an Internet pioneer, a nationally syndicated columnist, the creator of gourmet root beer, even a suspected former CIA spook. Who cares about food in company like this!

But there has to be something in it for Fred or connecting would be a waste of time, not something you would expect of a guy with a cell phone glued to his ear.

"It does two things. It helps a person who has a need, and second, once you've helped someone with a good contact, you occupy a higher place in his mind. You've got to remember that the hand in the giving position is also in the receiving position but you've got to serve first! The goal should always be to help the other guy first. Be patient. The karma bus runs in a circle. You'll get yours."

If there is a theme to Fred's networking technique, it must be the idea that you give to get. Fred likes to tell the story of his early days working for a dealership. When the store got too hectic to concentrate on the customer, Fred would drag the customer across the street to a juice bar where he would step behind the counter and personally prepare his prospective client's drink. Then, uninterrupted, he would focus intently on the needs of the customer.

One day his boss, called him to talk about what had become a juice phenomenon saying, "Fred, I've been keeping track of you and your trips across the street to the juice bar. Our typical closing rate is 20 percent. When you go out for juice, you are closing at 75 percent! Keep up the good work, Fred!"

Networking According to Fred

Networking, according to Fred Vang, has two simple steps:

- **Step one:** Recognize that you already have a network. Wherever you shop or pay your bills you have a network. You buy groceries, you take clothes to the cleaners, you stop for gas, and you go to the doctor. Everywhere you go, says Fred, you have a network that is easier to tap into than to create something from scratch. Make a conscious effort to let everyone know what you do for a living. (Remember your positioning statement?)

- **Step two:** Don't ask for a referral. Instead deepen existing relationships and the referrals will come.

> **MicroBranding Point**
> You should not ask for a referral until you have earned the right to be given one without asking.

When Fred opened his first dealership, it was on a four-lane highway with a narrow, bush-lined median. One afternoon a car caught on fire on the other side of the median. Noses pressed against the window of the showroom until Fred said, "Quick! Someone take him a fire extinguisher and a brochure. He's going to need a new car!"

One of Fred's believers quickly trotted across two lanes of traffic and did what he could to help. Then he introduced himself, handed the fellow a card, and waited.

In three days, the burned-out motorist appeared, insurance check in hand, saying, "I really appreciate the fire extinguisher. I had already been thinking about a new car; I guess I was lucky to be passing by your dealership!"

No Sale

Not everyone who holds a place in your network is a buyer. Some are even more valuable than buyers. These are the influencers. While a buyer may buy only once, an influencer can spin many sales in your direction. Spend time with the influencers and hope they don't buy! All the time and effort you spend with an influencer puts points of obligation into your account. They will feel psychologically obligated to send you solid referrals.

Fred says, "Don't ask for the sale. Wait for it to come through the filter of your network. Let your network filter out the flakes and the tire kickers. Network sales are programmed and massaged by the people who have already done business with you."

Fred tells the story of a high-powered, no nonsense San Francisco attorney who called one early morning and said, "I met a customer of yours on the plane last night, and he tells me you can get me the car I want at a good price with no hassle. Is that right?"

"That's what I do. I represent the customer."

"Good, then get me a…" and then he named a vehicle that Fred could not recommend.

"I can't do that."

"But I thought you could get anything I wanted."

"I can but I won't. That's not a good choice for you. Remember, I'm the customer's representative, and I won't get you a vehicle that isn't the best choice."

"Do you mean you will walk away from an easy sale?" growled the attorney, not accustomed to being told no.

"That's right. Now, maybe if you will sign a disclaimer that holds me harmless should you buy a vehicle that isn't right for you, then maybe I could help but I wouldn't like it."

"What do you think is the right choice?"

Fred told him and the next day the deal was done. One buyer. One influencer. Same person.

"The good stuff," says Fred, "is earned not asked for. The best sale is when you have spent enough time together and the customer asks you, 'When can you deliver?'"

■ ■ ■

For the latest tips, news, and worksheets to help
with your MicroBranding efforts, visit www.tscottgross.com
and choose the MicroBranding link.

CHAPTER NINETEEN

Just Wait

MARK MAYBERRY KNOWS EVERYBODY. If he doesn't know you, just wait. He'll get to you!

The big misconception about networkers is the stereotypical impression that they are glad-handers. They wear plaid sports coats, carry business cards in a holster, keep a Rolodex the size of a Volkswagen. Nope. That's not the case, and Mark Mayberry is poster child for the Networkers Antidefamation League.

Mark, a business consultant who speaks on the topic of entrepreneurship, is smart, low-key, and businesslike. He is also fun, outgoing, and a consummate networker.

I'm about to spill the secrets to his success so pay attention and you will learn something.

I met Mark, no surprise, at a cocktail party. This was in the days when I was too poor to pass up free hors d'oeuvres. It was also in the days when I was too stupid to understand the power of networking. Now, I no longer pass either a chance to meet someone new or a platter of munchies.

I became a networker at age forty-four after meeting Mark. But Mark became a networker when he was fourteen. I'll explain.

You couldn't tell it by talking to either of us, but Mark and I have something in common: we're both naturally shy. The difference is that Mark forces himself to cocktail parties and receptions. Sometimes I slip behind the curtain at first opportunity. Without Mark's lessons, I would give in to the lure of sitting cross-legged on the bed in my hotel room eating a two-piece mix from the local KFC.

Mark says that good networkers have to be there to win.

When Mark was fourteen, he was forced, make that dragged out of his shell, when his family moved to another part of the state. Moving a high schooler is seen as the kiss of death by many parents, but in Mark's case, it was the ticket to a skill that today serves him quite well.

Mark says that today his business comes nearly 100 percent from networking, and that it was the move at age fourteen that started him along that path.

Mark also benefited from a natural connector, a high school baseball coach who just happened to work as an umpire throughout the state. When the coach learned that Mark was going to leave, he let his network know that a young man with a great arm was on the move and advised the coach at the new school to watch for a kid named Mayberry.

Having attended thirteen schools myself, I can tell you that moving school-age kids makes them stronger not weaker. I can network. I just don't like it. While moving taught me how to use humor to fit in with one new group after another, Mark got good at networking. Speaking of the move, Mark says without hesitation, "It changed my life!"

Can you learn how to network? Mark says yes, that networking is more a matter of focus than technique. You have to focus on the other guy. Mark says that networking is not about winning or even keeping score.

"It's not about yourself at all, but it comes back to you. So in a way, in the long run, it really is about you. You just don't start with you in mind. I focus on the people I meet and think about where down the road I might be able to help them."

Asked about this idea of not keeping score, Mark says there are two reasons why you shouldn't be concerned about playing tit for tat. First, "if you are worried about scoring, you will lose focus. Second, there really is no way to put a value on a connection since all connections are not the same."

Like Fred Vang, Mark Mayberry seems to view networking and connecting as pure fun. Maybe the best networkers are just good people. Mark says that networking is as much a matter of personal pleasure as it is potential professional gain.

What you must do is be open and ready when a networking opportunity presents itself.

Mark, an avid golfer, was sitting in a Delta Crown room watching a tournament when he happened to chat up a fellow golf fan. It turned out that they were both on the same flight and both enjoyed the game of golf, more than you need for a good networking connection, says Mark.

Once airborne, Mark realized that they had not so much as exchanged business cards. "I thought, how stupid! And I walked over to his seat to say hello again. I wanted to send him a copy of my latest book just for being so much fun to visit with. Well, it turned out that I had been talking to Skip Barnett, the newly appointed CEO of Atlantic Southeast Airlines.

"When he saw my card, he asked what I did and then said, 'I could use a guy like you.' I turned a golf game into one of my biggest contracts, and I did it without anything in mind other than being friendly to a fellow traveler."

Profile

Is there a profile of a good networker? Mark says that while anyone can learn to be a good networker, there are folks who take to it naturally. Some (me for example) will walk onto an airplane and pray to be next to an empty seat. Others will hope for company. God forbid one type sits next to the other! Somebody is going to be disappointed!

Steps

Mark says to be careful not to make networking too scientific. He refuses to boil it down into steps giving instead a few key elements.

- ▪ **You have to be there.** You have to go to the reception. You have to attend the chamber dinner, the church mixer—you have to be there to play and you have to play to win.

■ **You have to put the other guy first.** Phonies or users can be spotted from a mile away. Mark says, "You have to listen with interest. You can't just go and flash your name badge. You have to be interested in the other guy. Think who you might know that the other guy should know. Think about who you know that might benefit from a connection. It's actually, fun!"

I think the really smart networker would go with a list in hand. A "who do you want to meet and why" sort of list. Mark gives that idea a cautious thumbs up with the warning that going by a list might also be an excellent way to miss someone really important to meet. And as you may suspect, Mark defines important to meet as someone who is fun, nice to be around, professionally interesting, and least, as well as last, might someday do something for you.

Maybe Mark is a bad example—he's a natural. Some of us might have to at least initially think about networking. But Mark says that when you are doing it right, you never have to think, "Boy, I'm really networking now!"

■ **Never get comfortable with your list of contacts.** I didn't get this one until Mark explained saying, "Notice how most people tend to stick with people who they know. They talk to people they know; they sit and eat with people they know. And that's a huge networking mistake."

Yes, but maybe we just happen to like these familiar faces. Mark thinks there are plenty of new faces that with a little effort will also join our list of familiar ones. Like Fred, Mark is always networking!

MicroBranding Point
Be there. Put the other guy first. Never get comfortable.

But, Ma!

I read a joke about a fellow who was awakened by his mother one Sunday morning.

"Wake up! You have to go to church!"

"But, Ma, I don't want to!"

"You have to, so get out of bed."

"But I don't want to. I hate going to church for two reasons: First, it's boring, and second, they always say bad things about me."

"I'll give you two reasons why you are going: First, you're forty-five years old, and second, you're the preacher!"

Networking takes at least a little chutzpah, and here's a hillbilly interpretation of chutzpah: The ability to risk looking foolish in order to get what you want. Like Fred, Mark has met CEOs, actors, and folks from nearly every walk of life. For two reasons: First, he was paying attention for networking opportunities; second, because he was willing to be rebuffed.

"Have you ever been turned down or put off?" I asked him.

"Absolutely!" Mark's answer was quick and certain. But when I asked by whom, he couldn't think of a single incident. What he could remember was a laundry list of folks who said yes.

"Isn't at least the prospect of getting turned down a bit intimidating?"

"I look at it as a matter of poor timing," Mark says. "People, even famous people, aren't going to turn you away unless the time is just not right. And that's not anybody's fault. Besides, think of the opportunities you could miss by holding back."

"Let me tell you a story. I got this story because of networking and it involves John Smoltz, the famous Atlanta Braves pitcher." (I knew that! Jock that I am, but just to be certain, Mark helped me with the spelling before continuing.)

"We were at a charity event. John is genuine. He's a great networker. He doesn't just show up and then hit the door. He takes time to visit because he understands that fans make him who he is. Besides, he seems to really enjoy meeting them.

"So, there we were. The dinner was over. Folks had headed to their cars when John asks me where the waitstaff might be. He said that he had promised them autographs.

"We found them in the kitchen, and John began to sign autographs and answer questions. The best question was, 'What's the pressure like to be asked to pitch in a World Series game?'

"Smoltz just smiled and never stopped signing as he said, 'Pressure is not pitching in the World Series. Pressure is being four years old, doing an accordion recital in front of your parents and their friends!'"

I guess in Mark's terms networking means to ask, no matter what, because there isn't really anything important at stake. You aren't four, and you aren't holding a junior-sized accordion!

"It's a matter of being determined," Mark says. "You have to invade the little cliques and stick out your hand. In a matter of seconds, you'll forget about being uncomfortable. Besides, it's too easy to be comfortable and that's why so many people are not good at what should be simple. I once networked with Ted Turner!"

"You did?"

"Well, not really. I saw him on TV, but so what? Networking is about learning from others, and I guess you can even do that vicariously. Ted said, 'Just because something is complicated doesn't mean it's difficult.' That's the way it is with networking. People only want to make it look difficult. It's not. It's natural."

I asked Mark (www.MarkMayberry.com) if there was anyone whom he had not yet met and like the rest of his answers, this one came quickly as if he had thought about it for years: "Someone who can invite me to play a round of golf at Augusta National Golf Club!"

No doubt, Mark will find him.

■ ■ ■

For the latest tips, news, and worksheets to help
with your MicroBranding efforts, visit www.tscottgross.com
and choose the MicroBranding link.

CHAPTER TWENTY

Networking Is...

NETWORKING IS NOT ASKING FOR FAVORS.

Networking is a form of marketing. It is a matter of establishing your brand.

Networking is a method for getting information. It is often a matter of going directly to or at least close to the source.

Networking is not a matter of creating shortcuts. It is a matter of discovering connections already in place.

Networking is a two-way exchange of information. The best networkers give more than they receive.

Author, speaker, deep-thinker Kare Anderson uses the term "Brief, Infrequent Encounters" to define what she thinks are some of life's great opportunities. The key thing to remember is that you can simply wait for opportunity to knock or you can go pound on the door. Which approach do you think will take you where you want to go?

Step-by-Step

There are six steps to effective networking.

❶ Be there.

❷ Target the mark.

❸ Preheat the contact.

❹ Control the transaction.

❺ Deliver value.

❻ Follow up relentlessly.

Be There

My first attempt to turn networking from art to science didn't include all six steps listed above. My friend Mark Mayberry looked over my list and said, "Not bad. But you left out the most important piece of advice. It happens to be the part of networking that you haven't quite mastered yourself."

I knew in a heartbeat what he meant.

> **MicroBranding Point**
> The most important step in networking is showing up!

My personal rule is to never do anything with a client that begins with a B (like bus, boat, or booze). I'd rather die than board a bus and go off with a partying convention group to a theme park or other attraction. Unless they give me the keys so I can go home on my schedule, I'm not getting on. Same applies to drinking with clients. I just don't do it. Being a little goofy on the platform sets me up for, "That guy's funny. But then, you should have seen him last night."

Nope. No buses, boats, or booze. On the other hand, I miss a lot of networking opportunities. While I'm back at the hotel reading *USA Today* over a chicken Caesar salad, Mark is out with the crowd networking his way to riches.

Mark is right. You've gotta show up.

The folks who golf like to crow that a lot of business gets done on the golf course. I wouldn't know. I don't have time to golf. That attitude has saved me plenty of time well spent with family, but there's also no telling how much it has cost me in lost opportunity.

My advice? If you are in a situation where the kids play golf, fish, hunt, shoot pool or craps—get with the program. There are only two other options: Get with the program or get left off the program.

Networking is simple—it's just not easy. To be good at it, you have to work at it. You have to plot and plan and prepare. Two thoughts to introduce you to the simple rules of networking are these: Smart networkers are hard workers, and they always bring something to the party.

Target the Mark

Party, plane trip, or business presentation, any time two or more people gather, there is the opportunity to network, to share information of mutual interest or benefit. The smart folks do two things the rest of us sometimes forget to do—think and plan.

If you know you might be in the presence of someone you want to meet or share information, make a plan. Be ready. It may be better to be lucky than good, but you'll notice that the better you are at thinking and planning, the luckier you are bound to get!

Never go to an event without a written list of individuals you hope to meet and what you would like to learn from them or share with them.

Preheat the Contact

In this world there are folks who love to connect people. They are natural born matchmakers. You may even be one of them. If you aren't, learn now!

Two key ideas. First, know who the matchmakers are and be willing to ask for the introductions you seek. Second, remember that matchmaking is a killer way to reciprocate.

Better add a third benefit: Matchmakers are often seen as a source of information. After all, they know who's who. They're in the know, and in this economy, knowledge is valuable. When you are recognized as a matchmaker, folks will seek you out bearing gifts of great information.

Find a matchmaker and let him know who you want to meet and why. Chances are he will be eager to make the introduction. If he knows what you want the meeting to accomplish, he is more likely to smooth the way.

"Bill, I found someone you are going to want to meet. This is Cindy, and she has a wonderful idea for a new business-to-business product."

See how that works? Instantly the conversation is targeted.

Notice that the matchmaker has a key role to play, instantly focusing the conversation in a manner that doesn't make either party uncomfortable.

"Bill, Cindy wants to meet you because she thinks you might buy her product."

Doesn't work, does it?

Matchmaking is a critical part of the transaction, and you would be wise to plan your matchmaker as carefully as you target the audience.

When the introductions are done, the matchmaker will usually fade away leaving you to fend for yourself.

Control the Transaction

If making the connection is half the battle, then getting what you came for is the other half. Simply meeting an individual may be a goal all by itself, but even then you must control the transaction. At the very least, you are after contact information that will make future interaction easy and natural.

One of the biggest networking mistakes is to lose control once the contact has been made. If you foist your card on someone and elicit a lukewarm promise to "call you sometime," you lose.

The only purpose of giving someone a business card is to get a business card. Who cares if you just placed your card in the hands of the King of Siam, if two steps into his hotel room, he tosses it in the trash? Giving a card is meaningless unless you get one in exchange, because now you have the information you need to follow up.

Deliver Value

The key to successful networking is to deliver value. You have to do or say something that lets your mark feel lucky to have met you. Obviously, you want to walk away with the information or commitment that you wanted in the first place. But, why not make the encounter a win-win situation?

We all like to seem smart and valuable, but the power players get all the attention they need and more. Besides, what's a burning issue to you might be small potatoes to them. Your job is not to get what you want and run. Folks who do this often get one shot but rarely two. No one likes to feel used.

Always try to deliver value of some kind. If your target gives you the winning lottery numbers, it will be tough to deliver a big enough thank you. But say it just the same. It truly is the thought that counts.

We are volunteers with Angel Flight, an organization that provides air transportation for seriously ill patients. One regular patient of ours makes frequent trips to MD Anderson Cancer Center in Houston from her home in New Mexico.

Now, there's no way a seriously ill cancer patient is going to be able to pay us for the time and dollars involved in her transportation. Multiply that times the number of other pilots and planes involved in her relay across the West and back and you will see that a dollar for dollar thank you just isn't going to happen. Then again, it's not expected.

Does a thank you count? You bet it does! We recently received a poem written by one patient's sister. (Here it is, in part.)

It is amazing how an illness can deplete you through the years
The loss of fun and function, treatment worries, money fears.

At times the thought of travel to the doctor far away
Is more than one can handle when they've barely made the day.

But the light of hope is brightened when an Angel phones to say
"I'll pick you up and fly you..." to the doctor on that day.

Now these are mighty Angels, you feel safe within their fold
For their wings are forged in metal and their hearts the purest gold.

There's more but I cry every time I reread it just like I cried on the day it first fell out of an envelope and landed on my desk. In the margins were the signatures of the family and friends of a patient we fly all too regularly. There was "April...oldest daughter" and "Ed and Irene...friends."

Do you think I will ever say no when this patient needs a lift to Houston? Not on your life.

See? Anyone can deliver value because value is not always measured in dollars.

> **MicroBranding Point**
> Smart networkers avoid completing the transaction in one meeting, because a single meeting does not a relationship make.

As great pool players will tell you, the way to win is not so much knowing how to put the ball into the pocket. No, the great players roll into position for the next shot. And that is a secret of networking that will serve you well!

He Hit Me

I never hear two bickering kids utter the words, "he hit me," without thinking of our son and the inevitable conflicts that young kids have while attempting to deal with bullies in a tough world.

It seemed that every day for the longest time our son would come home from school dragging his lower lip with a woeful tale about some big kid at the bus stop or on the playground who was just making his life miserable.

So it was no surprise when one day he came home in a cloud of misery, telling us that his teacher wanted us to call her about a small incident that occurred at school It seemed that, once again, there had been a little disagreement only this time it was our son who was in trouble.

"What happened?"

"Steve hit me."

"Why did Steve hit you?"

Now, you know what the answer was. It was a whined, "I don't know."

"Well, did you hit him back?"

"Yes, sir."

"I don't understand why you are the one who got into trouble. Is that exactly how it happened? He hit you. You hit him back?"

"I hit him back first."

Same with networking. You have to give before you expect to receive. Don't just bust into a relationship with a huge favor to ask. Trust me, folks in a position to dole out favors and information are already being hit so often they feel like punching bags. They know you're going to want something. They can often guess what it is long before you casually drop your hint into the conversational stew.

Here's the better approach. Hit them back—first.

Enter the transaction bearing gifts of information, entertainment, or introduction.

MicroBranding Point
Whatever you do, give before you expect to receive.

Unnatural Act

Too often targets of networking are asked to do something that while possible is awkward, perhaps borderline unnatural. Let's say that you would like to be introduced to the CEO of an organization for the purpose of pitching what you know to be a brilliant idea. And let's say that you are in a networking situation that will bring you nose to nose with an acquaintance of that elusive CEO. Are you going to ask for an introduction or possibly a good word on behalf of you and your project?

Maybe.

It depends on the relationship your target has to the CEO. Your target may not feel comfortable making the introduction. It could be that your target is herself attempting to promote a pet project or networking the CEO for an introduction to yet anther person. Whatever the reason, your target may not feel comfortable helping you out. It may be possible but yet not feel a natural step in her own relationship.

Should you ask anyway? No.

Follow Up Relentlessly

The most valuable asset in our office is our database. The names and numbers of thousands of purchasers of our previous books and tapes help us know, in a heartbeat, who is most likely to want our next book or tape. The names and numbers of the hundreds of meeting planners who have invited us to open or close their conferences represent a treasure of fee-qualified, quality-minded meeting planners who we know will want to have us back, if not this year then next, and if not next year then surely the year after.

Smart networkers do not rely on memory unless it's the kind you can buy.

I worry about telling you what to include in your database for fear of sounding manipulative and a user. But the truth is the folks who are careful to remember such things about a client or prospect as birthdays and hobbies are usually the kind of folks who actually enjoy remembering such seemingly nonsense.

> **MicroBranding Point**
> You can't be a serious networker without a serious contact database management program.

Check out ACT! or Goldmine. And if you really want to play the game, call the nice people at Hello Direct and get yourself a headset for your telephone.

While my clients talk, they hear the constant tap, tap, tap as I type notes into their contact record. What is important to them is important to me. I forget nothing. Even in this age of electronic everything, people are impressed when you remember something that is important to them. Maybe you did have a little help from Intel but at least you took the time to notice and enter the data.

When we started in business, we didn't have a hundred prospects to tend to. We used a three-by-five card file arranged by month. If I told you I would call you in October, I would file your card in October and never miss. But woe unto me if you called me in August! There was no way I could find your card in time to avoid sounding goofy.

Now, with a small computer network, we manage clients and prospects by the thousands and never miss a thing.

There is one best time to follow up—now! The chances of a follow-up being successful are inversely proportional to the time since the last contact. The longer you delay your follow-up, the less likely that it will be well received.

Have You Heard...

There is a down side to matchmaking; it's awfully close to that famous indoor corporate sport—gossip.

Face it. There are plenty of people who make their career out of ruining the careers of others. Connect information but never change it or filter.

The president of a company I once worked for decided to employ a presidential liaison. If knowledge is power, then controlling knowledge must be equally heady stuff. On many occasions when there was important but less than positive news the boss needed to hear, it was filtered carefully by the liaison. Once I sat at the presidential liaison's desk to make a quick phone call and was startled to see the minutes of a meeting where I had made a killer presentation to our top operating managers. A bright red X marked each mention of my name and beside it in delicate but just as red letters was printed the name of the presidential liaison. Because he controlled communication both to and from the boss, he thought he could get away with taking credit for my hard work. And he almost did!

> **MicroBranding Point**
> There is nothing more important than your communications. Don't let anyone change them or filter them—ever!

And when someone tries to match you to gossip or innuendo, don't walk. Run away!

Gossip is a form of lying because it is the passing of unverified information as though it were true. For something to be true, it can't be partly true. It must be 100 percent and nothing less true. Gossip usually is a partial truth which, by definition, makes it a total lie.

The Brief, Infrequent Encounter

Kare Anderson, probably the greatest thinker when it comes to managing business relationships, talks about what she calls a Brief, Infrequent Encounter. Kare believes that Brief, Infrequent Encounters are among the more important interactions that we have.

Luck is defined as when preparation meets opportunity. The implication is that we are often presented with lucky opportunities but fail to take advantage of them or even see them because we are unprepared. The greatest networkers always seem to get lucky. They are, but only because they are prepared.

Fred Vang (see chapter 18) was at the local post office on business when he spied a rather exotic automobile parked in the lot. A car guy through and through, Fred realized that this was a special automobile, one that would not have made it to the dealer network yet. That could only mean that it was being road tested.

Fred also knew that Denise McCluggage lived in his town, a world-class race driver and a syndicated columnist.

What did Fred do? He waited!

In a matter of minutes, he had struck up what would become a fast friendship with someone who he admired and with whom he shares an unabiding love, all things with wheels.

Me? I might have noticed the car. I might have gone home with a story about seeing a really cool car. Fred? He went home with a friend!

How did he do that? He managed one of those Brief, Infrequent Encounters.

MicroBranding Point
Be present, prepared, and forward. Be of service and
follow up.

Be present. You aren't going to get lucky staying at
home. If the group is going to a hockey game, tug on
your boxing gloves and tag along.

Be prepared. Think about who you might meet and
how you might be of service.

Be forward. Opportunity won't jump on you.

Be of service. Look for opportunities to serve. The
best opportunities are opportunities to make a
connection.

Follow up. When the ball is in your court, it's up to you
to make the next move.

Selling Yourself: A Four Step Process

There are four steps to selling any product even when the product is
yourself!

❶ Establish rapport.

❷ Discover the problem.

❸ Offer a complete solution.

❹ Cement the relationship.

Establish Rapport

Are you guilty of blowing a potential relationship right from the beginning? It's easy to do. In fact, there are two huge mistakes that most of us
make. Overcome these two, and you are on your way to creating a powerful, personal brand.

Mistake number one: Failure to be fully present. Most of us are so focused on introducing ourselves that we fail to focus on the other person. We go to a party and are introduced to a new face, and in an instant, we have forgotten their name. If you want to build a powerful personal brand, learn to be fully present. Listen. Listen to the name. Use it immediately. Ask how it is spelled. It tells the other person you are interested, and the process of spelling cements the name in your short-term memory.

Never offer an immediate exchange of business cards. Never.

If the other person offers a card, take it, study it briefly, and then return your attention to them.

Here's what you say about *your* card: "I'm sorry, I know I don't have a card with me, but I will be sure to mail one to you first thing."

The truth is—I don't have business cards!

Discover the Problem

Few of us love to sell as much as we love to serve. By nature, most of us are modest and feel awkward with those hard-ball selling ideas that have us throwing folks over the hood of their car and shaking them down for a sale or a raise.

There is a better way. Instead of selling hard, why not consider serving hard? It's the Law of Harvest that says what goes around comes around or as you sow so shall you reap or, simply put, the karma bus drives in circles. You can put yourself in the taker's position, and no doubt you will win a few. But put yourself in the giver's position, and you will win many.

The first step to receiving is discovering how you can serve others. Whether it is for free or for profit, it is better to discover a market looking for a product than to create a product and try to find someone to buy.

When you are networking, spend the bulk of your time and energy listening for ways you might be of service.

Offer a Complete Solution

Once you have discovered the problem, offer a complete solution. Don't just say, "You ought to meet so and so." Make the introduction. And what if you don't already know So and So? Introduce yourself by saying you have an idea for an introduction that will be valuable to both parties. Act as a connector and you will be connected! Neither party will forget that it was you who made the connection.

Follow Up Relentlessly

Here's where the amateurs get left in the dust. Pros forget nothing. Use your database to follow up and keep every promise.

■ ■ ■

For the latest tips, news, and worksheets to help
with your MicroBranding efforts, visit www.tscottgross.com
and choose the MicroBranding link.

CHAPTER TWENTY-ONE

e-everything

IN AN ONLINE WORLD, YOU HAD BETTER KNOW HOW TO GET AROUND THE DELETE KEY. Want a bit of advice for maintaining e-mail sanity? It is "delete quick and delete often." I take one quick glance at the sender and subject lines, and if there is no compelling reason to open the e-mail, I do what comes naturally—I hit delete.

Ask most folks who could easily be buried by their e-mail, and they will admit to reading their mail with one finger poised over the delete key.

Your problem is getting past the loaded digit. Here are a few good ideas:

- **Don't e-mail often.** When you have something important to say, the chances of your message getting read go up exponentially if you have a habit of only e-mailing when you have something to say of consequence.

- **Don't e-mail junk.** Cartoons, jokes, goofy quizzes, and idle gossip offend those of us who actually have a life. Save this kind of stuff for—well, I'd just not be involved anytime but at least keep this stuff away from the office.

◼ **Don't tease.** If the subject is serious, tell me what it is in the subject line. If the subject isn't serious, maybe you should reconsider sending an e-mail at all. Some folks like to put "no reply necessary" in the subject line of informational e-mails but that invites a quick, preemptory delete. If there is no need to reply, say so but save it for the end of your message.

◼ **Keep it short.** This applies not only to the message itself but also to the structure of the message. Paragraphs and sentences should be short and to the point. E-mail is an immediate medium. Save the prose for a handwritten letter where it is both appropriate and appreciated. Letters are for savoring; e-mails are inhaled.

Got your package. I still need the Brady Report.

Thanks.

◼ **Tell me up front.** If there are multiple topics, tell me. Otherwise, once I get the gist of the first message, I may assume that whatever follows is unnecessary additional information. You know what happens next—delete! Tell me, in the subject line, that there are "two topics to consider" and then deliver them short and sweet.

◼ **Be detached.** Or better said, avoid attachments. If the recipient is worried about viruses, the chances of an attachment being opened decrease dramatically. Make it easy and worry-free by putting your information in the body of the e-mail.

◼ **Leave me out.** If I am not directly concerned with the subject, there is no need to copy me. It's too easy to copy everyone in your address book. Way too easy. And there is no better way to burn a networking bridge than to send unnecessary cc's.

◼ **Let me in!** Never, ever spam. Instead, give folks a chance to opt in. Your lists will be shorter but more powerful. And make it as easy to leave a list as it is to join. Don't make folks scroll to the bottom to get off the list.

■ **Give me a goodie!** Make it worth my while to give you information or read your e-mail. Offer a special report or a "members only" section to encourage participation.

■ **Collect contact data relentlessly.** Everyone who visits you or your business, whether in person or otherwise, should leave behind a footprint. Collect as much data as possible. MicroBrands are built on targeted markets. The easiest way to get contact data is to simply ask.

■ **Get it right.** There is a reason why God made spell check. It's to keep people from looking like they can't spell. (They can't, but God thought it might be nice to make you look good in front of your peers.) But even God can't help your spelling if you don't use spell check. There may be no better way to kill your personal brand than to send e-mails to the world that are chock-full of typos and grammatical errors.

■ **Include me, maybe.** If there is one surefire way to get folks to block your e-mail, put them on a list without their permission. Not only will they remove themselves from the list; they will block your name as an eligible sender. Also, most savvy e-mail users filter the size of e-mails they are willing to receive. Send me a photo or other huge file, and my e-mail program will leave it on the server. I'll never see it!

Looking for the Connectors and Finding Kevin Bacon

Where have I been? It seems the entire world is playing *Six Degrees of Kevin Bacon!* The premise is simple. Supposedly everyone on the entire earth can be connected using six associations or less.

In other words, say you want to get a proposal into the hands of some powerful person that you don't know. According to the theory, you can give the proposal to someone you think is closer to your target who could (that's not to say would) hand it to someone who is closer still. In six hand-offs or less, your proposal would land on the desk, you get the deal, and everyone lives happily ever after.

The concept was originally the work of a well-known psychologist named Stanley Milgram. Milgram used what he called the "small world method" to find out how human beings are connected. Do we as individuals live in small, unconnected social groups, or are we, in fact, connected to the world at large?

Milgram decided to give a letter to 160 people living in Omaha and ask them to pass it from friend to acquaintance until it reached a stockbroker in Boston. None of the original recipients knew or had heard of the stockbroker but all could at least think of someone who might know someone who did.

It turned out that most of the letters were eventually delivered, and most were delivered in only five or six steps.

The surprise is that the majority of the letters that finally made it came from one of only three individuals. These individuals we call connectors, people who seem to know everybody. (You can read more about this phenomenon in *Tipping Point* by Malcolm Gladwell.)

Milgram did the hard work and then a fellow named John Guare wrote a play called *Six Degrees of Separation*, which, in turn, inspired three inebriated Albright College frat brothers to suppose that every actor living or dead could be likewise linked to actor Kevin Bacon.

And, thanks to the Internet, the idea has spread like wildfire. Check out the Oracle of Bacon Web site and you will see that with the help of a computer with too much memory to burn, Mr. Bacon is connected to nearly a quarter of a million other thespians including Elvis and E.T.! The Oracle has also computed that there are nearly seven hundred other actors much better connected than Bacon.

Small world.

Here's the big question: How connected are you?

Here's an even better question: How much better connected could you be if you tried?

I had my own dumb luck encounter with the small world method when I wrote my first book, *Positively Outrageous Service*. Without thinking about making a connection, I happened to mention to a friend that I had encountered quite a few examples of Positively Outrageous Service while flying Southwest Airlines.

"I bet they'd love to read your book," she said.

"Read it? I'd kill for a cover quote from them."

"Well, I don't know anybody at Southwest, but I know someone who has a friend who just might be able to make the introduction."

Talk about your long shot. I hated the thought of wasting an expensive manuscript copy to send to a friend of a friend who might know somebody. But I didn't want to disappoint such good intentions so I headed to the copy shop, spent a few more bucks I didn't have, and bundled up a manuscript copy of *Positively Outrageous Service*.

About a month later the phone rang.

"It's someone named Sherry Phelps…says she's with Southwest Airlines."

My heart stopped.

"Hello, this is Scott!"

"This is Sherry Phelps with Southwest Airlines and before this conversation goes one word further, we have to get something straight." Good Lord, they hate my book and they've found some reason to sue me!

"Yes, ma'am."

"Have you been up studying our company?" She meant had I been roaming around the halls doing unauthorized research. I hadn't, but now that she mentioned it, it seemed like a good idea.

"Yes, ma'am, I have. But not like you think. I've been studying your company at thirty thousand feet from the back of the bus."

Now followed a long pause.

"Good! How do we get ten thousand copies?"

Small world.

Ideas are like a virus. They even spread like viruses, so a little research in a seemingly unrelated field might be just what the doctor ordered to boost the health of your MicroBrand.

Small World Epidemic

There was an interesting study by an Argentinian by the name of Guillermo Abramson and his sidekick Marcelo Kuperman. (See *Physical Review Letters*, March 26, 2001). Abramson and Kuperman were investigating the spread of disease and made a discovery that I believe applies directly to MicroBranding.

It turns out that for a disease to spread through a population, more than the number of contacts is at play.

Abramson and his colleagues tracked the spread of disease through a social setting where individuals were rigidly connected, interacting only with their immediate neighbors. They also studied a society where everyone can loosely contact anyone else.

They discovered that the number of contacts needed to create a "small world" in the rigid society was nearly double the number needed when individuals freely connected to anyone.

In the rigid society, epidemics would flare up and then quickly settle to small pockets of the group. In the society where connections were loose and fast, epidemics tended to flare and ebb, and then flare up again cycling repeatedly.

Now, here's the kicker. Where slightly more than two out of ten people knew each other, epidemics would or could take hold. But when less than that magic two-plus out of ten knew each other, epidemics would not take hold.

In marketing, we are attempting to create an epidemic of ideas. We may be spreading the idea that John's Diner is a great place to eat or that Tisha's Fashions are the coolest.

What's this mean to you? It means that for your networking and other brand-building activities to have value, they must be consistent and range as far from your close association as possible. You have to connect with a lot of people outside your normal circle of influence. That's what effective networking is all about!

We are currently working on a project that takes us well out of our circle of influence or so we thought before we learned about the small world method. Critical to the success of the project will be an introduction to a particular television producer. Of course, we could simply smile and dial in hopes of finding the right person at the right time and then send our pitch along with the thundering hordes for "consideration."

Or we could count on the world really being a small world.

Last week we mailed out several hundred letters to folks in our database who know our work and had been identified as being well connected. We made one simple request: If you enjoyed reading our last book, would you do us the favor of connecting us with Mr. Big? It turns out that so far no one seems to know Mr. Big. However, we did get a call from someone who knows his boss and will be happy to make the introduction.

Small, small world!

Bringing Home the Bacon

The fourth step in building a MicroBrand is to cement the brand with multiple, quality impressions. Notice that there are two qualifiers for impressions: gotta be quality and gotta be plenty of them.

MicroBranders pay as much attention to the quality of impressions as they do the quantity. MicroBranders look for the connectors, the influentials. Don't tell just anybody. Tell someone likely to talk. Tell someone who will do your marketing for you.

In the movie industry, they market not to you and me but to the frequent moviegoers. The attempt is to give a movie legs. Legs as in "people will walk out of here (on their legs) and tell others about it." So the trailers (previews) that we see in the theater are not necessarily targeted to us. The target is the influentials, the connectors, the ones most likely to talk and whose opinion is most highly valued.

> **MicroBranding Point**
> The strength of a MicroBrand is focus. MicroBrand marketing is more efficient than mass marketing, because MicroBranders know exactly who is their customer and exactly where they live.

Want to know the best part? With PR, your qualified prospects find *you*!

In the ad world they call making multiple impressions "breaking through the clutter." Depending on the message, the media, and the target market, it can take from one to a dozen or more impressions before the viewer/listener/reader actually notices the message.

In our business, the office staff has as their goal to get me out of their hair. Nothing makes them happier than to have me gone! So they focus all their efforts on booking speaking engagements, the longer, the better.

Several years ago, we did an informal study to find out how many impressions it took to book the average speaking engagement. What's your guess? Two? Four? More?

It turned out that our median number of contacts was to us an unbelievable 8.05 impressions!

What does this mean?

First, it means that even in our business it takes a lot to break through the clutter where your offer can be received. There are thousands of folks who want to keynote conferences. Many of them will do it for little more than expenses and exposure. And if you are a meeting planner, all of them seem to be calling you.

Now some guy from Texas calls and wants the same job only he wants to be paid.

It takes a lot of impressions.

What else does our little research mean? It told us that if we stopped calling after four contacts, we would likely lose 50 percent of our business! Give up (in our case) after four tries and kiss half of your business good-bye.

What is the clutter count in your business?

One other thing we discovered: There is a critical mass at which your MicroBranding efforts become self-perpetuating.

Having worked for some years entertaining and educating audiences, a certain amount of our business just shows up on our doorstep. Our median number of contacts, our clutter count, is lower than when we first started.

Kevin Bacon strikes again! Once you have made enough marketing impressions to hit critical mass, then every impression counts for more.

This also means that starting and stopping your marketing efforts is counterproductive. Making one impression now and waiting months to make another is worse than useless; it's a costly marketing mistake.

MicroBranding Point
Once you have begun your MicroBranding campaign,
don't stop!

■ ■ ■

For the latest tips, news, and worksheets to help
with your MicroBranding efforts, visit www.tscottgross.com
and choose the MicroBranding link.

CHAPTER TWENTY-TWO

POS Marketing

WHEN ALL IS SAID AND DONE, when the consultants and sales trainers have packed up their charts of closing techniques and powered down the Power Pointless, there are only two reasons why anybody does anything: They either want to feel good, or they want to avoid feeling bad. If you are ever lost in a marketing decision, forget the research, throw away the statistical analysis, and ask yourself this question, "Will this make my customers feel good?"

Every decision, and it doesn't have to be a branding, marketing, or management decision, every decision is a psychological estimation that calculates the odds of feeling good or feeling bad on the basis of the next action or lack thereof. It's that simple.

When you marry, you are thinking about all the good things that are going to happen as a result of your decision. You weigh in the bad things and net-net, if you think the balance is tipped in favor of feeling good, you say "yes!"

When you take a job, you go through the same analysis.

When your customer buys from you, it is only because she thinks the purchase is going to make her feel good. Or not.

The other side of the equation is avoiding feeling bad.

While setting up for a seminar at a Midwestern hospital I chatted with a pleasant woman charged with room arrangements.

"Will you be staying for the seminar?"

"No, but I'd love to. I have a report that's due."

"Aww, let it wait," I teased.

"I'd like not to do it at all, but they think it's important."

"It's not?"

"Not at all. I doubt anyone actually reads it, but they expect it on the table at the start of the staff meeting. So every week I crank it out. I probably could just change the cover, and no one would notice. But I wouldn't dare. And if I don't do it today, I'll have to do it over the weekend."

I noticed a ring on the left hand and ventured, "And no doubt your husband wouldn't be too happy about that."

"Not really. I'm kind of like that report. I doubt he would notice if I were there or not."

Uh, oh, I had stepped in it. A smart guy would have let it drop.

"You don't sound like a happy camper to me. Why did you marry a guy who wouldn't notice if you were home or not?"

"I'm over forty, and I just got tired of being poor." (Don't wanna feel bad.)

The same applies to some employees. They don't love the work; they just need the income. For them, coming to work is not a matter of fulfillment and joy. It is a matter of avoiding the bill collector. By the way, do you think these folks are among the most or least productive employees?

What about customers? Do you want customers who buy from you because they love you or because you are the only or cheapest game in town? Trust me, the high-priced, quality provider is having a lot more fun than the bottom feeder.

Suddenly, it struck me that in light of the previous statement I'm going to have to explain Southwest Airlines, the low cost provider of air travel. (The modifier is actually low cost provider of *quality* air travel.) That's the difference. Low cost is not necessarily schlock.

Southwest flies clean, modern, meticulously maintained jet aircraft operated by the industry's best and brightest. Inexpensive does not equal cheap.

Every decision is a matter of feel good vs. don't want to feel bad. Every decision.

Why do men wear ties? Is that a feel good decision? I think not. What normal adult male would get up in the morning and say to himself, "Give me some colored cloth, put it around my neck, tie it real tight, that'll feel good"?

I don't think so.

The only reason why men wear ties is because they don't want to arrive at an engagement and discover that they are the only one without one.

And women! I have it on good authority that there's not a female on the planet who wakes up in the morning and says, "Hot, damn! It's a pantyhose day."

Feel good vs. I don't want to feel bad.

Or what about airline food? These days in the back of the bus you aren't about to get real food. You may get a Bistro Bag or a Sky Deli. And what are those? Approximately sixteen ounces of crap. There's nothing in those bags that you would actually choose. But do you take one? Of course, you do! Why?

Because you are afraid that if you skip the cart, the guy next to you will open his Bistro Bag at thirty thousand feet, and, for the first time in airline history, there will be something in that bag that looks good. And you won't have one! (Don't want to feel bad.)

Think about how this applies to you as a husband or wife, a Mom or a Dad. How does it apply if you are an employee? What does it mean to your MicroBrand?

For a preview of where we are headed with this thinking, let's say this:

MicroBranding Point
It takes an enormously confident and competent individual or organization to have fun whether it's at home, at work, or in the marketplace.

Awareness vs. Feel Good

Carry the argument just a little further and we see that there are, basically, only two approaches to marketing: There is awareness marketing, and there is feel good marketing. (The fancy folks call feel good marketing, "relationship extension" marketing, but I like feel good—it makes me feel good!)

Awareness marketing is typically left to the amateur marketer, while the big boys beat their brains out with feel good marketing or at least a combination of awareness and feel good.

Say you are in the business of selling toilet paper. Do you really think you can sell it cheaper than Sam Walton? Of course not! Heck, you'll be lucky if your supplier can sell it to you cheaper than you could buy it at Wal-Mart!

So what does the MicroBrander do? You either don't sell toilet paper, or you sell a premium grade toilet paper that makes behinds feel so good that their owners are willing to pay a bit more. Feel good.

And what does the average independent do? Cuts margins to the bone and tries to run price ads against the world's largest retailer. And that is just plain goofy.

MicroBranders go where the competition isn't, and when they get there, they use feel good marketing to tell their story.

Awareness marketing focuses on price, product, packaging, and place.

Feel good marketing focuses on the promise of feel good. Come down, eat in our restaurants, stay in our hotels, drive our rental cars, let us do your dry cleaning, and we're going to make you feel good!

Need proof? I logged on to Superbowl-ads.com and here are the top six according to their surveys:

#6 Pepsi—Bob Dole's Little Blue Helper

#5 Bud Light—Cedric the Entertainer

#4 Bud Alien Dog "Whassup?"

#3 E-Trade Monkey Cry

#2 Bud What are You Doing?

And the number one, Super Bowl XXXV commercial—EDS Run with the Squirrels!

Check them out. Every one of the top six are feel good commercials. Every one.

Bob Dole on the beach talking about his little blue helper. The Western world just knew he was pitching Viagra. What a hoot when it turned out to be the blue can of Pepsi! Made you feel good.

Cedric, the hapless everyman, had a killer babe waiting on his couch for a cold Bud Light. In the kitchen, we watched Cedric, Mr. About-to-Get-Lucky, shaking himself and his beer with joy only to watch his chance for romance dissolve in a shower of suds when he opened the shaken can and sprayed Ms. Wonderful.

All of them were feel good commercials. Not one pitched price.

EDS, formerly Electronic Data Systems, used feel good to show that this buttoned down geek-oriented Dallas company could boogie with the best of them when they showed frightened townspeople running with the squirrels in a hilarious takeoff of the running of the bulls, famous to Pamplona, Spain. (This was a follow-up to the previous year's commercial, which featured cowboy cat herders.)

Feel good. The amateurs pitch price, product, packaging, and place.

In the real world, the one-on-one world, this translates quite simply: People do business with people they like. They will justify paying a higher price or driving a few miles out of the way or bending corporate rules to promote someone they want to do business with.

This also explains how ugly guys who are funny often marry pretty women. We make them laugh and laughing feels good.

Was Super Bowl XXXV a fluke?

I think not.

The top ten Super Bowl ads of all time were all feel good ads.

Do you remember the 1993 ad in which Larry Bird and Michael Jordan made successively more difficult shots from further and further from the net until finally they were shooting from the tops of skyscrapers?

Or how about the 1980 Mean Joe Greene spot where the small boy gives up his Coke to a game-weary Greene who in turn hands over his jersey?

In 1999, there were the two Dalmatians separated at birth. One grew up to ride a fire truck, while the other made it all the way to the Budweiser Clydesdale beer wagon!

And finally, it was 1984 and you remember this one. It was the Apple Computer commercial and the introduction of the Macintosh. Killer!

And all of them were some version of feel good. Not one mentioned a price or promotion. Feel good.

Awareness-Feel Good-Image

Too bad that marketing is not a precise science. It is easier to define marketing terms than to see them at work in the wild. There probably are awareness ads that are strictly awareness ads. The same may be true for feel good ads. But probably not.

More likely there will be elements of both in any ad. In fact there is a third type of marketing, and that is image marketing, something of which the average MicroBrander does little. Why? Hold still, "I'll esplain it, Lucy."

Awareness ads tend to focus on features. Feel good tells us why or how the features will impact our lives. In both awareness and feel good, the media is doing most of the thinking. Image ads leave it all up to the customer to fill in the blanks. When you see a Nike ad stuffed with images of athletes in Nike gear, it's up to the customer and the position that Nike owns uniquely in each viewer's mind to fill in the message.

Image ads are risky business, especially for a developing brand. For most MicroBranders, they are not an efficient use of precious media.

Advertising vs. Marketing

I know half my advertising is wasted, I just don't know which half.

—JOHN WANAMAKER

We're going to talk for a moment about advertising and marketing as though they were absolutes. They are not. You cannot always, if ever, cleanly draw the line between advertising and marketing, but a good working definition is:

> **MicroBranding Point**
> Advertising builds product awareness, while marketing builds a personal relationship.

More than thirty years ago, Donald O. Clifton of Selection Research, Inc. talked about it in these terms: He said that there are four nontraditional ways to evaluate the strength of a business. The traditional measures would include sales, profits, inventory turns, and return on investment. But from a marketer's point of view there are at least four other measures: awareness, preference, frequency, and relationship extension.

To Clifton's list of four, I would like to add the concept of share. Customers who buy from you regularly may still be saving their big dollar purchases for someone else.

More in a moment but first these interesting numbers: The value of the brand Coca-Cola is estimated at more than $70 billion dollars. MicroSoft Windows is nearly the same while IBM, if you could buy just the brand not the physical assets, would set you back more than $53 billion. Ford, Disney, Intel, and the most valuable non-U.S. brand, Nokia, would all run in the high thirties.

What is the dollar value of your brand?

You do have one, and it does have a value. For years, even small businesses have been sold on the basis of the value of their brand. It's called "goodwill." Notice when a business is sold there is often a listing of assets by market value plus a guesstimate of the value of the brand. It's always been there. We've just been calling it something else.

Awareness

You could get a simple measurement of your brand by asking for directions to your business. Step onto any street corner and ask passersby where you are located. If the majority of them can, without hesitation, give you directions to your place, you can say that you are doing just fine in the awareness category.

Up the ante just a tad and ask what time your place opens and perhaps add a question or two about your product or service. Or get really fancy and ask strangers if they know where to find the product or service that you provide and see if your name comes up.

"Excuse, me. I was told that there is a good car stereo shop around here. Can you help me out?"

"Oh, that would be Rod's Stereo Sounds. You're close. It's about a mile in that direction on this side of the street. You can't miss it. It's a long white building with a bunch of cars in front."

Now, in terms of awareness, that was good. Let's try something a bit more challenging.

"Thanks! Do you suppose they are open this early?"

"Oh, sure! I know they close early on Saturday, but they should be open now."

Here's the pro-grade question: "Great. I'm looking to buy one of those new Nokia telephones."

"You'll find it at Rod's. He has all the best brands. Even if he doesn't have what you are looking for, he will either find it for you or have something you'll like better."

Go ahead. Take a walk. And don't come back until you have a good idea of how you measure up in the awareness department.

If your awareness is low, you need to do more advertising.

USP

Brand awareness all by itself is worthless. Whether it's a personal or corporate brand, having the market know who you are is a nice but meaningless form of standing out. What counts is if the market knows what makes you stand out in a way that matters to the market. What is the singular point of difference that makes your offer better?

This is your unique selling proposition, your USP.

Can you say it in a few words? If not, back to the drawing board!

Preference

Preference is simply the number of potential customers who would choose your product or service over that of the competition. It may be a little harder to measure, but you can still get a fairly good idea simply by asking.

> *"If you were in the market for lawn services, would you be more likely to call Golden Eagle or Maldonado's?"*

> *"Would you rather eat at Church's or KFC?"*

> *"If money was not important, would you rather stay at the Westin or the Hyatt?"*

> *"How much more would you be willing to pay to fly on American?"*

That's a little more complicated step in the preference department. Try it with your own business.

Got it? Preference is a good measurement of perceived value. If you are low in the preference department, you had better crank up both the advertising and marketing.

Frequency

Frequency is a measure of how often your average customer will buy.

When we ran our fried chicken franchise, it was determined that chain-wide, the average customer visited 1.1 times per month. If frequency could be improved to 1.2 visits per month, that would represent a 9.1 percent increase in sales. Think about it. If you could encourage your customers to think about you just a few hours sooner since their last visit, you could move the sales meter significantly. And notice, that's with no new customers!

If you could do something to make the customers you already have think of you twice as often, you could double your sales without seeing a single new face.

A little side bar here. While this book is not about customer service, we have to remind you that managing the customers you already have is without doubt cheaper than all the marketing and advertising campaigns you could ever launch.

Studies show that it is significantly cheaper to market to the customers you already have than to find new ones.

The issue of course is churn. In any business, there are always new customers coming into the business as old customers are leaving.

Naturally, you aren't going to keep every customer. Some are going to die or move or have changing needs. But many are going to leave for greener pastures. Some savvy competitor is going to discover a weakness in your operation or offer and pick them off one by one.

Two points: First, if you knew which of your customers was next to leave, what would you do? Second, if you were competing with you, what weakness would you exploit?

Now, go do something!

Share

The grocery business talks about share of stomach. They realize that their customers don't always cook at home. They also realize that there is more to groceries than cooking.

In fact, the trends are strongly in favor of meals that are either ready to eat or almost ready to eat. Anywhere along the continuum between scratch and ready to eat there is a product to meet the need.

Instant potatoes have been around forever. (They even taste like it!) But we were shocked to discover that you can purchase prepared whipped potatoes. Then we noticed that in the produce department you can buy peeled and cubed potatoes in a package that also contains the ingredients you need to make whipped potatoes. Of course, in the deli department you can buy hot, ready-to-eat whipped potatoes. And here's an idea for the gourmand—it's still possible to buy whole, raw potatoes.

We can't imagine why you wouldn't want to peel and mash your own potatoes. God only knows how long the ones in the deli case have been there. And isn't it the height of laziness to buy peeled and cubed potatoes? Well, I guess not. You can buy salad mix, marinated pork loin, even cored and peeled pineapple. Why not potatoes?

How do you like 'em? Cooked from fresh? Already prepared? Or somewhere in between?

The grocers want your potato business. All of it!

Are you getting all of your customer's potato business?

Ask!

"Where else do you shop for…"

"When you aren't close to us and you are looking for…."

Relationship Extension

The final measure is often called relationship extension by marketers. I just call it feel good. The evidence of feel good is also difficult to measure empirically, but you can get a good sense of how you are doing by watching a few transactions.

Stand back and count how many customers seem to be treated as unique human beings. Are there any visual or verbal cues that might let the customer know that he or she was recognized? The obvious is calling a customer by name. But just as good might be someone saying, "Hey! Nice to see you again! Did you manage to get that old Chevy running?"

Remembering my order or asking about my kid is just as powerful as remembering my name. Yesterday we stopped at the soon-to-be-world famous Burger Basket. The new waitress, Zoe, didn't call us by name but when she came to our table she had a large iced tea for me and a smaller one, no ice, for Buns. She extended the relationship, let us know we were known, treated us as unique human beings—awww, heck, she just made us feel good.

When it comes to marketing yourself or your ideas, there are four additional key concepts to keep in mind: desirability, believability, exclusivity, and convenience.

Eaten By Tangibles

Of two customers sitting in a fast food fried chicken restaurant we used to own, one takes a big hunk of jalapeno pepper in his teeth followed by an even bigger hunk of hot, juicy fried chicken as he says, "That's the best fried chicken I have ever put in my mouth." He now takes another bite of pepper and another chunk of chicken. His buddy, sitting across the table, does the same as he says while chewing, "Well, it oughta be. They marinate this stuff for twenty-two hours."

Now, here's the truth. If you just whacked off two big bites of fiery jalapeno, you'd be lucky to identify anything about the rest of your lunch. If you knew you were dealing with chicken, you'd be doing better than most. Describing it as the best chicken you ever put in your mouth would be a stretch. Unless, of course, you knew, even before you took a bite that you were about to get world-class, deep fried bird.

And how could they have possibly tasted the marination?

They didn't. But they did know it was great chicken, and they did know it had been marinated for twenty-two hours. How?

I told them. Repeatedly.

Day after day, I had been on the radio inviting people to come in for "great fried chicken, marinated for twenty-two hours for flavor all the way to the bone. It's fresh, never frozen, and we hand cut it every day and then marinate it for flavor all the way to the bone."

Here's the question: If you do something for the customer and the customer doesn't know you did it, does it add value? No! It may add to the cost, but it doesn't add a thing to the value. To add value you must make what you do real to the customer. You must tangibilize it!

A few months ago, Buns was laughing at a cartoon. The caption read, "If a man speaks in the forest and there is no woman there to hear him, is he still wrong?" Judging from the laughter, Buns seemed to think he would be. Your mission?

MicroBranding Point
Tell the customer when you do something that adds value to your brand.

If you made soup from scratch for your sweetie, better say so or it could have just as well come from the can.

If you have special training that your boss isn't aware of, better spill the beans if you want to be considered for that special project.

If your company is one of only a few that are certified installers of your main product, let the customer know before you lose the bid based on price alone.

Get it? If you add value without making it tangible, real to the customer, you've added nothing more than cost.

Making something already there seem real and valuable is an important part of MicroBranding. In fact, adding a story or other relevant information to a product or service can go a long way towards enhancing value. It can also be a matter of significant competitive advantage.

Which would you rather have—a rug mass produced by a huge plant in China or a carpet handwoven in a Mongolian village following designs handed down from generation to generation? The first is something to keep your feet warm. The second will warm your heart. Both are rugs no matter how you describe them, but one comes with a story.

Two of our dearest friends purchased a carpet in Morocco. We have been stepping on it for years every time we walk down their hall. One night they told us the story of how that carpet wound up in their home in Chattanooga. It was a wild and wonderful story. We stepped into the hallway for a closer look at this piece of wool that was no doubt not worth the price they had paid—except for the story.

Now, when we walk down that hall for breakfast, we always stop and admire a rug-turned-masterpiece.

MicroBranding Point
Tangibilize to add value.

AT&T has gone to work wiring remote Alaskan villages for the Internet, closing the digital divide and bringing the world to the Eskimo people. (I checked. You can use the word Eskimo.)

Turns out that there is a Seattle company named Viatru that does business as market2market.com. Its specialty is connecting native artisans with buyers everywhere. The technique involves telling the stories of the craftspeople who sell from Viatru's site. Like the rug in our friend's house, each of the items sold comes complete with a story or other interesting information about the who, what, when, and where of manufacture.

In my office, there is an interesting carving of a moose antler in the shape of a female shaman. It was crafted by Inuit Indians who live in the far reaches of Canada. Of course, the carving is beautiful, but what makes it special is the story that the dealer wrapped around it. When folks admire the piece, I always take the opportunity to point out that they are looking at a shaman, a spiritual healer as known and revered by the Inuits.

In a wired world where anyone can and will compare price on the Internet, you had better get good at cutting costs or adding value. But remember, value is not in the product. It is in the mind of the customer. That's where you have to go to make things right and to make the sale.

Desirability

A thing is worth whatever the buyer will pay for it.

—PUBLILIUS SYRUS

If you want to make big bucks or win a heart or earn a promotion, you have to create a brand that is desirable. Desire, a measure of value, is in the mind of the customer.

> **MicroBranding Point**
> Products people need are sold on price. Products that people want are sold on emotion. When something is desirable, price takes a backseat.

Believability

At the age of twelve, I was asked not to return to the Kentucky Diner in Latonia, Kentucky. No, I hadn't misbehaved. I didn't steal the silver. I just took the restaurant up on its all-you-can-eat fried chicken offer. Mark Patterson, Gary Shetly, and I had come into a few bucks and decided we would go out for dinner.

I wasn't all that hungry but I do like chicken, and it was an all-you-can-eat offer. So, shyly I asked the waitress, (we called them waitresses back then not servers or as the Hilton calls them, waitrons) if I could have another piece of chicken.

Whoa! You would have thought I had smacked the poor woman.

She *did* bring me a scrawny excuse of a chicken leg that she plopped onto the table with such a noise that everyone in the joint stopped to see what was the matter.

Gotta say it tasted pretty good. And, even though I was not all that hungry, I do like chicken and she had been so nasty at my previous request that I thought maybe I should give her a chance to redeem herself and asked for another round.

Poor old Gary Shetly. I thought the kid was going to crawl clear under the table. Especially when I asked for yet another serving. It was about then that he and Mark decided to wait out on the sidewalk under the big green clock on the bank building. They waited and I ate. They waited a little longer; I ate a little more.

The next day the restaurant's neatly lettered sign that had announced All-You-Can-Eat Chicken Special $1.09 disappeared, never to be seen again.

MicroBranding Point
If you are going to make an offer, make it believable.

A couple of years ago McDonald's launched what was called the "55 Campaign" to promote the Big Mac. The idea was to celebrate the thirtieth anniversary of the double-decker, cholesterol delivery system, and McDonald's did it by discounting it to $.55, the same price as originally introduced.

I believe that in most places a Big Mac will set you back in the neighborhood of two bucks so this promotional price represented a discount of almost 75 percent. You would think that customers would have knocked down the doors for such a huge discount. They didn't. They stayed away in droves.

Why? I think it was that, at such a deep discount, the promotion did not seem believable and suddenly the flagship of the Mickey D menu no longer seemed either desirable or exclusive.

Exclusivity

People will buy anything that's one to a customer.

—Sinclair Lewis

Robert Cialdini calls it the Law of Scarcity. When there are few of an item, the value goes up. This is even true for items that no one would or should want.

Take the Edsel. In 1959 that would have been "take the Edsel, please." Because in 1959, there were too many Edsels; it was one of the biggest flops ever made by the Ford Motor Company. So, not many were made, not many were bought, and the Edsel was just a dog, a marketing idea gone down the tubes.

Today, if you had an Edsel in good condition, it would be worth in the neighborhood of $5,000, considerably more than it was brand new.

And what if we had started with something really cool like a '57 T-Bird with automatic transmission, power steering, power seats, and power brakes. You'd be looking at $41,000.

The opportunity for MicroBranders is this: We have to turn our small size or numbers into an advantage.

One way is to use price as a measure of scarcity. In the mind of the consumer, high price usually equals good.

"I took her to a high-priced restaurant."

"She's the most expensive attorney in her field."

"We bought the best one we could afford."

I have often told folks that if I cut my speaking fees by 80 percent, I would starve to death. Not necessarily from lack of money but from lack of sales. At 20 percent of my fees, no one would hire me. Why? Because, they would reason, at those prices, he must not be good.

Think about a client who wants to bring 250 of its top salespeople to the Hyatt Regency Maui for a sales meeting. The client decides to hire an outside speaker, and because this is also a reward for good performance, sessions are only scheduled in the morning. The rest of the day will be time off for play.

Start totaling what it costs to put those 250 bodies in front of the speaker for a couple of hours. There is salary and airfare, meals, shuttle, and the Hyatt isn't what you would call cheap. Soon you're talking some serious buckos. You could easily be toting up a number in the neighborhood of several hundreds of thousands of dollars.

Is the company going to hire a $500 speaker?

Is a $50,000 speaker necessarily better than a $500 speaker? Well, you can definitely say that one is a better marketer, but you really can't tell from fee which the audience will love the most.

What you can imagine is this conversation after the speaker bombs...

"Where in hell did you get that guy? He was awful!"

"The bureau said he was highly recommended. He's one of their highest paid speakers."

And that settles it. Expensive is at least supposed to equal good. And it definitely equals exclusive.

Your job is to do a little price comparing. Find out where your product fits in range of prices. You don't want to be the cheapest, because it's for sure you won't be perceived as the best.

If you aren't the best, then think about selling your product or yourself at the low end. Why? Because there is only one place worse than the bottom and that's the deadly middle. In the middle, you get beat up on price and you are looked down on in terms of quality.

If you decide to compete on price, forget any idea of exclusivity and focus instead on believability and convenience. Bill yourself as "the low-cost alternative" and console yourself to dealing with the bottom feeders of the market. They won't be the best customers, but you can have them all to yourself.

Convenience

In retailing there is an old saying that the most important three ingredients for success are location, location, and location. What that really means is this: You have to make it easy for your customers to buy.

Will you take their check? Are you open hours that are convenient?

Are your return policies a hassle? Is it easy to call you on the phone? Ask yourself what you might be doing to make doing business with you difficult—and then eliminate the obstacles.

MicroMarketing

Smart MicroBranders create MicroMarketing events to draw attention. You have to think. You have to be willing to take a chance, and most importantly, you have to be confident enough to handle the occasional failure.

The four steps to creating MicroBranding events are:

- Have fun.

- Involve your product.

- Be location sensitive.

- Do something good for others.

Have Fun

Fun gets attention. It's as simple as that. Have fun and people will be drawn to you. On an individual level, you'll notice that folks are drawn to people who tell great stories, always have a smile, and seem to be enjoying themselves.

Fun is natural, and people are drawn toward fun like moths to a flame. They want to be a part of it, if not personally at least vicariously. At a party, folks will gravitate to the person who seems to be having the most fun. They may not be willing to do whatever he is doing, but at the very least they want to be near in case fun will rub off on them.

Think of the best commercials. They often involve humor, and there is always a story line. My favorite Super Bowl commercial is the one where a patient is wheeled into the emergency room. A nurse yells out, "Doctor! This patient has money out the wazzoo!"

I keep watching for that commercial to be replayed. It was fun.

Keep in mind that fun can be enjoyed vicariously. Often folks don't want to participate personally, but they are perfectly happy to watch others enjoy themselves.

We once held a sidewalk art contest where we gave great prizes to amateur artists invited to create chalk art on our parking lot. The event attracted artists by the dozens but spectators by the hundreds. Everyone had fun, whether they were on hands and knees creating serious art or standing at a distance enjoying the event.

Involve Your Product

The goal of all marketing is to get trial. If the result is anything other than trial, or perhaps an on-the-spot sale, then your marketing is a failure. Introducing customers to your staff or new location is nice but worthless unless there is trial leading to a sale.

If you have a good product and your price and terms are fair, then why do you need to market? Trial.

Too often businesses are asked to contribute to great causes without any benefit to the business. If you have money to burn, fine. No, I take that back. Even if you have money to burn, there is no point in contributing to an event that will not in some way also benefit you or your business. Why? Because there are too many worthy endeavors that you can participate in to be blowing limited time and energy on promotional opportunities that have no value to you.

Be Location Sensitive

Being location sensitive when it comes to marketing efforts is an extension of involving your product. Smart business operators understand the value of getting customers to their property.

If you want to contribute to the Little League, fine but ask them to hold the player sign-up at your place. At the very least require parents of interested kids to pick up the registration form at your place.

It makes no sense to spend good money on promotional events that happen elsewhere. Especially since it's so easy to get people to your place where they can see and even try your product.

Do Something Good for Others

Smart MicroBranders understand that doing good for others is often the ultimate selfish act. You should make it your business to do good for others. Do this if you are the nicest person on the planet. Do this if you are the scum of the universe. Do this because it works. It works for you, and it works for others. You cannot come in second, if you put others first.

Years ago when we still owned the restaurant, I was disappointed to see a young woman waiting for a carryout order. I am a bug about fast service and can't stand to have our customers wait.

"Hi, I'm Scott Gross and I'm sorry to see you waiting," I said by way of introduction.

"I know who you are, and I don't mind the wait. They told me they were cooking it fresh, and it would be worth an extra couple of minutes."

"Well, I'm glad you feel that way. I still don't like to keep you waiting."

"I probably shouldn't tell you this," it seemed like I was about to hear something I would rather not know and was pleasantly surprised when she continued by saying, "I'm glad you have good food because I'd eat here even if it wasn't."

"You would? Why?"

"Because of all the good things you do for this community. I sort of feel obligated. So I don't mind a few minutes wait, especially since I know it's going to be delicious!"

The karma bus takes a circular route.

March...

I remember the time the folks from the March of Dimes visited our little restaurant and asked if we would be willing to help sponsor their annual fund-raising walk. They wanted a contribution of $300 for printing T-shirts for each of the participants.

The idea was that sponsors would get their logo printed on the shirts.

"No. But thanks for asking," was my answer. It didn't require much thinking, as clearly this request wasn't even close to meeting our four standards for promotion.

The young woman visitor was clearly surprised. She had expected us to be easy targets as evidenced by her reply, "But you sponsor everything!" She was incredulous.

"Yep, but I won't sponsor this!" I started thinking about how I could say yes.

"Why not?" She asked more surprised than unintentionally rude.

"Because there is no way I am going to spend $300 for people to walk on the other side of town. Now," I was thinking almost out loud, "if you want to make a little adjustment in your event, I think I can help you.

"We start and end the march here at our parking lot. I'll put a tag on our regular commercials to help promote the event. We can even use our changeable sign to let folks know, and we can do some kind of bounce-back coupon to get right to our regular customers.

"Let's start the march about 9:30. It should take about two hours. I'll help you lay out the course.

"We'll start the folks off with one of our hot, honey butter biscuits. That will give them a nice boost of energy for the walk. I'll get the Chicken Man to lead them in a few warm-up exercises, and then he can get them started on the walk."

"You can do that?" She was impressed.

"I know him personally," was my reply.

"Then," I continued, "when they get back to the parking lot, I'll have someone here to give them a nice cold cup of iced tea. How's that sound to you?"

Trust me, I was an instant hero. From "Hell, no!" to "Let me help" in one easy step.

Now, so much for Mr. Goodguy.

The march started at our place, but more importantly, it ended there. And what time did it end? About 11:30 a.k.a. lunch!

I gave each marcher a killer, hot, honey butter biscuit. And what is that? Trial! I believed that if I could get my product into your mouth, I would own you for life.

I also gave them a small cup of iced tea on their return. Most would drink the tea and then, surprise, order lunch! Why tea? Because there is nothing in tea! If you have high iron content in the water, you hardly have to put the tea in tea!

I had the Chicken Man lead the march. Why? Because if you are the photographer assigned to cover this event, what would you take a picture of? Three or four hundred people in look-alike T-shirts or a guy in a chicken suit?

I rest my case.

By the way, it was a cool suit. Green knee socks; yellow shiny shorts;

an orange top; white, custom fur wings; a rubber beak; wraparound mirrored sun glasses; and a white hard hat on which we had stuffed and mounted a real chicken.

It was a cool suit.

When we sold the restaurant several years ago, we kept the suit. Buns likes me to wear it around the house occasionally.

The Holstein Stroll

USA Today picked it up. *National Public Radio* turned it into a feature. And the charming woman who fielded my call to the Building a Better Brattleboro could not understand how a simple comment at a recent membership meeting had managed to attract national media attention.

> *Brattleboro, VT—Business leaders want some national attention for their town so they are considering copying the traditional running of the bulls held in Pamplona, Spain…(it) would be the running of the heifers."*
>
> —*USA Today*

The event would take place on the first Saturday of June to kick off National Dairy Month. It would be a natural for a town like Brattleboro, Vermont, where the dairy industry literally anchors life in this small but surprisingly sophisticated town. The National Holstein Association is headquartered at the north end of the picturesque Main Street while a three-hundred-head dairy farm holds down the southern end.

Here's what happened. A local woman got the wild idea that a running of the heifers would be fun and might generate plenty of lighthearted publicity. She mentioned it to a local dairy farmer who agreed. The fun-loving duo mentioned it at a meeting of the Building a Better Brattleboro Association.

Typical of most reporting on local civic groups, the meeting failed to make the front page of the *Brattleboro Reformer*. But the heifer run did. The editor of the *Reformer* thought the story was fun, so he plopped it (no pun intended) right on page one. The rest is history. Before long, half the media outlets in the country was running the story.

Think about it. You don't get a more outrageous hook than the idea of a herd of heifers stampeding down Main Street sweeping up camera-toting tourists as they go.

The nice lady on the phone couldn't understand how they had managed to attract national media attention by accident when it was so difficult to get media attention on purpose. "It was the hook. Running heifers is outrageous," I told her. "You are well on the way to building a MicroBrand."

Brattleboro is about more than cows, strolling or otherwise. It has a large Yuppie community and is a mecca for high-tech research and development. Sort of a Birkenstock-with-white-socks crowd.

"The cows are important to the culture," I told the woman. "Everybody wants to feel like they are living in the country and close to nature, even the ones who would rather die than milk a cow. It's an important part of the positioning for your town."

"Funny, we just developed a new logo, and it doesn't have a single cow in it."

"Better change it right away!"

■ ■ ■

For the latest tips, news, and worksheets to help
with your MicroBranding efforts, visit www.tscottgross.com
and choose the MicroBranding link.

CHAPTER TWENTY-THREE

Nothing But Web

THERE ARE FOUR INGREDIENTS TO SUCCESSFUL MARKETING ON THE WEB and, surprise, they aren't much different from traditional retailing.

❶ **Make it easy to understand the product.** One way to add value is through knowledge. If the customer does not understand the product, she isn't going to buy. One advantage of a great brand is that it serves as a shortcut to the buying process. When the customer understands the brand, she will intuitively understand the products offered under the brand umbrella.

A Web site should offer an opportunity to try the product: Read the book, see the item on a model, watch a video clip of the product in use. Use media to give close-up, insider knowledge to make it easy to imagine using the product or benefiting from the service.

❷ **Make it safe to buy.** Smart people worry about Internet security. Make certain that your site is safe—and tell the customer what you have done to ensure that safety. State your policy on privacy right up front. Remember, if the customer doesn't know you did it, you didn't do it!

❸ **Make mistakes penalty free.** Make returns simple and hassle-free.

❹ **Wrap an experience around the transaction.** Be mindful of the total experience of using your site. Give me video and audio. Involve me through surveys or even chat rooms where I can meet other customers. Occasionally communicate without the intention of selling. Keep me informed. Educate me on new and innovative uses of your product. Express concern with me that transcends the sale.

Make your site exciting. Become the sole source for interesting, fun, or useful lists such as the top ten best sources for something your customers want or the top twenty-five money-saving tips that involve your product.

Turn your Web site into a resource that your customers can use. Post links to useful Web sites. Post engineering data that advanced users might find helpful. List important events that your community of users might find interesting.

Timely, relevant, interesting content is what makes a Web site valuable. In other words, create a site where users want to come even when they are not buying.

Connect

Connect your Web site with as many other sites as your users will find interesting or useful. Make certain that the other sites link to your site. The whole idea is to create a site that your market will consider a valuable resource and to have other sites where customers who fit your profile will find you.

Connect II

Customers are often loyal to a product, but they are just as likely to be loyal to you. Customers want a relationship, and your Web site is a great place to get up close and personal. Invite customers to e-mail with their questions. Give them a place to post their comments, and don't be too quick to edit out negative comments. Better to deal with negative comments on your own Web site than to face the possibility of "anti-you" Web sites springing up everywhere.

Give customers a chance to connect with other customers. Check out what *FastCompany Magazine* has done to create mini-cells of customers in major cities everywhere. Can the magazine control what its Company of Friends groups do? Would it want to? Not even! Putting customers in control gives them ownership and moves your MicroBrand from product to lovemark.

Provide Updates

If you are offering a product that may evolve or grow, use the Web to provide updates. This could be a source of revenue, but it could just as well be free depending on the product. Every morning at 9:15 my computer checks in with the MacAfee Web site to see if there are updates to my antivirus software. I pay an annual subscription for the service, and MacAfee gets a free shot every day to sell me additional products.

We'll do the same with this book. There will be tons of material that won't make it past Buns in the editing process. So you can get it free at www.tscottgross.com along with any new ideas and stories that might be valuable to a MicroBrander.

Offer Samples

There is one key objective when it comes to marketing—get trial. The premise is simple: Given a taste of a great product, you will want more. Use the Internet to sample product. Be liberal. Don't worry about theft. You can't stop it, and besides, that's why there's hell!

One great way to sample intellectual product is through an e-zine. Ask for e-mail addresses of visitors and communicate regularly. Make it even easier to get off the list than it was to get on, and don't communicate too often. How often is too often? When you notice subscribers jumping overboard, that should be all the sign you need to cut back.

Don't .com Your Brand

The easy way to get to the Internet is to add a .com to your brand name and throw up a Web site. Be sure to make it easy for customers to order and take plenty of bandwidth to tell your company story.

NOT!

Here's why: If you want to move from product to lovemark, you have to be willing to let the relationship with the customer be more important than a potential immediate sale. The idea is to allow the customer to bond with the brand so that whenever the need arises, it is your brand that gets first and, perhaps, only thought.

If the site looks like a commercial, the customer is going to abandon the visit in an instant.

So, what do you do?

Name the site according to the way the customer thinks about the product category. If the product is dry cleaning, then the name might be stainremoval.com. If the product is gardening tools, then maybe yourgarden.com might be a good start. And while you should not hide your sponsorship, at least be smart enough to promote yourself in small case. Use the site to solve customer problems. Give lots of useful advice. Maybe provide a free sample in exchange for contact and other demographic information.

But above all, let the customer come to you.

Back to that site name for a moment. Consider your tag line as a Web address. If the tag line is on target, it is a concise statement of your brand promise. A well-constructed brand promise defines the customer's needs in customer terms (i.e., myachingback.com).

The Internet moves branding from a one-way commercial to a two-way conversation—if you use it properly.

■ ■ ■

For the latest tips, news, and worksheets to help
with your MicroBranding efforts, visit www.tscottgross.com
and choose the MicroBranding link.

CHAPTER TWENTY-FOUR

Freedom Begins With Me

Men are born equal, but they are also born different.

ERICH FROMM

THIS CHAPTER IS RESERVED. It's reserved for that special few who understand that work and life cannot be separated. That being true, if the work you do is working you, then you'd better make certain that you are doing work that fills you up and contributes to your human beingness while you are in the process of your human doingness.

Okay, I admit, that's too close to Zen to be productive. Instead, let's just say this: There are few companies that put people first. Southwest Airlines is one of them. You are about to discover that brands can come *inside*.

You may have seen their commercials, Southwest Airlines bringing Americans the freedom to fly. I love the last line in the commercials where what we assume is the captain speaking in a disembodied voice says, "You are now free to fly about the country."

Cool!

Remember Sherry Phelps, the sprite working at SWA? No power suits, no Mont Blanc pen. She is…just Sherry. The kind of person you want to know. Oh, and did I mention that she is smarter than the average bear? Actually, she's smarter than a family of bears, and it was probably her studied feel for the pulse of an airline that helped SWA embark on an internal branding program.

The idea is simple—be brand congruent to include those *internal* customers that everyone talks about but only great companies like SWA actually do something about. Sherry says that it's critical for a company, at least her company, to be brand congruent. She says SWA "makes sure that everything we deliver is in agreement with who we say we are and what we say we can do."

I read an internal SWA memo that commented that any airline can get airplanes and counter space. It takes something special to stand out. (These SWA folks are MicroBranders in spite of their size!) The intention behind SWA's internal branding program was several-fold: attract new employees for growth, retain valuable employees, and reinforce the brand promise to customers in a way that Positively Outrageous Service is delivered.

It was a pretty keen observation to notice that the same folks who fly Southwest are often the same ones who work for Southwest. So why not use what they know about marketing outside to love on the folks working on the inside?

Sherry says that too often employees would call with problems for which there was already a solution. Maybe when they first heard about it, they weren't ready to notice or maybe, says Sherry, "we weren't doing a good enough job of communicating."

So they saddled up and rode off to their agency, GSD&M, and asked for help in creating an internal branding campaign that would benefit both employer and employee by cementing the SWA brand promise.

A People Service Center complete with an 800 number and intranet presence was created to serve as a one-stop shopping experience where employees could get answers to their problems and where the SWA internal brand could find living embodiment.

The program falls under the tag of Southwest Airlines: Freedom Begins With Me!

There are eight SWA employee freedoms:

- ■ Freedom to pursue good health.

- ■ Freedom to create financial security.

- ■ Freedom to make a positive difference.

- ■ Freedom to work hard and have fun.

- ■ Freedom to stay connected.

- ■ Freedom to create and innovate.

- ■ Freedom to grow and learn.

- ■ Freedom to travel.

Like all good branders, SWA understands that for products and programs to have value, they must be communicated. So, off they go with Freedom Expos in all of their regions of operation. Internal departments set up booths and treat their internal customers like—real customers! This is a form of tangibilizing, the making real of benefits provided but often not seen so as to add value.

It's hard to act small when you are so big and growing so fast. But Southwest Airlines does it, and internal branding is part of its secret.

Oh, ask Sherry why she shares so freely and she just laughs. It is a Texas laugh. There is a trace of accent even where there are no syllables to drawl as she says, "You can't copy Southwest Airlines!"

I'll put it a little differently. Knowing is not the same as doing. You can learn their secrets, but only the exceptional company will go to the effort to put them to work.

You're now free to give it a try.

MicroBranding Point
Your internal brand is as important as your market brand.

■ ■ ■

For the latest tips, news, and worksheets to help
with your MicroBranding efforts, visit www.tscottgross.com
and choose the MicroBranding link.

CHAPTER TWENTY-FIVE

Brand Champions

Be All That You Can Be

WWW.GOARMY.COM

ONE OF THE KEY PRINCIPLES OF MICROBRANDING IS THE IDEA OF BRANDS WITHIN BRANDS. Your corporation has a brand but then so might your department. Of course, you personally have multiple brands. There is the brand you present to your boss as well as the one saved special for your spouse. Your marriage is branded in the eyes of your friends, and, if there are kiddos at home, no doubt they have a completely different brand moment when they hear your name.

Still it was with a bit of surprise to crank up the tube and find myself face-to-face with an "Army of One." "Army of One" replaces "Be All That You Can Be" and, even for a MicroBrander, it is a bit of a shock. "Be All That You Can Be" has been around since 1981. It is, according to *Advertising Age*, the number two ad jingle in history. (McDonald's "You Deserve a Break Today" is number one.)

What in the world is an "Army of One"? How does that fit with the concept of strict obedience and precision response in do or die situations?

I did not expect to find a governmental example of MicroBranding, but I did.

Faced with an extremely competitive labor market, the U.S. Army took a long, hard look at its long-running recruiting campaign. It did the smart thing and looked from the viewpoint of the potential recruit and much to its surprise, it discovered that what made the old campaign so popular with recruits of a now older generation was received much differently by the current crop. And the perception was not good.

If the parents of today's recruit-age persons think "Be All That You Can Be" is just what the doctor ordered for a generation of sheltered and self-centered young adults, the kids themselves think just the opposite. While "Be All That You Can Be" sounds like a promise of self-potential realized, to the kids it sounds like something you do simply to please Mom and Dad.

The old campaign was viewed as a college program. The old program had a "this will make a man out of you" tone that the youngsters on a good day could barely relate to. The kids see "Be All That You Can Be" as an education program, a quick way to earn cash for college.

Research showed that "Be All That You Can Be" is one of the most memorable ad messages of all time. It also showed that memorable is not nearly the same as motivating. And worse, it was seen as merely a way to "make your parents proud."

Contrast this to surveys that show that confidence in the military is at an all-time high, 43 percent in 1999 compared to 27 percent in 1971, and you see a generation that is just waiting for the right message. What is the right message?

First you have to study the market.

Today's recruit age prospect is:

- **Self-sufficient.** They are latchkey kids and have grown to prefer being in control.

- **Entrepreneurial.** They think they have the best solutions.

- **Team-oriented.** They have strong team instincts and tight peer relations.

- **Tolerant.** They strongly believe in individual freedom.

- **Connected.** They view the worst part of military service as being away from friends. Remember, this is a cell phone, Internet generation.

What the Army and other armed services are trying to do is understand the target audience.

The Navy is building new ships with hundreds of ports for high speed Internet access. New galleys will feature menus that closely approximate food served at familiar chain restaurants. Even the bunks will be roomier and mattresses more comfortable. Why? Because the target market is changing, and so must military service if it is to compete with the private sector.

More recruiting is being done online. Why? Because as Willie Sutton might say, "That's where the people are." Someone in the armed services has realized that just because you were once eighteen doesn't mean you understand eighteen-year-olds.

Since the start of the campaign, visits to the goarmy Web site are up 167 percent.

And the Army has taken on a more human face as the new campaign features real soldiers and invites you to meet them online. The new campaign shows exactly what boot camp, the scariest part of the commitment, is really like as filmed live and on location.

To the old-timers in and out of the service, this "Army of One" seems totally out of place. To them, the slogan seems to encourage a Rambo-mentality that is unlikely to be effective in the heat of battle. To older Americans, the theme seems to be the very antithesis of teamwork. It is self-centered and not military at all.

But the kids listen to the same slogan and hear a completely different message.

What they hear is not an "Army of One" but an Army where the individual is important, an army where you are given individual preparation that allows you to contribute to the team.

"This," said a young person referring to the new offer, "tells you how you can be a better person and helps you plan for your future."

When today's potential recruits hear the message, they get that in the Army their contribution will be valued. They hear that the Army's greatest strength comes from the combined efforts of individual soldiers.

In other words, "Army of One" is a message that resonates with the only important audience— the target audience.

> **MicroBranding Point**
> The target audience is the ONLY audience that counts.

Da Mayor

If a MicroBrand is a powerful, personal, and often local brand, I can think of no better example than the brand that is associated with a big city mayor. So why not look at a mayor's race from the viewpoint of a MicroBrander?

San Antonio is the ninth largest city in the United States. Sounds like a big megalopolis but there is one small hitch. It is the thirty-fourth or so largest metro area in the U.S. What that means is that when you are out of town in San Antonio, you are really out of town. Unlike Los Angeles, which is often referred to as seventy-seven suburbs in search of a city, San Antonio is one big happy family all clumped together on a high spot between the Edwards Plateau and the beautiful Texas Gulf Coast.

Actually, that's not really one big happy family. There are two, and they are often not happy with the other guys or even with themselves.

On the north side of town lies the golden arch of shopping and suburbs and the sprawl that always seems to accompany the idea of urban. On the south and west side is the other "real" San Antonio, the predominantly Hispanic communities that have traditionally been un-der-served and under-represented. Oh, did I mention that the north side is where the growth can be found? Also the money. Also the major-ity of Anglos.

The Hispanic community suffers from under-employment not to mention a school dropout rate that is nothing short of scandalous. (By the way, dropping out of school is in some respects a cultural issue with Hispanics who find it natural, perhaps expected to start work early in order to support the family. If there is one thing Hispanics bring to the party, it is a healthy work ethic.)

There sets the stage for the mayoral race between two soon to be former city council members who are vying for a job that pays all of $50 a week.

One is Tim Bannwolf, who hails from the prosperous north side of town. The other is Ed Garza, a boy from the barrio who regardless of the outcome of the race "made good."

The drama begins late in the race when an April 17th *San Antonio Express News* headline declares that current mayor, Howard Peak "may abandon campaign neutrality" because he is displeased with Bannwolf ads. Bannwolf, running behind in straw polls, had gone negative with, among other things, a TV ad featuring grainy black and white footage of Garza and the allegation that Garza had played a seamy role in a recent city scandal.

The commercial was snide. How else do you describe a dialogue that paraphrases Garza and then has the announcer sneering, "Oh, really?"

Smart marketers know that positioning is always "against" something or someone else. But in this case, the position was not in the form of a positive; it was a negative. Considering that following the commercial introduction, Garza remained strong in the polls, even gaining in some, would you score this as point Bannwolf or point Garza?

On April 19, Garza runs a second (also negative) series of commercials in response to the Bannwolf attacks. In Garza's ads, Bannwolf is portrayed as an empty chair at city council meetings. That same day, Roddy Stinson, curmudgeon at large and popular *Express News* columnist, takes a swipe at Bannwolf. According to Stinson, if Bannwolf had pledged to "fight special interests," he only had to look at his own list of campaign supporters.

What does a MicroBrander say about staking a position? If you grab the high ground first, it is awfully difficult for the competition to take it away from you. Bannwolf ceded the high ground to Garza with his attacks that were perceived by many in the community as unfounded and examples of "politics as usual," which the American people had pretty much vetoed in the national primaries of 2000.

Bannwolf gave Garza the high ground.

The next day, April 20, a letter to the editor sums up community feelings calling Bannwolf attack ads a "smear the opponent tactic." In spite of relentless negative commercials, Garza holds his ten-point lead in straw polls conducted by local television stations.

MicroBranders know that once you own a position in the mind of the market, it is difficult to change or lose that position. One key reason is that the market "needs to be right." And, having made a decision about you or your product whether favorable or not, changing their mind is an admission of being wrong.

This explains why once the public has decided that you are a good guy, charges, even proof of wrongdoing, rarely stick. For you, there will be an excuse. You will be seen as a hapless victim.

On the other hand, if you own the position of bad guy, additional charges will bear the weight of further proof that you are a snake, and the market, again, will be right.

In the OpED (Opinion/Editorial) section, Ed Garza was forgiven when he launched his second negative ad in response to Bannwolf. "Bannwolf played the bad boy first and Garza followed, thus casting the mild-mannered mayoral hopeful as an opponent who would not take a punch laying down."

Most voters simply yawned. Somehow the negative ads had made both leading candidates seem irrelevant. By April 25, and nearly a million dollars of ad funds, early voting had nearly dried up.

Good marketing demands that we send a message the market wants to hear—or they simply won't hear at all.

On April 27, the *Express News* rebuked the fair-haired boy from the north for a direct mail piece that featured a banner and a headline from the paper, "...the copy underneath, which harshly attacks Garza, was not printed in the *Express News* as the layout leads readers to believe...(it) distorts the truth..."

In the same issue, columnist Rick Casey makes the interesting statement, "Smart negative ads leave mud sticking to their target. Stupid political ads find the mud being blown back into the face of the thrower."

One day later, the OpEd page put it bluntly: "Tim Bannwolf is now definitely the underdog."

Four days before the election, thanks to Tim Bannwolf, Garza had only one thing to do—convince the heavily voting, north side Anglo population to support him. Fair or not fair, the market will be comfortable with people who look, act, and even vote like themselves. That might be the only thing that earns Bannwolf his $50.

May 3rd and the headlines read "Polls Show Garza Leads by 22 Points." Garza has gone to all-positive advertising.

Sunday May 5th. The headline on the *San Antonio Express News* screams, "Garza in Blowout." (Garza received 59.51 percent of the vote, Bannwolf 28.17 percent.)

MicroBranding Point
Position is always against something. Make sure you control this something.

The Biggest Duck

There must be a market for everything. Who could imagine an athletic shoe with a plastic plate in the arch of the sole? And if you imagined it, what would you do with it?

For one thing, if you were a boy between the ages of six and sixteen, you would Soap. That's a verb. It means "to grind using only your shoes." If you are still confused, it's obvious you aren't sixteen.

Soaps are a new brand of shoes that the kids use to slide themselves along curbs and handrails. It looks dangerous, and it probably is. Still, when you see it you'll think it's cool, (or rad, a different, edgy kind of cool). You may even want to give it a try.

Notice that the brand name is its own special lingo. Can you imagine someone saying, "Let's go for a nice, long Nike?" I don't think so. But young people do say, "Hey, dude! Wanna Soap?"

All great or soon-to-be-great brands have to have a legend, and Soaps do not disappoint. The story, and it may be true, goes that someone slipped on wet pavement and said, "This feels likes sliding on soap." From there it was a natural for the California inventor to say, "Wouldn't it be cool if we could do this all the time?"

And then there were Soaps.

Soaps are a brand managed by In-Stride, a San Antonio company that has MicroBranding down to a science. Its vice president of marketing and development, Brad Beasley, has always used the principles of MicroBranding to do Goliath marketing on a Lilliputian budget.

"At first we had to." Small companies don't have mega-budgets.

"But then when we did have a budget, we realized that sometimes not having enough money is often better than having too much money. It forces you to be creative.

"The big guys with infinite ad dollars do more of a branding campaign than we do," Beasley says. "Sometimes you don't even see a pair of shoes in their commercials. Anything we do has to generate immediate sales."

The core market was not targeted as much as they were simply found. Soap marketing is centered on The Soap Tour, two full-sized vans equipped with metal soaping rails and staffed by a crew young enough to relate and foolish enough to demonstrate this fad-turned-product called Soaping.

The Soap Vans stop at beaches and ballparks drawing a crowd that will result in many converts. Says Beasley, "Soaps has a cult following. They want to be involved. So we stay in touch. We e-mail the kids regularly. That builds brand loyalty."

I guess it does! How often do you hear from the people who make *your* shoes?

Young people want to be leading edge. They want to be invincible, and in an interesting way, Soaps helps them be and do just that. Beasley says that Soaping is much easier than the outrageous things you see the skateboarders on television doing. Only a handful of skateboarders worldwide can do what you see on TV, but Soapers can at the very least give the impression that they are just as radical.

The box that Soaps come in is not much more than a huge warning label, and, of course, the plate on the bottom of the shoe has a label. And isn't that just perfect for attracting a kid who is dying to look dangerous?

In-Stride recognizes that the young audience is searching for identity, and it is there to help them do just that. According to Beasley, not everyone who purchases the shoes actually uses them for Soaping but they do scuff up the plate to make themselves look dangerous!

Soaps were never imagined as a Nike killer. They will be happy to be a big duck in a small pond. And if that's not MicroBranding, I don't know what is!

This year there is another Soap World Tour in the works. A new version of the shoe will be available for those who don't want to Soap but who want the clean, fashionable look of Soaps made popular the hard way.

The marketing coup will be a video game by Sega that will feature Soaps. There will be Soaps ads in the game, and, of course, the game characters will Soap their way to adventure.

Beasley says that successful entrepreneurs have to have at least a touch of P.T. Barnum.

Why do we MicroBranders have to be different? Because different helps us stand out in a message-cluttered world. But Beasley cautions that different is not enough. "You have to have a unique product—with a purpose. Just because your product is unique doesn't mean that people will need it or (worse) want it."

Does the Soap brand of marketing work? I could give you numbers, but perhaps the best response comes in story form.

After Beasley took on the Soap brand he was visiting his father in the Midwest when out of the blue his dad asked if he had heard of the new shoes that the kids were wearing. They were doing something called Soaping!

"I couldn't believe that my dad knew what they were! I thought it was the end of the world!"

Mrs. Smith Calling

"We're well trained. We're fast. We're going to be nice to you." I could give you a month, and you would never figure out that this is the brand statement of a fire department.

In the fire business, there is one name that turns heads, the Phoenix Fire Department. And this idea of well trained, fast, and nice is their mission statement, values statement, tag line, and logo. If success is any measure, it proves that branding doesn't have to be a big hairy deal.

Focus on one simple idea. Play it over and over again to the troops as well as the market, and you are set up for a MicroBranding success.

Think about it. You can't get much more local than a single city, even if it is one the size of Phoenix. In an age where government is looked upon with suspicion, the Phoenix Fire Department (PFD) stands out. (Having worked with them while researching another book, *Borrowed Dreams*, I can tell you firsthand that they do more than stand out; they are outstanding.)

Captain Bob Khan, deputy chief public affairs says, "We try to keep it simple. We're well trained. We're fast. And we're going to be nice to you. Then we walk the talk through empowered firefighters." And I know that is more than the public affairs guy talking the company line.

The Phoenix fire stations are in firefighter terms, Taj Mahals, complete with fitness centers, sleeping quarters that are actually comfortable, and all the fire-rescue equipment an engine could possibly carry.

And training? There is mountain rescue, confined space rescue, swiftwater rescue, and, believe it or not, palm tree rescue! While I was there, one of the company members was being trained to operate heavy equipment in the event there was an emergency on a construction site. The men and women of the department love it!

What's more important, the market loves it.

The market for fire rescue services in Phoenix has a name—Mrs. Smith. To keep the department focused tightly on its mission and brand, Mrs. Smith serves as a metaphor for the customer. The entire department is focused on keeping Mrs. Smith happy with the understanding that if Mrs. Smith is happy, everybody will be happy. The city council, the chief, the firefighters, everybody. And when Mrs. Smith is happy, funding for training, salaries, equipment, even Taj Mahals flows freely.

Asked if the department has a logo other than the official fire axe and shield so typical of the fire service, Khan at first says, no, then remembers, the bumper sticker. If you live in Phoenix, you've seen it. A red sticker with white letters that simply says, BE NICE under which is the department slogan, Our Family Helping Your Family.

PFD teaches us that branding doesn't have to be complicated. It must be focused, and that means everyone on the team must buy in to the message. Even the guys who drive the huge ladder trucks that sport a sign that reads "Ladder Boys Rule" or the snorkel engine that is known as "The Tower of Power" (and we can't leave out the hazmat crew a.k.a. "The Glow Boys").

Captain Khan wasn't all that clear or concerned with the terminology of MicroBranding. He, like his department, didn't want to get hung up in the details of branding, only the results. He says that PFD is not all that different from Nordstrom and Mercedes.

"When you are delivering good service all the time and you have good, empowered people, when you talk about it, you really aren't marketing. You're delivering quality."

Brand, MicroBrand, multibrand. Go figure!

It's Joe Albertson's…

You would think that MicroBranding is strictly the province of small business, something more suited to the entrepreneur than to a corporate giant. Well, maybe MicroBranding is how the giants got to be giants. Read about the early days of Wal-Mart when Sam Walton gave pony rides outside his then struggling mini-chain.

Then there is Albertson's Supermarkets based in Boise, Idaho. In 1976, Albertson's ran an ad campaign that people still remember. "I can't get on an airplane, tell people who I work for, and not hear it!" says Craig Peterson, vice president of advertising for Albertson's. Craig wasn't there when the fabled Joe Albertson's campaign was launched, but he hears about it often.

Do you remember it?

"It's Joe Albertson's…supermarket… but the produce department is mine."

Local versions featured local department managers. Photos of department managers began to show up in the stores. Small children would come to the stores, spot their now-celebrity managers, and begin to sing the song.

Oh, the song! Simple, almost juvenile but catchy as the devil himself. Pam Beaumont, who was vice president of marketing (and present at Joe Albertson's birth!…the company, that is), recalls boarding airplanes, having their corporate luggage tags spotted by the flight attendant, and being serenaded via the PA system.

There was even a piano bar in Seattle where Albertson's employees were greeted with the lounge version of the tune.

What was unique about the campaign is that it superimposed a strong, personal, local brand on top of a strong, corporate regional brand.

The idea was more inspiration than hard core research, says Beaumont. The idea behind the campaign was simple: Find something to differentiate Albertson's from the rest of the pack. In those days (we're talking 1976), there were no photo labs, few pharmacies, fewer still floral departments. Groceries simply had perimeter departments.

Basic research indicated that groceries were hard to differentiate other than by price and that perhaps the best opportunity was the produce department and the other departments such as meat and deli that lived along the perimeter of the store.

It was in the produce department that Albertson's enjoyed a clear lead and that is exactly where the company started, eventually working around the store until finally, after rave reviews on the campaign, even the grocery guys got in on the excitement.

The campaign lasted only fifteen months when changing conditions in the industry signaled that it was time to move on. Joe Albertson's was replaced by more traditional price advertising, but he wasn't forgotten. If a big chain like Albertson's can put a public face on the produce manager, why can't you do the same with yours?

It's Joe Albertson...MicroBrander...but the B.I.G idea is mine!

■ ■ ■

For the latest tips, news, and worksheets to help
with your MicroBranding efforts, visit www.tscottgross.com
and choose the MicroBranding link.

CHAPTER TWENTY-SIX

Brand Management

Managing the Brand

MANAGING THE BRAND MIGHT BE BETTER DESCRIBED AS MASSAGING THE MESSAGE. It is as much a matter of listening as it is a matter of talking.

Most of us think of communications as sending when in fact the best communicators are those who listen hardest. The best brand managers are hard listeners. What do they want to hear? They want to hear what the customer is thinking about their product and the product of the competitors. The truth is:

> **MicroBranding Point**
> B.I.G. ideas often come from little details.

Last night I saw the first commercial for Game Boy Color and a new game called Tilt 'n Tumble. If you've ever played a Game Boy, you know it is a small, hand-held electronic game machine. Slip in a game cartridge and the palm-sized device becomes a computer platform for any one of a number of arcade-style games. The action is controlled by a couple of buttons and a toggle pad that acts like a joystick. It's fun.

But the Tilt 'n Tumble works a little differently. You control the game by tilting the entire device.

Now where did the idea to tilt the device come from? My guess is that some bright researcher noticed a very retro game (pinball) and saw players attempting to fudge the silver ball with not-so-gentle shakes of the machine. Someone said, "Why can't we do a computer version of that?"

What does a brand manager want to know? Well here is a short list of questions we might want answered by our customers:

- **Why do you shop with us?** You may be surprised. What if the only reason was because they live close? It might tell you that competition could easily take your share of market.

- **Where else do you shop? Why?** You might be able to easily duplicate a service or product offered by the competition allowing you to get a larger share of customer.

- **How often do you shop with us?** You need to know how often the average customer shops. Doubling the frequency could double your sales with zero additional marketing dollars.

- **How often do you shop with our competitor?** What is the other guy doing that promotes frequency? What does this question tell you about share of customer?

- **What similar products do you buy?** What products could you add that might attract incremental sales?

- **With whom do you shop?** Are the shopping partners potential customers? Are they children or spouses who might have unmet needs?

- **Who influences your buying decision?** Women do 85 percent of the shopping in America. They buy 50 percent of the cars but influence a whopping 70 percent of the sales. Thirty percent of women out-earn their husbands, and women are starting companies at a faster rate than men. Even when couples shop as a couple, it is often the woman who has the most influence on the buying decision.

■ **What could we do to attract you more often?** It may be something simple, something you've overlooked. Maybe extended store hours. Maybe delivery service.

> **MicroBranding Point**
> Don't ask, don't sell.

And be prepared for answers that may be unexpected. Remember the goal is to provide the products and services that your customers will buy, not just what you get a kick out of selling.

Step inside the modern Stockbridge-Munsee Health & Wellness Center, and you could be in any health services facility in the world. Except you aren't. In fact, you are on Reservation property at a facility owned and operated by Native Americans also known as Mohicans. Yes, if you are wondering where are the last of the Mohicans, I can tell you. They are in Bowler, Wisconsin, and doing quite well, thank you very much. (By the way, Indian seems to be quite the acceptable term if you are worried about being PC.)

When the center services were being considered, they included the usual suspects such as radiology, pharmacology, and a slew of services you would expect of your local general practitioner. The Behavioral Health Department offers a daunting list of services from Anger Management to Parenting Skills. But the customer said that wasn't quite enough.

Ask and you can participate in smudging, talking circles, pipe ceremonies, sweat lodge ceremonies, and song services.

Ask. Be prepared to listen.

How Long Are You in the Store?

The surveys say again and again that the longer they shop the more they buy. Sometimes putting the high traffic items in the back of the store will bump up sales. But you won't know unless you ask and, in this case, it may mean following customers with a stopwatch.

One big mistake is to talk to buyers while ignoring shoppers.

From the people who leave without making a purchase you may want to know:

■ Why did you decide not to buy?

■ Do you plan to purchase later?

■ Where do you plan to purchase and why?

■ What factors will influence the purchase decision?

The goal is to find out what is important to your customers. Discover what their larger problems are. Ask what keeps them awake at night and at least consider letting your brand be there and waiting when the future arrives for them.

It would be nice if you could look into their pocket. Do they have pictures of their wife or husband? Photos of the kids or grandbabies? Maybe it's their dog or goldfish. Will you find folded cash or only a few coins to jingle? They will have keys to what is important to them. A sportscar. A pickup truck with a gun rack. Maybe a bass boat or a mini-van. Would there be gum wrappers, beer can tabs, or granola bars? If you could look into your customer's pockets, you could learn a lot.

But you can't. So find other ways to look. Start by asking as much and as often as you can without being obnoxious. You can never learn too much about your market. Ask and ask often. Be prepared to be surprised.

Find out everything you can about your market.

Of all the things you might want to know about your customers, who they are, where they live, and what they buy have to be the three most important. (Okay, we can argue about that.) The reason I choose these three is that they are critical to establishing a relationship. For non-customers with whom you want to have a relationship, the first two are top of the must-know list.

Brand managers will do anything to acquire accurate customer and shopper contact information.

Many Web sites will not allow access unless you fork over your contact data. (Of course, there is more subtle technology for tracking Web traffic.)

At the very least you want contact information because that is the minimum you need to begin a relationship. Smart marketers stay in touch. *The Today Show* invites you to frequent todayshow.com. Barbara Walters ends her show saying, "We're in touch so you be in touch," all in an attempt to further the dialogue.

> **MicroBranding Point**
> Whatever your business, don't let anyone escape without obtaining contact information.

Those who have shopped with you once are more likely to shop or buy from you again. They are pre-qualified prospects. Losing them is no different than flushing marketing dollars down the drain. Why? Because previous customers or shoppers are the low-hanging fruit, ripe for an offer of a new product or service. With these folks, you already own brand awareness and can spend your efforts telling them about what's new without going through the time-consuming, costly efforts of introduction.

How can you get contact information? Ask!

You may have to promise privacy protection and you may have to offer something in exchange, but most customers will give you what you want so long as you ask properly and tell them why you want to know and how they might benefit.

"We'll be sending you advanced notice when we run specials.

"We want to include you on our monthly e-zine, which is full of the latest user information."

"There will be a drawing for a free..."

You get the idea. Get the information no matter what!

The Brand Message

One of the goals of brand management is keeping the product and organization in alignment. You cannot do this without first getting agreement about the organization values, mission, vision, and short-term goals. Keeping the brand focused is key to brand management. Otherwise, it is too easy to create products and services that may make short-term sense but spell long-term disaster.

Sandy Anglin, a friend and management consultant, mentioned that 69 percent of the American population could correctly be identified as "true blue" when it comes to their personal and social values. I wasn't sure where she was going with that until she mentioned the ad campaign for Oldsmobile that said, "It's not your father's Oldsmobile."

So?

So if the vast majority of Americans identify with traditional values, maybe their father's Oldsmobile is exactly what they want!

Great brand managers are concerned that corporate values are aligned with customer values. That doesn't necessarily mean that if customer values change, you have to. It does mean that you should at least be aware of changing values and have the option of following your customers.

Buns and I like to shop at Kids R Us, most of the time. It has good products, fair prices, and helpful people who can interpret when grandparents have trouble figuring how to buy a shirt for a kid we can only describe as "he's about this tall and kinda skinny." But buying shorts there, or anywhere, is a bit problematic because now the gangsta look has spilled into mainstream and shorts are no longer short. Instead, they are long almost to the knee and make boys and men look so out of proportion that they resemble those bear characters at Disney.

Was Kids R Us on the right track when it went to the gangsta look? Who knows? But one thing is certain. Some buyer decided, correctly, that this was the way the market was going and didn't want to be left behind.

Too Much?

There may be a point at which collecting more information about your customers is not worth the effort. The biggest mistakes belong not to those who ask too much, but to those who don't ask the right questions.

Remember New Coke? What was the question? "Which do you like better (in a blind taste test), Coke or Pepsi?" Taste tests showed that Pepsi was the preferred flavor. So common sense would tell you that Pepsi should be the hands-down winner when it came to sales, but it wasn't.

There must have been other reasons behind the choice. There were but, apparently, the folks at Coke got obsessed with the fact that Pepsi seemed to be beating them in the taste tests. They got so obsessed they forgot to ask customers, "Why do you buy Coke or Pepsi?"

Asking some of the questions can be as dangerous as not asking at all if it leads you to a false conclusion.

When we opened our restaurant many years ago, we selected our soft drink based on a simple question to the grocery manager at our local HEB Supermarket. "Which of the two soft drink powerhouses gets the most shelf space based on sales?" From that information we made our choice.

Twice, based on that same simple research, we switched from one to the other.

Our practical experience taught us that folks who asked for Pepsi would happily accept Coke. When Pepsi was our featured drink, those who ordered Coke would often switch to Dr. Pepper when told we carried Coke. Why? I have no idea. And that's the point: There are many factors that influence buying behavior and often they are not obvious at all.

MicroBranding Point
If you want to know, you have to ask.

One day my appendix fell out and Doc Jim sent me to the hospital. I was there for a week of torture that arrived three times daily on a tray at my bedside. One gray and miserable afternoon I was doing time ungraciously when a young woman knocked at my open door saying tentatively, "Mr. Gross?"

"Yes," I probably hissed.

"Do you have time to answer a few questions for me?"

"Time? Lady, time is all I've got. Come in?"

"I'm from the Dietary Department and we're doing a little survey…"

"Great! You are just the people I've been waiting for! I'd love to tell you what I think."

She decided to stay but chose the chair closest to the door. "Are you satisfied with portion size?"

"Yes, ma'am." Texans are polite even when ticked off.

"Does the hot food arrive hot and the cold food arrive cold?"

"Yes, ma'am."

"Are you happy with the variety? Are you able to chew the food?"

"It was my appendix not my jaw, and variety is not an issue. Thank you for asking."

"And thank you, sir." Texans are polite even when they suspect an attack. She rose to leave but I arrested her with a firm…

"Please sit down! Don't you want to know how this stuff tastes?"

She looked over her form clamped firmly to the hospital issue clipboard and said, "No, sir. That's not one of the questions."

"Well, it is today! If I were colorblind, I would not be able to tell any difference in it all! Some of it is red. Some is white. Most is a pasty gray color and all of it tastes exactly the same, like a blend of old shortening and Play Dough. Would you mind writing that on my sheet? And would you mind letting them know that if the International Red Cross happens by, I will be charging cruelty, ma'am." (I added ma'am because I am a Texan, and we are always polite.)

What did it matter if I could chew the food but hated it?

Asking only *some* of the questions is dangerous.

■ ■ ■

For the latest tips, news, and worksheets to help
with your MicroBranding efforts, visit www.tscottgross.com
and choose the MicroBranding link.

CHAPTER TWENTY-SEVEN

Protecting the Brand

I'm Going to Disneyland!

WE WATCH THE SUPER BOWL EVERY YEAR. Sometimes it is the only football game we watch the entire year from start to finish. We like the halftime show, we love the commercials, and it's always fun to watch the camera zoom in on a winner's face and see who gets to go to DisneyLand.

Super Bowl XXXV was a bit of a surprise. The MVP was MIA.

Baltimore Ravens' middle linebacker Ray Lewis was undeniably the MVP of the game. But that was on the field. Off the field was another story entirely. Off the field Lewis carried baggage rather than balls.

Lewis and what the papers labeled, "associates," had been accused of a stabbing murder outside an Atlanta strip club following the previous year's Super Bowl. Lewis managed to get off with misdemeanor obstruction of justice while his "associates" were found not guilty.

Well, guilty or not, Disney wasn't about to send this "winner" to DisneyLand, and Wheaties decided to make the historic cover of its box a team sport rather than risk the potential fallout from a Lewis solo appearance.

Wheaties said that "the players on the Ravens' Wheaties box represent the entire team and reflect its historic accomplishments this season." A Disney official allowed even less, saying, "I can only tell you that we never talk about how we reach our decisions. It would take away the magic."

And putting the wrong face on the box would have been magic of the worst kind.

A brand is a precious thing to waste. You put your brand at risk with every chance association. Choose wisely or you will be like Ray Lewis who was reduced to saying, "When I get back home and sit down, I'll go over a couple of things with the marketing people and hopefully get some things set."

Creating a brand and building a brand are only part of the process. If you want your brand to maintain its value, you must do more than prevent it from becoming tarnished. You have to polish it on a regular basis.

But this chapter is about protecting your brand—and sometimes you have to get downright aggressive!

Bad Tape

A few years ago and rather late one evening our phone rang.

"Hello, this is Scott!"

"Are you the same Scott Gross that does Positively Outrageous Service?"

"Yes, I am."

"Well, my wife heard you speak a couple of years ago." There followed a long pause that I was reluctant to step into. My first thought was that somehow I had offended his wife and now, having finally completed the gun handling course, he was calling to defend her honor.

"Ohhh-kaay," I waded in hesitantly.

"She recorded your speech."

"Well, that's alright. People sometimes do that. How can I help?"

"When she played the tape for me, I said, 'I can do that!' and I've been giving that speech ever since. I don't mind telling you I'm really good at it."

Now I have become the one in need of a speech, but the words refused to come and I decided to just wait this one out.

"People really like it! They laugh in all the right spots and all, but I have one little problem…" Now, I've still not decided if this guy is an attorney toying with me or just some goof or maybe some goof of an attorney. So I cautiously take the bait without setting the hook.

"And what is that?"

"There's one part where the people are laughing so hard that I can't understand the line that follows and it gets a good laugh too so I hate to leave it out. I want to do this thing just right."

I won't share the remainder of the conversation. For now just get this: The only thing worse than having someone steal your material is not having material that folks want to steal.

You have to protect your brand. You have to protect it from others, and you have to protect it from the worst enemy of all—yourself.

Remember Domain

Brands are property. They have value and legal standing but only if you take the first step to protect them.

From the moment you begin to think brand, think protection. If you don't tie up a great name or idea, you can bet that someone else will.

The first step in brand defense is Internet offense. When you first realize that you are onto something, tie up the URL. There is no point in developing a killer MicroBrand only to discover that you haven't covered your bases.

In addition to .com, there are plenty of new suffixes available and that's the bad news! There is .com, .biz, .edu, .info, .pro, and more. And if you want to be protected, you have to tie up them all! Register your domain with the Internet Corporation for Assigned Names and Numbers (ICANN) and don't forget the United States Patent and Trademark Office. Until you have made your mark with patent office, you may own the URL but still have no trademark protection!

Copyright

Record industry asks Napster to block 135,000 songs.

USA TODAY

Possession is nine-tenths of the law.

YOUR MOTHER

When it comes to intellectual property, having it and keeping it are two different things. In the book business, it is common to be advised to take almost any offer you can get when it comes to foreign rights. No point, they say, in negotiating because if you deal too hard, they'll simply print your book anyway.

In the United States, things are a bit more civilized but not much more. Any original work of authorship is granted copyright protection. You don't even have to mark it as copyrighted, but then how will you defend it? Even though you have a valid copyright, the moment a work is produced without registration, defense is a near impossibility. (Check out http://lcweb.loc.gov/copyright for complete information.)

Trademark

Trademarks are like copyrights for ideas. You can trademark a word, phrase, symbol, or design. You can even trademark combinations of the above so long as you are referring to a source of goods or services. You can trademark colors and shapes, possibly even scents and sounds. Harley attempted to trademark the roar of its motorcycles. (It didn't succeed, but it was brilliant for trying!)

Trademark registration is relatively inexpensive, but it does require a careful search before you file.

When it comes to protecting intellectual property, here is the best advice: Get advice—competent—legal advice!

■ ■ ■

For the latest tips, news, and worksheets to help
with your MicroBranding efforts, visit www.tscottgross.com
and choose the MicroBranding link.

CHAPTER TWENTY-EIGHT

Killing Your Brand

Oh, Baby!

KILLING A BRAND TAKES FAR LESS TIME THAN BUILDING ONE. Cash out-of-pocket is a lot less, too. Sometimes it takes but a few simple words uttered at the wrong time or even a simple misinterpretation of the boss's desires.

"Hold down costs this coming quarter," could easily lead to unintended cuts with unanticipated results.

Operations executives of a national chain restaurant were reminded that because sales were soft, there seemed to be only one way to make bonus: Put a tight lid on unnecessary expenses. Their response? Close regional warehouses so store personnel could not requisition replacement parts for critical cooking equipment. And what was the result of that? Hand-lettered signs in some of their restaurants apologizing for being out of a few popular products. And the result of that? Even lower sales!

Last week while driving into town to attend a concert, my pager went off announcing that a woman was in labor a few miles back along the highway. We did a U-turn and followed a highway patrol officer who was flashing by at a high rate of speed.

Imagine this branding moment from the perspective of a soon-to-deliver pregnant woman moaning in a mini-van that had broken down at the side of the road stranding her, one frantic husband, and her five bewildered children.

I jumped from our vehicle pulling off a lamb's wool sports jacket. I am middle-aged with silver hair. I walked to the passenger's window, stuck out my hands as Buns gloved me for the task about to present itself, ready or not. I walked briskly to the mini-van, calmly introduced myself as I asked the children to quickly move from the van to the patrol car.

How would you describe this branding moment? Middle-aged man with silver hair, must have delivered babies by the hundreds, "Honey, we're in luck."

Of course, what I was thinking was, "Good Lord, woman. Please don't have this baby now. I've never done this before!"

Would have ruined my brand in a heartbeat!

Or how would you like to be a Firestone dealer? Good people selling what must have been great tires by the millions. Ma and Pa owners/operators who depended on the folks at corporate to protect their brand which, by extension, is their livelihood. Then someone makes a decision to hurry tire inspectors and maybe a few imperfect tires make it into the system.

Kind of a so-what, isn't it? If a tire is bad, it gets returned. Heck, it's probably a rarity that tires are ever pushed to the edge of their rating. Sounds almost logical. Sounds almost defensible. Unless, of course, it was your tire on your SUV that rolled over. Da, da, da, da... another brand bites the dust.

More than unsuspecting motorists were injured in the Firestone fiasco. A brand went too, threatening to take along with it the lives and livelihoods of thousands of folks whose very existence were wrapped around the Firestone logo sewn above their shirt pockets.

Today Bridgestone-Firestone announced a new ad campaign featuring CEO John Lampe along with the launch of tiresafety.com. The campaign involves Lampe telling the Firestone safety story and includes giving out $5 tire gauges (2.5 million of them) to customers who buy Firestone. All this after earnings fall 80 percent.

Tell me. Which would have been cheaper? Millions spent in an attempt to save a valuable brand or getting it right the first time?

THE TEN BRAND "NEVERS"
❏ Never attempt to do too much under one brand name.
❏ Never settle for second best when it comes to marketing materials.
❏ Never forget that at every point of customer contact your brand is defined.
❏ Never confuse image with brand.
❏ Never take an action that is not in support of the brand—even when doing good.
❏ Never choose a name that doesn't work hard.
❏ Never fail to defend your brand position.
❏ Never make an unbelievable claim.
❏ Never attempt to define your brand yourself.
❏ Never use marketing to drive sales against a poor offer.

There is a reason why smart business owners do not throw a grand opening party on the first day of business. They aren't ready. Now, if that is obvious then why is it also not obvious that marketing should not begin until the product is ready?

Look at the automotive industry. Time after time automakers have rushed a potentially good product to market and ended up killing sales with massive recalls for problems that could have/should have been fixed before product release. The dealers were ready and crying for product; marketing was anxious to let loose a killer campaign. Everything was ready except—the product.

Think about the early version of the Pentium chip. Was it ready? Well, in spite of a glitch that created errors when performing large calculations at high speeds, the product did just fine. For all but the tiniest handful of potential users, the chip was the best thing since sliced bread. Unless they were told, chances were that few would ever experience the slightest problem.

Unfortunately, someone told.

The news got out that defective chips had been knowingly delivered to unsuspecting customers. Suddenly, folks who would never in their wildest dreams push their computer chip to the max felt betrayed and angry that they had been sold a bill of goods. Suddenly, the fastest chip they had ever used turned, in their eyes, into worthless junk.

This was good marketing driving sales against a poor offer.

Never use marketing to drive sales against a poor offer. You are spending money to hurt yourself.

How should you spend money? Well, the obvious is to wait until the product is just right before spending precious marketing dollars. But spend on what?

MicroBranders will spend on traditional marketing, of course. They will also focus on clever activities to make those dollars stretch. But to really go to market effectively, MicroBranders will spend carefully on hiring and training.

Great hiring and careful training multiply marketing effectiveness.

Traditional marketers sometimes spend dollars on sales contests with the intention of buying the enthusiasm of the team to promote the new product. Sometimes they buy secret shopper services to check that the crew is suggesting the new product to every customer.

That's a fine idea even though it's a dumb idea—unless the entire campaign is supported by great hiring and careful training.

Here's the worst—badges. Some marketers think that if they make a clever badge and hang it on the employees that they will somehow get excited about the program.

Wrong.

One early morning on a drive to the Texas coast, my dad asked me to stop for coffee.

"Drive-through okay, Dad?"

"Sure, son. Anywhere."

"Good morning. Welcome to…. May I help you?"

"Yes, ma'am. We need a small cup of coffee. Black. Please."

At the pick-up window, I could not help but notice a badge pulling on her top. It was huge and shouted the words "WE CARE" in bold print. The sucker had to have been six inches across. Someone was really trying to make a statement and I, ever the corporate trainer, felt morally obligated to be supportive.

"So, what is it that you care about?"

She looked puzzled then noticed that I was nodding toward the badge that was lowering her center of gravity. She grabbed at it with both hands, pulled it away from her shirt, and turned it to read as if for the first time saying, "Oh, this? It just means we give a shit."

At a rental car counter in Boston one cold winter morning, I tried again inquiring about a badge as big as a saucer. Some clever marketing drone had spent no doubt days thinking up a rather forced list of platitudes that somehow turned pride from an idea into an acronym.

Professionalism, respect, integrity—sorry, I'm getting bored in the telling.

"Good morning! What's with the badge?"

She slapped her hand to her chest, quickly covering the kelly green badge that hung from her shirt. It was clear that she was uncomfortable with me or anyone reading it.

"Awww, it's just something from corporate." She turned and walked away. Another marketing buck bites the dust.

■ ■ ■

For the latest tips, news, and worksheets to help
with your MicroBranding efforts, visit www.tscottgross.com
and choose the MicroBranding link.

CHAPTER TWENTY-NINE

Conversational MicroBranding

STREET MEDICS ARE TAUGHT EARLY ON not to burst onto a scene without first sizing things up. It's an act that only takes seconds, but one that can easily save lives including that of the medic. There's no telling what you might learn in those few seconds. One of the most important signs to look for is something we call guarding. You don't need to be a trauma doc to interpret guarding. Victims hold where it hurts. And, since there are so many signs of pain other than tears, an experienced eye will quickly conduct a mental triage taking the medic almost automatically to the patient most in need.

Corporations guard, too.

Where there is weakness or hurt, corporations guard. They are tending corporate cows, those sacred animals that for one reason or another are carefully guarded in spite of the tremendous pain they often cause. Just as the medic makes a beeline to the guarded body part, the MicroBrander must head to where the corporation hurts most.

In times past, it was possible for organizations to put off seeing a doctor for the longest time. Markets moved slowly, products tended to evolve rather than innovate, and corporate insiders were easily kept from the public, hidden behind multilayered organization charts.

You can't do that any more.

You shouldn't want to.

The solution is conversational MicroBranding.

> **MicroBranding Point**
> Conversational MicroBranding is the art of putting the whole brand, and nothing but the brand, right out in the open where the public that loves it and owns it can protect it with ideas.

At lunch today, we tuned in to CNN and watched the continuing saga of Firestone and Ford with Firestone firing an incredible shot, announcing that it was no longer willing to provide tires to Ford, ending a partnership that goes back the better part of a century. Why did Firestone do it? No doubt Firestone customers had spoken and were finally being fully heard.

If you are just starting to build your MicroBrand, begin a conversation with your market and then continue that conversation. If you are rebuilding a brand, the market is the first place to start.

> **MicroBranding Point**
> The market speaks—whether you want them to or not.

Look at the Web sites devoted to slamming otherwise well-respected brands. Beam yourself over to www.Planetfeedback.com and see what I mean. And don't forget to check out the ever-elegant, www.ScrewedCentral.com. Is there one company you love to hate? No doubt someone else hates it with you.

I keyed in Denny's, a favorite of mine but clearly not of everyone, and in two clicks, I had a nutcase du jour, who wrote: "Naturally, I had to come by and set the record straight. I am known on local systems as the King of Denny's, because I have achieved that honored goal of being banned from the Denny's in Warminster, Pennsylvania, for life. *For life.*"

But not all complainers are nuts, and even those who are have economic value. I once had a competitor sneer about a rather goofy customer of mine saying, "That guy's an idiot." All the while I was thinking, "He may be an idiot but he's my idiot!" The guy did business with us at least twice a week. Send the rest over!

Back to Denny's. This company has it figured. Listed at the renegade site was an opportunity to click directly to the corporate site where you could talk to a Denny's spokesperson. I hit the link and, sorry, was sent to Planetfeedback. So I tried again and got the corporate site and selected an 800 number, offering English and Spanish. Now there's a smart move!

The folks who answer the phone are "specialists" and I didn't resist asking. "I'm a specialist in guest assurance," announced an accent that was clearly Southern and definitely nice. She clarified adding, "That's customer service."

"Can you tell me how many good calls you get relative to the ones with complaints?" I knew I was pushing her beyond the script, but I asked anyway.

She checked with her supervisor and returned with the bad news pleasantly delivered. "Sorry, sir. But we can't answer that here. You'd have to talk with our public relations department."

"No problem. Can you give me their number, please?"

Back to the supervisor.

"I can give you their fax number, but you can't call them directly. That would only be for the media."

Here's a suggestion. Raise the price of a Grand Slam a nickel and get those PR folks a phone!

I hate to criticize. Handling complaints is a tough thing to do. Successful MicroBranders will do it, however, if they want a real relationship with their market.

Here's a tip. If you can't trust your employees to talk to the market, you may need to do a better job of hiring and a much better job of training. Tightly scripted media responses often do more harm than good. When you script a conversation, it is no conversation at all.

Years ago I decided not to fly Continental Airlines. This was long before Gordon Bethune took over as the chief and miles before Continental started winning all those awards for on-time performance and accurate baggage-handling. Back then, I wrote a letter about two flights that were diametric opposites.

My flight to LAX (Los Angeles International) was textbook perfect. On time, killer cabin service, and our expensive video equipment was treated as if it were a cargo of Fabergé eggs. That was outbound. Inbound everything including the service was a 180-degree difference. So I wrote.

It was about six weeks before the response came, and clearly Continental was ill-equipped to handle a positive comment. All that was promised was to hunt down the offending flight crew and see that they were disciplined.

Form-speak doesn't cut it in the age of instant communications. The market wants a human conversation. Not many years ago, it was an effort to write to someone across the street. Now, in an instant, you can make your feelings known around the world.

Don't wait for the market to talk to you. Talk to the market first and always. Talk to the market openly. Lie and the market will know. Lie and the market will tell you they know.

Do this:

- Make giving feedback easy. Ask for it, both the positive and the negative.

- Share feedback throughout the organization.

- Make employee training a sign of commitment to their success.

- Train employees in how to talk to the market and then encourage them to do it.

- Avoid handling customers by script. No scripted greeting; never a scripted sales pitch.

- Form letters should be consigned to the delete key. Compliments and complaints are personal matters; handle them personally.

- Connect customers. They often are strongly loyal to other customers and, by extension, to your brand.

- Don't admit to mistakes. Announce them. Be proactive because you will be caught. Put the welfare of the customer and your relationship to him or her ahead of short-term profits or the potential for embarrassment.

MicroBranding Point
Don't *try* to be the best brand in the world. Be the best brand for the world, and the market will reward you richly.

And, while you are at it, have fun and make the world a better place!

■ ■ ■

For the latest tips, news, and worksheets to help
with your MicroBranding efforts, visit www.tscottgross.com
and choose the MicroBranding link.

CHAPTER THIRTY

MicroBranding Toolbox

MicroBrand: *A precisely targeted, highly focused personal or local brand built through strategic use of public relations and calculated networking.*

A MicroBrand is:

- **Efficient:** Little brand-building efforts spill into nontargeted audiences.

- **Personal:** Likely to involve an individual personality.

- **Local:** Usually restricted geographically or by industry.

Lesson One	In the land of the blind, the one-eyed man is king.
Lesson Two	You never know when you are going to touch someone in an important way.

TEN KEY PREMISES OF MICROBRANDING

1. You already have a brand. You just may not know it.

2. You don't need a globally recognized brand to compete.

3. A MicroBrand is, in many ways, more powerful than a global brand.

4. You are multiply-branded, and chances are you are focusing on the wrong one.

5. You don't need leading edge technology or global reputation to create loyal, profitable customers.

6. Building a MicroBrand costs less than you now spend to be mediocre.

7. All brands are MicroBrands.

8. It is much easier to destroy a brand than to build one.

9. Building a powerful MicroBrand is easily accomplished on a microbudget.

10. MicroBrands may not always be outstanding, but they always stand out.

THE BRAND BUILDING PROCESS

Truth or Dare
- ❏ Foundation values: what really matters
- ❏ Mission: the purpose for which you come to the party
- ❏ Vision: where you are going
- ❏ Snapshot: where you are at this instant

Value Discovery
- ❏ Position: what you want your customer to think about you
- ❏ Billboard: your brand promise in six words or less

Conscious Creation
- ❏ B.I.G. Ideas: what will set you apart from the crowd
- ❏ Image: what the customer sees
- ❏ Name: we save a critical step for last, where it belongs!

Cement Yourself
- ❏ Ink & Air
- ❏ Positively Outrageous Service Marketing

THE BRAND STRENGTH QUIZ

So you think you've got a great brand? Here's a quick quiz to get you thinking. There is only one correct score—and that's any score greater than your competition. Score your brand, and then run your competition's brand through the quiz. Compare the results and then get to work! Answer 1-10 for each question.

____ Can you define your brand in a few words?

____ What percentage of your potential market has an awareness of your brand?

____ Are you and your brand synonymous? Do clients look for the brand instead of you?

____ When offered with another brand, is yours the brand of choice?

____ Is your brand defensible, so unique no one could challenge?

____ Can your customers easily define or identify your brand?

____ Are you brand congruent? Does everything you do support your brand?

____ Is your brand valuable? Does it define something the customer will pay for?

____ Is your brand timeless?

____ Is there room to grow within the brand?

POS DEFINED

Positively Outrageous Service:
- ❑ Is random and unexpected.
- ❑ Is out of proportion to the circumstance.
- ❑ Invites the customer to play (or be otherwise involved).
- ❑ Creates compelling, positive word of mouth.

THE TEN BRAND "NEVERS"

❑ Never attempt to do too much under one brand name.

❑ Never settle for second best when it comes to marketing materials.

❑ Never forget that at every point of customer contact your brand is defined.

❑ Never confuse image with brand.

❑ Never take an action that is not in support of the brand, even when doing good.

❑ Never choose a name that doesn't work hard.

❑ Never fail to defend your brand position.

❑ Never make an unbelievable claim.

❑ Never attempt to define your brand yourself.

❑ Never use marketing to drive sales against a poor offer.

GREAT PR NEEDS FOUR THINGS

❑ A ticking clock.

❑ An innovative hook.

❑ A What's-In-It-For-Me.

❑ And finally, a sedative.

SIX STEPS TO EFFECTIVE NETWORKING

1. Be there.

2. Target the mark.

3. Preheat the contact.

4. Control the transaction.

5. Deliver value.

6. Follow up relentlessly.

FOUR STEPS TO CREATING MICROBRANDING EVENTS

1. Have fun.

2. Involve your product.

3. Be location sensitive.

4. Do something good for others.

FOUR STEPS TO SELLING ANY PRODUCT

(*even when the product is yourself*)

1. Establish rapport.

2. Discover the problem.

3. Offer a complete solution.

4. Cement the relationship.

WEB SITE EVALUATOR

There are no right answers, just plenty to think about. The Web is so new and markets are so different that evaluating your Web marketing is really a matter of letting he who is without sin cast the first stone. At least this will get you thinking!

____ Do you focus on expertise or personality?

____ Do you offer a reason to visit again?

____ Are you easy to find?

____ Can a visitor get what she wants easily?

____ Is the site congruent with your brand?

____ Are there lots of links to your site?

____ Is there plenty of quality content?

____ Do you have multiple sites where appropriate?

____ Do you link to related sites?

____ Are there things to do on your site? Surveys, quizzes?

____ Does the site benefit you? Is there a call to action? Are you mining information?

____ Can visitors buy product?

____ Is the site interactive? Can visitors establish a relationship with you?

MICROBRANDING POINTS

Fundamental MicroBranding Points

- If they know you at all, you have a brand.

- Ma and Pa. Make it your mantra for branding success.

- All business isn't good business. Own your island.

- Do what you love and the money won't matter. Better yet, do what you love, and it will show.

- Don't confuse your personal brand with your corporate brand.

- A strong brand takes the emphasis off quality.

- When you know what is really important, you will always know where you are.

- Choose an island that, if you owned it, you could achieve all of your goals and then set out to own all of it. Leave the rest of the world to the other guys. So long as you own your island, there will be plenty to go around.

- Brands are emotional statements.

- The target audience is the ONLY audience that counts.

- The market speaks—whether you want them to or not.

- Don't *try* to be the best brand in the world. Be the best brand for the world, and the market will reward you richly.

Products and Customer MicroBranding Points

- Customers want a relationship. Give it to them.

- If you are going to create a product, first ask the market. Otherwise, the product will remain just that, a product. It will never mature into a brand.

- Better to make a modest promise that you can keep than an outrageous promise that leads to certain disappointment.

MICROBRANDING POINTS

■ Industrial-strength showmanship should never, ever make the customer uncomfortable.

■ Industrial-strength showmanship should allow the customer to choose whether or not to participate.

■ Whatever your theme, play it to the hilt.

■ Since consumers pay with money, time, and feelings, you'd better deliver an experience that rewards all three.

■ Products people need are sold on price. Products that people want are sold on emotion. When something is desirable, price takes a backseat.

■ If you are going to make an offer, make it believable.

Corporate Brand Face MicroBranding Points

■ How could you become a personality in your business? How could you give your business personality?

■ Is your brand as well developed as your image? Does your image accurately reflect the brand you want to build?

■ Your brand is a promise. Your brand is a story. Never vary from either.

■ The stories told about a brand define the brand as much for those who own it as for those who want to own it, the customers.

■ What is your story? Are you telling it?

■ It takes an enormously confident and competent individual or organization to have fun—whether it's at home, at work, or in the marketplace.

■ Whatever your business, don't let anyone escape without obtaining contact information.

MICROBRANDING POINTS

Mission Statement, Values, Vision & Position MicroBranding Points

■ The least productive approach to foundation values would be to order up a corporate retreat, negotiate a few rope-and-obstacle courses, and come home with a declaration to force-feed to the troops and hang on the lobby wall.

■ Having a mission statement and living it are two distinctly different things.

■ You have different brands that are your life, so why not have different mission statements?

■ A clear vision is what holds the dream in place. Start without a vision and your branding efforts will be an eternal surprise—and failure.

■ Position is in the mind of the collective market. Reality hardly counts.

■ The "position statement" describes the position you want to own.

■ Positioning describes the mental real estate you actually hold.

■ Advantage is always defined by the customer.

B.I.G. Ideas MicroBranding Points

■ Incompetence kills innovation. MicroBrands are built on standing out. Standing out begs for innovative thinking.

■ B.I.G. ideas often come from little details.

Image MicroBranding Points

■ Generic names encourage generic business.

■ The logo, or image, is what the customer sees. The brand is what the customer thinks.

■ The *last* MicroBranding step is designing a logo!

MICROBRANDING POINTS

Managing the Brand MicroBranding Points
- Brand values naturally lead to a brand commitment.

- Discover what your customer values. Make common values known.

- Your internal brand is as important as your market brand.

PR and Networking MicroBranding Points
- Once the market is targeted, it is time to hit it again and again with clever public relations.

- Humor is a key element of great publicity.

- For networking and public relations to be effective, they must be continuous.

- You should not ask for a referral until you have earned the right to be given one without asking.

- Be there. Put the other guy first. Never get comfortable.

- The most important step in networking is showing up.

- Smart networkers avoid completing the transaction in one meeting, because a single meeting does not a relationship make.

- Whatever you do, give before you expect to receive.

- You can't be a serious networker without a serious contact database management program.

- There is nothing more important than your communications. Don't let anyone change them or filter them—ever!

- Be prepared. Be of service and follow up.

- Once you have begun your MicroBranding campaign, don't stop!

MICROBRANDING POINTS

Marketing MicroBranding Points

■ The strength of a MicroBrand is focus. MicroBrand marketing is more efficient than mass marketing, because MicroBranders know exactly who their customer is and exactly where they live.

■ The MicroBrander approach to marketing is to let the market come to you.

■ Until you tightly define the market, you cannot efficiently build your MicroBrand.

■ Advertising builds product awareness, while marketing builds a personal relationship.

■ Tangibilize to add value. Tell the customer when you do something that adds value to your brand.

■ Position is always against something. Make sure you control this something.

MAKING WORK FUN

(Yes, if you're going to have a brand, you might as well enjoy it!)

❑ Decide if you are working at a job you love. If not, you know what to do.

❑ Be competent. Nervous bosses aren't much fun.

❑ Choose time to play carefully. Be serious when appropriate.

❑ Help the boss build a team of winners. Losers aren't fun to work with.

❑ Think of fun names for products, processes, and policies.

❑ Create job titles that reflect the mission of that job.

❑ Schedule play time, create celebrations, and learn to party smart.

❑ Learn to read the cues and clues to know when a customer is ready to play.

❑ Keep score.

❑ Have fun at home. Play on a winning team.

A P P E N D I X

Web Addresses

Albertsons	www.albertsons.com
American Airlines	www.aa.com
American Cancer Society	www.cancer.org
Anglin, Sandy	www.Brain-Dancing.com
Boston Globe	www.Boston.com/globe
Bridgestone-Firestone	www.bridgestone-firestone.com/
Cisco	www.cisco.com
Crate & Barrel	www.crateandbarrel.com
Dell Computer	www.Dell.com
Denny's	www.Dennys.com
East Pasco Medical Center	www.epmc.com
Executive Jet Aviation	www.netjets.com
FAO Schwarz	www.fao.com
FastCompany	www.fastcompany.com
Fiesta Texas	www.sixflags.com
Ford	www.ford.com
Game Boy	www.gameboy.com
Globe and Mail	www.GlobeandMail.ca
Habitat for Humanity	www.habitat.org

Hooters	www.hooters.com
IHOP	www.ihop.com
Jewell Food Stores	www.webvan.com
Kelloggs	www.kelloggs.com
KFC	www.kfc.com
LA Times	www.latimes.com
Levenger	www.levenger.com
LL Bean	www.llbean.com
Longaberger	www.longaberger.com
Macaroni Grill	www.macaronigrill.com
Mayberry, Mark	www.MarkMayberry.com
McAfee	www.mcafee.com
MD Anderson Cancer Center	www.MDAnderson.com
Menke Manufacturing	www.ducktape.com
Miami Herald	www.miami.com/herald
Mohican	www.mohican.com
NASCAR	www.nascar.com
NBC	www.nbci.com
New England Spa & Sunrooms	www.nespas.com
Nine Inch Nails	www.nin.com
Nokia	www.nokia.com
Old San Francisco	www.OSFsteakhouse.com
Outback Steakhouse	www.outback.com
Pike Place Market	www.pikeplacefish.com
Pizza Hut	www.pizzahut.com
Plow and Hearth	www.plowandhearth.com
Proctor and Gamble	www.pg.com
Ralph Lauren	www.polo.com
Ronald McDonald House	www.rmhc.com
Ruth's Chris	www.ruthschris.com
San Antonio Express News	www.mysanantonio.com/expressnews
Sizzler	www.sizzler.com
Smashing Pumpkins	www.smashingpumpkins.com
Soaps	www.soapshoes.com
Sportif USA	www.sportif.com
Streetfighter Marketing	www.streetfighter.com

Sysco	www.sysco.com
Taco Bell	www.tacobell.com
Today Show	www.NBCi.com
ToysRUs	www.toysrus.com
Vang, Fred	www.fredvang@earthlink.net
Victoria's Secret	www.victoriassecret.com
Waffle House	www.wafflehouse.com

I N D E X

About the Author

T. Scott Gross speaks frequently at conferences across the nation and around the world. He is best known as the creator of *Positively Outrageous Service* and, now, *MicroBranding*. Scott is a master at unraveling marketing mysteries and known for a gentle humor that keeps audiences laughing while they learn fistfuls of practical, put-them-to-work-today ideas.

To contact Scott, please visit www.tscottgross.com or call his office anytime at 830-634-2122.

For information on booking T. Scott Gross for speaking engagements, contact Leading Authorities Inc. at 1-800-SPEAKER or your favorite speakers bureau.